Programming Your GPU with OpenMP

Scientific and Engineering Computation
William Gropp, Series Editor

Ewing Lusk and Janusz Kowalik, Previous Editors

A complete list of books published in the Scientific and Engineering Computation series appears at the back of this book.

Programming Your GPU with OpenMP
Performance Portability for GPUs

Tom Deakin and Timothy G. Mattson

The MIT Press
Cambridge, Massachusetts
London, England

This book was set in LATEX by the authors and was printed and bound in the United States of America.

Library of Congress Cataloging-in-Publication Data

Names: Deakin, Tom, author. | Mattson, Timothy G., 1958– author.
Title: Programming your GPU with OpenMP : performance portability for GPUs / Tom Deakin and Timothy G. Mattson.
Description: Cambridge, Massachusetts : The MIT Press, [2023] | Series: Scientific and engineering computation | Includes bibliographical references and index.
Identifiers: LCCN 2023010386 (print) | LCCN 2023010387 (ebook) | ISBN 9780262547536 (paperback) | ISBN 9780262377737 (epub) | ISBN 9780262377720 (pdf)
Subjects: LCSH: Graphics processing units–Programming. | OpenMP (Application program interface)
Classification: LCC T385 .D45165 2023 (print) | LCC T385 (ebook) | DDC 006.6/8–dc23/eng/20230515
LC record available at https://lccn.loc.gov/2023010386
LC ebook record available at https://lccn.loc.gov/2023010387

10 9 8 7 6 5 4 3 2 1

We dedicate this book to our wives, Hannah Deakin and Pat Welle, who have been seriously neglected as we spent countless hours writing this book.

Contents

III Beyond the Common Core

Series Foreword

The Scientific and Engineering Computation Series from MIT Press aims to provide practical and immediately usable information to scientists and engineers engaged at the leading edge of modern computing. Aspects of modern computing first presented in research papers and at computer science conferences are presented here with the intention of accelerating the adoption and impact of these ideas in scientific and engineering applications. Such aspects include parallelism, language design and implementation, systems software, numerical libraries, and scientific visualization.

William Gropp, Series Editor

Preface

Heterogeneity is here! The days of High Performance Computing (HPC) systems that utilize only a single-processor architecture are long gone. Modern computers are composed of multicore CPUs, vector units, Graphics Processing Units (GPUs), and all manner of accelerators. To get the most performance from these systems and have programs run fast, we need programs that effectively utilize all the different processors in a system. We need programs that run each part of an application on the processor most suited to it.

GPUs are almost ubiquitous in modern HPC systems. Originally specialized to accelerate the rendering of images, they are now fully programmable and boost performance for a wide variety of data parallel workloads in scientific computing, machine learning, artificial intelligence, computer vision, cryptography, and much more.

OpenMP started long ago in 1997 with a focus on symmetric multiprocessor systems. It defined simple mechanisms to parallelize loops and run programs across multiple threads running in parallel. It did this through compiler directives and a collection of functions from the OpenMP Application Programming Interface (API). Over the years, hardware and applications have diversified dramatically, and OpenMP has responded by going well beyond parallel loops.

In 2013, about a decade before our writing of this book, OpenMP added support for heterogeneous systems. This was in response to an urgency to respond to systems based on GPUs. While general-purpose GPU programming (GPGPU) had been around for years by that time, the 2012 announcement of the first GPU-based system at the top of the TOP500 list got a lot of attention [1]. It drove the HPC community to realize that GPU-based systems were inevitable, that software had to adapt and get ready for heterogenous systems. This drive to embrace GPUs has not waned in the intervening years.

It's an old quote, and the original source is lost, but the sentiment that "software is permanent, hardware is temporary" still resonates today. Applications must evolve to embrace accelerators. The trend to heterogenous computing won't end with GPUs. Additional disruptions in processor architectures are inevitable. Programmers must respond. This is why OpenMP, with its ability to manage work across heterogeneous processors, is crucial. OpenMP's goal is to deliver portable and performant parallel programs. Its high-level model and directive-based approach is a perfect fit for many programmers.

This book will help you learn how to program a GPU with OpenMP. The first part of the book provides the background you need to understand GPU programming with OpenMP. We start by reviewing hardware developments that programmers need to understand. We explain the GPU, its differences *and* similarities to the modern CPU. Next, we include a chapter that summarizes how to use OpenMP to program multithreaded systems (i.e., multicore systems with a shared address space). With this background in place, you will be ready for our core topic: how to use OpenMP to program heterogeneous systems composed of CPUs and GPUs.

GPU programming is the topic for Part II of the book. Parallel programming is hard. Just as the original version of OpenMP made it easier to write multithreaded code, modern OpenMP greatly simplifies GPU programming. With 10 items consisting of directives, runtime functions, and environment variables, you'll be able to write programs that run on a GPU. In many cases, these programs will run with performance on par with that from lower-level (and often nonportable) approaches. We call these 10 items the *OpenMP GPU Common Core*. Explaining the GPU Common Core is our main goal for the second part of the book. After covering the items that make up the GPU common core, we close Part II with a discussion of the key principles of performance optimization for GPU programming: the so-called *Eightfold Path* to performance.

Given the wide scope of parallel computing, many interesting and challenging algorithms have been developed. Some of these require detailed control of the system that goes well beyond the GPU common core. This is the topic of the third part of this book. Data lives in different discrete memories with computation spread out across different processors. OpenMP provides ways for programmers to take explicit control of the distinct features of a heterogeneous system: device selection, data movement, and coordination of computation, all in an asynchronous manner. It gives us constructs to run on multiple devices alongside the host CPU. It gives us the means to control the movement of data through a complex memory hierarchy. As no program stands in isolation, OpenMP supports integration with an existing code-base, fitting into the lively ecosystem of optimized libraries that modern programmers depend on.

An important theme throughout the book is portability. OpenMP was created by, and continues to be shepherded by, a diverse community of leading hardware and software vendors, academics, compiler writers, supercomputing centers, and governmental laboratories and agencies. The OpenMP community is dedicated to cross-vendor standards that express parallelism in a portable, performant, and productive way. The directives and API functions from OpenMP are supported by industry, so we can be confident that our programs will be able to run across a diverse range of processors, including (of course) CPUs and GPUs.

Acquiring the skills required for heterogeneous computing can seem daunting. Our approach, established from years of teaching GPU programming, has been shown to work well. We first establish the relatively simple core of OpenMP to get you started. This common core is all most programmers need and is sufficient to support serious application work. Then we build on that common core, adding detailed control of the system. The key to the success of this approach is that it gets you writing code as soon as possible. This is key. To really master GPU programming, you must "learn by doing" and write lots of code. This makes for an exciting journey as you gain the skills you need to write software that takes full advantage of heterogeneous systems. With this book, we hope to join you on that journey as you learn how to program your GPU with OpenMP.

Acknowledgments

We have many people to thank for making this project possible.

Eric Stotzer provided the initial push for this project and was a source of valuable advice in the early days of the effort. Simon McIntosh-Smith provided access to Isambard and the HPC Zoo heterogeneous systems that were invaluable for developing the example programs shared in this book. The members of the OpenMP Language Committee helped us with our queries on the specification. The OpenMP compiler and runtime developers who have worked tirelessly and thanklessly to implement each OpenMP standard as it is released. Without their hard work, the GPU constructs in OpenMP would be nothing but words on a page. None of this would be possible without them. We are grateful to our reviewers and the team at the MIT Press, who have been so supportive as we wrote this book. Thanks also to our copyeditors, who helped us prepare and improve the final manuscript. And finally, we thank our families for putting up with lost evenings and weekends as we worked to pull this material together.

I SETTING THE STAGE

Fully programmable GPUs emerged around 2006 and have become an important element of high performance computing. A well-rounded programmer must know how to write software that runs on a GPU. A GPU, however, is almost always associated with one or more CPUs. Hence, to utilize the full capabilities of a system, you need to exploit both the GPU and the CPU.

OpenMP is a well-established programming interface for writing multithreaded software for a CPU. With OpenMP 4.0 (released in 2013), constructs were added for programming a GPU. We did this because we believed combining GPU programming and CPU programming in a single programming language was the best approach for our multi-device (CPU, GPU, and more) world.

In this book we will show you how to program a GPU using OpenMP. This requires that you start from a solid foundation in OpenMP and the world of heterogeneous systems. We could point you to other books [2, 3], but we believe a book should stand on its own. Hence, we open with two background chapters to set the stage for our journey into GPU programming.

We start with a discussion of heterogeneous systems in Chapter 1. Our goal is to explain the essential elements of GPUs while showing how they relate to (and differ from) CPUs. We then move on to Chapter 2, where we cover the basic elements of OpenMP. If you have already mastered OpenMP, you can probably skip Chapter 2, though you may want to skim it just to make sure you understand the specific jargon we use when discussing OpenMP.

1 Heterogeneity and the Future of Computing

How do you summarize over 40 years of computing history in a few pages? Picture a pendulum swinging from one extreme to another. The pendulum spends very little time at the low point where forces are balanced. In fact, that point is precisely where the pendulum is moving the fastest and those trying to follow the motion must struggle the most to keep up.

This mental model is a good way to think about the history of computing. We could start with the works of Babbage and Lovelace or much later with Turing, but for the sake of brevity, let's start with the era of computing that emerged with the microprocessor. In those days (the late 1970s and early 1980s), a programmer needed to understand the low-level details of the system. In a normal workday, a professional programmer wrote in low-level languages, regularly dropping down to assembly code as needed. Programming was a matter of understanding hardware bottlenecks and then working at the lowest level to work around them and get those computers (primitive by today's standards) to do what was needed.

As the 1980s progressed and the full force of Moore's law kicked in, the game changed. With microprocessor performance doubling every couple years, a programmer was actually punished for spending too much time optimizing code for a particular system. The pendulum had swung from a world where the programmer was almost a hardware engineer to the opposite. The ability to add new features instead became the focus. Productivity and portability were the driving concerns, and programmers came to think of themselves as software engineers working to make ever more complex programs correct and full-featured.

In the early 1990s with the introduction of out-of-order execution for a microprocessor's instructions, the pendulum had reached an extremity where the need to write assembly code fell to the side. Object-oriented programming and other high-level concepts were the focus for software engineers. Performance was truly the job of the hardware, and we all rode the coattails of Moore's law into a bright future of ubiquitous computers filling every facet of our lives.

Pendulums, however, keep moving. In the early 2000s, the ability to manage static effects such as electrical leakage came to dominate. Power densities made cooling a major problem. Manufacturing microprocessors was harder. Moore's law was still with us, but it could no longer be used to double performance every couple years. As Herb Sutter famously observed, for software engineers "the free lunch was over."

This is all ancient history at this point. Multicore chips emerged. Core counts were small, cache hierarchies were simple, and Dynamic Random Access Memory (DRAM) cost models were relatively flat. People had to write multithreaded programs. While OpenMP was created to program supercomputers in the years before multicore chips, the transition to ubiquitous multicore chips pulled OpenMP into the mainstream. This was great for old-timers who still remembered the bygone days of hardware-centered programming (that is, the sort of people who created OpenMP in the first place). For the masses of programmers, however, these were dark days. Understanding hardware and utilizing that deep understanding became a requirement once again to write performant code.

We hoped the pendulum would swing through the low point in its journey and that language/compiler technology would take us back to a time when programmers didn't have to spend their days coding to low-level features of the hardware. We were wrong. The pendulum swing into hardware-aware programming was just getting started. First, there were the many-core chips with non-uniform memory cost models that required programmers to understand where their threads executed and how they lined up with memory. Then chaos struck the life of programmers again with the advent of heterogeneous computing.

The idea is simple, though the software response is anything but simple. Hardware specialized to a specific task is more power-efficient than general-purpose hardware. If your application does computations that look like a graphics pipeline, use a GPU: a processor specialized for graphics processing. If you are operating over high-dimensionality arrays containing dense blocks (a pattern commonly found in deep learning applications), use a Tensor Processor Unit. If you are coordinating execution over a wide range of storage, networking, and computational elements, use an infrastructure processing unit. A system composed of heterogeneous hardware elements is a system that, for a fixed amount of power, runs faster. This is called *heterogeneous computing*. It's not about moving the work from a CPU onto a GPU and then, once there, keeping the work there (something we call *offloading*). It's the old game of organizing a computation so the "whole is greater than the sum of the parts" by matching each part of your program to the hardware for which it is best suited.

And this is where the pendulum sits today. Programmers need to understand a great deal about the hardware. Programmers need to know which classes of algorithms map to which types of hardware. Programmers need to understand how to target one block of code to a throughput optimized device (e.g., a GPU) while another block of code asynchronously runs on another device that may be latency optimized (e.g., a CPU).

The pendulum will swing back. Some day, the tools programmers use will hide those details from them. That day, however, is not today. When the pendulum swings to the blissful extreme of programmer productivity where hardware is hidden behind layers of abstraction, we know it will someday swing back again. That's just how computing seems to work.

In this book, we will explore heterogeneous computing and how you can write programs that exploit heterogeneity using OpenMP. We are in a world where you have to understand hardware and how software maps onto it. OpenMP is an explicit API. You tell the compiler what to do through directives and a supporting API, and it does what you say. Some OpenMP directives are more prescriptive, stating exactly what should happen, and others are more descriptive, giving the compiler and runtime freedom to "do the right thing." In this book, we will explain how all of that works and, in the process, tell you about the key design patterns used in heterogeneous computing.

Our journey begins with this chapter. We set the stage with a brief description of the hardware we use when running programs written with OpenMP. Even experienced parallel programmers with detailed knowledge of parallel hardware should skim this chapter to make sure we are on the same page concerning the jargon used for describing hardware.

1.1   The Basic Building Blocks of Modern Computing

Computer architecture is a fascinating field. If you want to master it, read the famous text book we all learned it from (Hennessy and Patterson [4]). For our purposes, we will simplify the problem by thinking in terms of three basic processor building blocks:

- The CPU

- The SIMD vector unit

- The GPU

We skip many important developments in computer architecture with this simplified view of hardware, but it turns out that most of what you need to know as an application programmer working in heterogeneous computing can be addressed in terms of these three basic building blocks. We will consider each in turn.

1.1.1   The CPU

A CPU is a device optimized for latency-sensitive computing. You click your mouse and expect something to happen immediately. Of course, there is always a delay, which is a span of time we call the *latency*. As long as this latency is small on a human time scale (less than 50 microseconds), the user feels the computer is delivering results instantaneously and all is well.

Low-latency computing is difficult. The time to reference an item in memory (DRAM) is around 100 nanoseconds. This latency seems quite small, but not when you consider that a modern CPU completes basic arithmetic operations in well under a nanosecond. With orders of magnitude differences between the speeds of the CPU cores and the performance of memory, a CPU keeps high-speed blocks of memory (Static Random Access Memory or SRAM) close to the cores in a CPU. These are organized as a cache hierarchy to maintain a window into DRAM memory. As long as the items needed from memory reside in cache, all is well and low latencies are provided.

We show a typical server in Figure 1.1 with a common configuration of CPUs. We use this figure to drive home the fact that the cache hierarchy is complicated. The design of the CPU is optimized around managing memory to deliver low latencies. Each core may support a number of hardware threads (in the figure there are two: HT_0 and HT_1). By switching between the two threads while the core executes, the various Arithmetic Logic Units (ALU) are more likely to be fully consumed. On each core is a pair of L1 caches, one for instructions (L1I\$) and one for data (L1D\$). They share a unified L2 cache. Those caches keep data close to the CPU cores to hide the latency to main-memory (which is accessed through the pair of DDR memory controllers on each CPU). The speed differences between memory and the cores is so great, however, that we often find another level of cache. This is the L3 cache broken down into blocks and spread out around the chip. And that's not all. There are cache coherency protocols that run between the pair of CPUs (in the CPU in Figure 1.1 this is through the QPI ports, a bus that connects the two sockets), so our windows into memory are consistent between the two CPUs. These two CPUs and all their cores share a common view of memory. Ideally this view is the same from any one core to any location in memory. This arrangement is

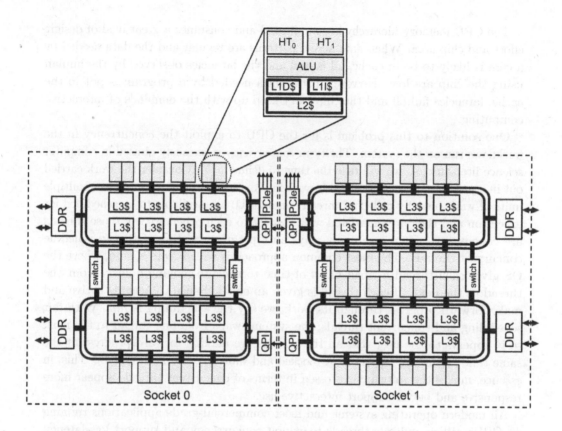

Figure 1.1: **A block diagram of a typical server** – Each server consists of two sockets with each socket holding a CPU. Each CPU has 16 cores, the details of which are shown for one core. Source: [2].

often called a Symmetric Multiprocessor (SMP). Note, however, that SMP is an idealization and the fact of the matter is that due to multiple memory controllers (DDR) and the cache hierarchy, the cost function for a memory-access is anything but uniform. Therefore, the system in Figure 1.1 is more accurately understood as a non-uniform memory architecture (NUMA).[1]

---

[1]We won't explore NUMA issues in this book, as it is discussed at length in the context of OpenMP in *Using OpenMP — The Next Step* and *The OpenMP Common Core*, both published by the MIT Press.

The CPU memory hierarchy is complicated and consumes a great deal of design-effort and chip area. When data access patterns are regular and the data needed by a core is likely to be in cache, all is well and the latencies observed by the human using the chip are low. However, if the data needed by a program is not in the cache, latencies fall off and the chip can't keep up with the demands of interactive computing.

One solution to this problem is for the CPU to exploit the concurrency in the workflows run on the system. The term *concurrency* is seriously abused in computer science literature, so we will take the time to define it [5]. Consider the work carried out in a program. We can break this work into distinct units of work. When multiple units of work (usually called a "thread" on a CPU) are available to be scheduled for execution and they are unordered with respect to each other, we say those threads are concurrent. There are many ways an Operating System (OS) can schedule concurrent threads. The most common approach is called *time-slicing*, where the OS gives each thread a small block of time to execute moving quickly from one thread to the next. If each thread is given an equal chance to become active and make forward progress through its work, we say the scheduling is *fair*. With fair scheduling and concurrent threads, the system swaps from one thread to the next, so it appears to the user that all the threads are making forward progress at the same time (assuming they are not blocked and waiting on some resource). This, in essence, makes the software expressed in terms of concurrent threads appear more responsive and better support interactive use.

All modern operating systems and most commercial-grade applications running on CPUs utilize multiple threads to exploit concurrency and support low-latency, interactive computing. When there are large numbers of threads to schedule across a CPU, we can increase the speed at which the threads complete their work by adding multiple cores, thereby supplying the threads with more physical hardware resources. When a workflow has concurrency (to support multiple threads) and we exploit that concurrency by running on multiple cores, we say that that workflow is running *in parallel*.

Concurrency and parallelism are closely related but different. Concurrency deals with unordered units-of-work available for execution on a system. Parallelism takes those units-of-work and runs them at the same time. Concurrency is used even on one core to support responsive computing, so work can proceed from one unit-of-work while another is blocked waiting on some resource (such as memory). Parallelism is only at play when multiple units-of-work are *actually* making progress at the same

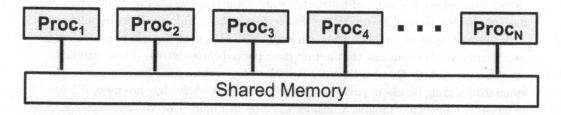

Figure 1.2: **A simple representation of a symmetric multiprocessor system**
– Most OpenMP programming views a CPU in this simplified way with the processors
($Proc_1$ to $Proc_N$) as the cores of the CPU. Source: [2].

time. We will have much more to say about concurrency later when we talk about
synchronization between units-of-work on a GPU.

We now have a good understanding of the CPU and how the components that
make up a CPU are organized. If programmers had to think in terms of systems
as complex as that shown in Figure 1.1, very few multithreaded programs would
be written. Fortunately, a programmer can often write code thinking in terms of
a much simpler model, leaving the complex details for later when optimizing a
working program. The simple model used with OpenMP is that of a SMP as shown
in Figure 1.2. This is a vast oversimplification, and it won't work when reasoning
about optimizations for the NUMA features of a chip. For writing initial code, and
frankly, for most programmers writing all their OpenMP code, this is the level of
hardware abstraction used. The fact this simplified architectural model works as
well as it does is one of the reasons the CPU with OpenMP has been so successful
for multithreading.

1.1.2 The SIMD Vector Unit

We use the term *high performance computing* for applications where performance is
a feature of the application. The goal is to complete a fixed body of work in less
time or, conversely, to complete more work in a fixed unit of time. In both cases, a
key ingredient is to increase the rate at which operations complete.

A CPU does this with multithreading; that is, concurrent threads running in
parallel across a collection of cores. Another approach is to use parallelism that is

in the data, where a stream of instructions are applied in parallel to a collection of data elements. We call this SIMD or *Single Instruction Multiple Data* parallelism.

A common type of problem that can exploit SIMD parallelism is one expressed as a sequence of operations that act on data packed into vectors. These problems are common enough that SIMD units optimized for vectors have become one of the standard building blocks of parallel architectures. To see how they are used, it helps to consider a specific example. Consider the loop in Figure 1.3. We add vector A to vector B to produce the result in vector C.

```
1   #define N 4000
2
3   int main()
4   {
5
6       double A[N], B[N], C[N];
7
8       init(A,B,C); // initialize arrays ... code not shown
9
10      for (int i = 0; i < N; i++) {
11          C[i] = A[i] + B[i];
12      }
13  }
```

Figure 1.3: **Vector Add program** – This program will add two vectors of length N to produce a third vector.

A computational element called a *vector unit* will use SIMD parallelism to execute blocks of instructions between elements of these three arrays. Let's consider a case where our vector unit is 256 bits wide, so we can process four 64-bit floating point operations in each instruction of the vector unit. We will convert our vector addition program into a vectorized program in two distinct phases. First, we transform the code so the loop matches the one you'll need for the vectorized code. That means we need to modify the loop so the loop body carries out four additions of the vector elements per loop iteration. We do this by *unrolling the loop*. We show our loop unrolled by four in Figure 1.4.

In the second phase of our vectorization process, we replace the operations in the body of the unrolled loop over scalar values with vector instructions. We will use the well-known Advanced Vector Extensions (AVX) introduced in 2008. The

```
1   #include <assert.h>
2   #define N 4000
3
4   int main()
5   {
6       double A[N], B[N], C[N];
7
8       init(A,B,C); // initialize arrays ... code not shown
9
10      assert(N%4==0);
11
12      for (int i = 0; i < N; i=i+4) {
13          C[i]   = A[i]   + B[i];
14          C[i+1] = A[i+1] + B[i+1];
15          C[i+2] = A[i+2] + B[i+2];
16          C[i+3] = A[i+3] + B[i+3];
17      }
18  }
```

Figure 1.4: **Vector Add program unrolled** – We unroll our vector addition loop by four, meaning the loop body acts on four elements of the data (four 64-bit numbers for a 256 bit wide vector unit). For simplicity, we require that N can be evenly divided by four.

resulting vector code is shown in Figure 1.5. In this code, we use the following AVX intrinsics:

- __m256d: the type for the 256-bit vector registers to hold (in our case) four 64-bit floating point numbers.

- _mm256_loadu_pd(): loads four doubles (*pd* or "packed double") from an address that may not be aligned on a 32-byte boundary (the "u" in "loadu").

- _mm256_storeu_pd(): stores four doubles to an address that may not be aligned on a 32-byte boundary.

- _mm256_add_pd(): adds two vector registers holding double precision floating point numbers to return their sum in another vector register.

We would compile this code with the GNU compilers as *gcc -mavx*. The above operations assume the data is unaligned. For best efficiency, the arrays A, B, C should be aligned to a 32-byte boundary, enabling the use of other (not shown) AVX instructions that assume alignment. We can do the former by allocating the memory for these arrays using the following statement:

```
double *A = (double *)aligned_alloc(32,N*sizeof(double));
```

When the workflow in a program maps onto a vector unit, the performance benefits
can be substantial.

```
1   #include <assert.h>
2   #include <immintrin.h>
3   #define N 4000
4
5   int main()
6   {
7       double A[N], B[N], C[N];
8       // 256 bit vector registers to be packed with double precision numbers
9       __m256d Avec, Bvec, Cvec;
10
11      init(A,B,C); // initialize arrays ... code not shown
12
13      assert(N%4==0);
14
15      for (int i=0; i < N; i=i+4){
16
17          Avec = _mm256_loadu_pd(&A[i]);
18          Bvec = _mm256_loadu_pd(&B[i]);
19          Cvec = _mm256_add_pd(Avec,Bvec);
20          _mm256_storeu_pd(&C[i],Cvec);
21      }
22  }
```

Figure 1.5: **Vector Add program with vector intrinsics** – We use vector intrinsics
to compute four additions in parallel across the lanes of our SIMD vector unit.

Most programmers, however, do not write vector code directly. The compiler
unrolls the loop, organizes the instructions for SIMD execution, and replaces them
with specialized vector instructions. In an ideal world, that would be good enough.
Indeed, for a simple case such as vector addition, the compiler does quite well. In
practice, however, codes do not so directly map onto vector instructions and the
exploitation of the vector units are often quite poor. To help the compiler with the
transformations needed to support vectorization (such as loop unrolling) OpenMP
added a SIMD construct and a collection of clauses.[2]

---

[2]SIMD in the context of OpenMP is discussed at length in *Using OpenMP — the Next Step*
and *The OpenMP Common Core*, both published by the MIT Press.

Vector units for SIMD parallelism are rapidly evolving. The widths of the vector units are commonly 256 bits on lower-end CPUs and have climbed to 512 or even 1024 for CPUs used in high-end servers. There is no reason the concept must be restricted to one-dimensional vectors. SIMD units for two-dimensional arrays have appeared on the market optimized for the matrix-multiply operations common inside deep learning pipelines.

Vector instructions operate on vector registers to operate on multiple data elements in parallel. There is a second (and equivalent) way to think about vector instructions. It's a perspective where you transpose your view and think in terms of scalar operations happening on lanes of the vector unit, or the *SIMD lanes*. For example, the sequence over packed doubles with 256-bit vector instructions:

```
Cvec = _mm256_add_pd(Avec,Bvec);
Dvec = _mm256_add_pd(Avec,Cvec);
Fvec = _mm256_add_pd(Bvec,Dvec);
```

can be considered as four SIMD lanes:

```
SIMD-Lane0: C[0] = A[0] + B[0]; D[0] = A[0]+C[0]; F[0] = B[0] + D[0];
SIMD-Lane1: C[1] = A[1] + B[1]; D[1] = A[1]+C[1]; F[1] = B[1] + D[1];
SIMD-Lane2: C[2] = A[2] + B[2]; D[2] = A[2]+C[2]; F[2] = B[2] + D[2];
SIMD-Lane3: C[3] = A[3] + B[3]; D[3] = A[3]+C[3]; F[3] = B[3] + D[3];
```

As far as the hardware in concerned, the computation is the same in both cases. Thinking in terms of SIMD lanes, however, is a useful abstraction for programmers trying to understand their vector code, especially for more complex streams of instructions. In essence, the vector lanes act like scalar processing elements of the vector unit that run in parallel. Execution occurs in lock-step through the stream of instructions, so all elements of the vector are processed together.

1.1.3 The GPU

The CPU is optimized for latency. It does this with help from a complex memory hierarchy integrated with the cores inside the processor. Another option is to optimize a processor for throughput. Consider processing a stream of images in a computer-generated video. The problem defines a certain frame-rate for image updates so the video appears smooth to the human observer. The time to display any given pixel in an image is immaterial. What matters is the time to update the entire image so the frame-rate of the video can be supported. This is the classic throughput computing problem.

Graphics Processing Units (GPUs) have been an important component within personal computers since the late 1990s. They consisted of large numbers of simple processing elements specialized to graphics operations. Complex memory hierarchies were not needed since, if the update of a pixel is stalled waiting for data, the processor could shift to other pixels while waiting for updates from memory. This meant most of the "real estate" on the chip was dedicated to computing rather than caches, leading to high compute densities.

The first papers about using graphics processing hardware for general computing appeared in the mid 1990s; right around the same time GPUs were appearing on the market. The term GPGPU for general purpose GPU programming appeared in the early 2000s, but the field of GPGPU programming really took off with the introduction of CUDA™ [6] in 2006 (for NVIDIA® GPUs only) and the open standard for programming GPUs, OpenCL™ [7], in 2008. These programming languages were designed in close collaboration with GPU architects who created fully programmable graphics pipelines.

The idea behind a GPU builds on the SIMD concept. A stream of instructions is broadcast to a set of processing elements that execute as lanes in a large SIMD unit. The mental model is that an *index space* is formed, analogous to that defined by the N-dimensional range (NDRange) of a vectorizable loop, and a function corresponding to the loop body (a *kernel*) executes as a distinct *work-item* at each point in the index space. The programmer writes serial code for the kernel, and the parallelism emerges from the fact that the kernel executes in parallel at each point in the index space.

The analogy to the SIMD vector parallelism continues when you consider how the index space is managed. The index space is broken into groups that execute together. These work-items inside a work-group are active at the same time and hence can interact. Individual work-groups, however, are streamed through the GPU concurrently (to hide latency to memory) and therefore cannot directly interact. These work-groups are fundamental to understanding a GPU. They are made up of one or more blocks of work-items that physically execute across a set of processing elements just as the lanes of a SIMD vector unit execute together. This width is the GPU's natural block size for execution. It is in essence the *SIMD width* or *subgroup* size or *warp* of the GPU. For high-performance code, you want the work-items in a sub-group to execute "as if" in lock-step (a *converged* execution flow).

A modern GPU optimized for throughput provides high compute densities. We show a block diagram for a typical (and somewhat idealized) GPU in Figure 1.6. The GPU is divided into a number of compute units that are driven by a stream of SIMD instructions. It acts much like a multiprocessor optimized for streaming SIMD instructions (hence why in CUDA™ this is called a *streaming multiprocessor*). Each compute unit contains a block of SIMD lanes driven by a single stream of instructions from a *SIMD Thread Scheduler*. The sub-groups are dispatched to run a number of work-items together corresponding to the width of the device (16 in this case). The SIMD lanes execute on their own set of registers (private memory) that resides in the register file. They share, however, memory local to the full work-group that resides in the L1 cache for compute unit.

The GPU contains multiple compute units (16 in this case) that together share memory global to all of the SIMD lanes (or processing elements). As shown in Figure 1.6, the arrangement of compute units is not flat with respect to memory. They are hierarchical, and therefore optimizing code for a GPU requires many of the techniques familiar to programmers working with OpenMP for a NUMA system.

A modern GPU is even more complicated than what we show in Figure 1.6. In addition to the replicated SIMD lanes, a compute unit often has load/store units, special function units, and other specialized processing elements. The presence of these additional hardware elements, however, does not change the basic programming model as they are just local accelerators for instructions within a work-item, hence including them at this point in the discussion is not helpful.

In this discussion, we've shifted between different terms for many aspects of GPGPU programming. This is a fundamental frustration of GPU programming. GPUs for GPGPU programming are young compared to CPUs. While the terms used with CPUs are well established, the terminology of GPUs varies widely between different GPU vendors and programming languages. To help pull the concepts together, we review the terminology from three different sources in Table 1.1: Hennessy and Patterson [4], NVIDIA®'s CUDA™ [6], and OpenCL™ [7] from the Khronos® Group. By pulling these terms together in one place, we hope that readers from different foundations in GPGPU programming will be able to follow our discussion. In this book, we tend to use the OpenCL™ terminology since it was cross-vendor from the beginning, though when discussing specific features of GPU architecture the terminology from Hennessy and Patterson [4] is sometimes preferred.

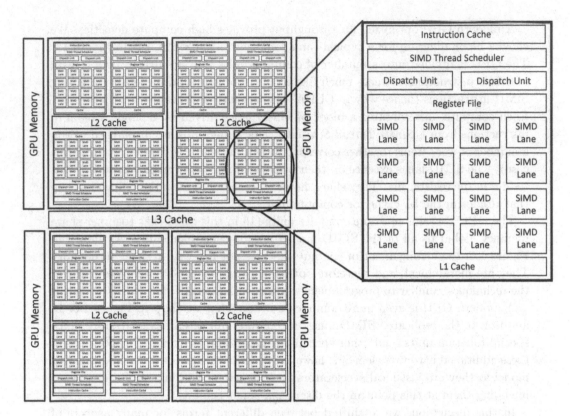

Figure 1.6: **A simplified block diagram of a typical GPU** – The computing within the GPU happens in the SIMD lanes of a multithreaded SIMD processor, which in addition to the SIMD lanes often includes load/store and special function units (not shown in this figure). The multithreaded SIMD processors are organized hierarchically around caches and on-device GPU memory.

Few programmers would undertake the task of GPGPU programming if the full complexity shown in Figure 1.6 needed to be fully embraced when writing code. Much of what a programmer does can be done using a much simpler model. Consider the abstraction of a GPU shown in Figure 1.7. While a GPU has multiple levels of hierarchy, a programmer typically thinks in terms of a basic host-device architecture with a three-level hierarchy on the device. A host (generally a CPU) offloads kernels onto a device for execution. Data moves between the device memory and the host

Table 1.1: **GPU Terminology** – GPU Terminology from Hennessy and Patterson, CUDA™, and OpenCL™. The one uncertain match is the last row; a sub-group usually corresponds to a warp, but a conforming implementation of OpenCL™ may use a sub-group to refer to smaller blocks of work-items that make up a warp.

Hennessy and Patterson	CUDA	OpenCL
Multithreaded SIMD Processor	Streaming multiprocessor	Compute Unit
SIMD Thread Scheduler	Warp Scheduler	Work-group scheduler
SIMD Lane	CUDA Core	Processing Element
GPU Memory	Global Memory	Global Memory
Private Memory	Local Memory	Private Memory
Local Memory	Shared Memory	Local Memory
Vectorizable Loop	Grid	NDRange
Sequence of SIMD Lane operations	CUDA Thread	work-item
A thread of SIMD instructions	Warp	sub-group

memory. Once on a device, instances of kernels (a work-item) run at each point in an index space (NDRange). Work-groups run on compute units (CUs). Work-items run on Processing Elements (PEs) or, in some cases, down an additional layer in the hierarchy to the lanes of a SIMD unit inside a PE.

The device memory is shared and available to all processing elements in the GPUs hierarchical structure. Each Compute Unit might in addition provide a layer of memory available only to those Processing Elements contained within it. This we will call (as in OpenCL™) the local memory. The Processing Elements in each Compute Unit can access this memory, however it is not accessible by Processing Elements outside the Compute Unit. We will address using this local memory in OpenMP in Section 7.4.

This book will show how to program a GPU device using OpenMP. In later chapters, we include case studies to show the abstract device model and the concepts in OpenMP come together and are applied to real hardware.

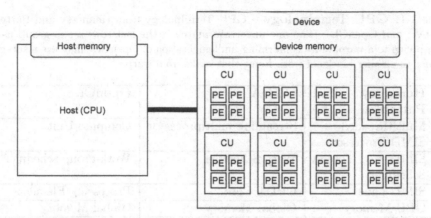

Figure 1.7: **A typical GPU platform** – A target device is always connected to a host, which behaves like a CPU. The device is composed of a number of Compute Units (CU). Each CU contains a number of Processing Elements (PEs). A PE may execute as SIMD lanes or, in some cases, may provide an additional level of hierarchical parallelism by executing vector (SIMD) instructions.

1.2 OpenMP: A Single Code-Base for Heterogeneous Hardware

Heterogeneous systems are typically composed from these three components, CPU, SIMD vector units, and GPUs. A programming language such as CUDA™ is designed to move computation from the CPU and onto the GPU. This is the idea of "offloading" work from the CPU. The problem is that the CPU is a powerful processor and to leave it idle while all the work happens on the GPU is a waste.

The goal, ideally, should be heterogeneous programming where a problem is decomposed into parts that run on a GPU, parts that run on the CPU, and parts that run well on the SIMD vector units. By mapping each portion of a problem onto the hardware best suited to it, you end up with a situation where "the whole is greater than the sum of the parts."

To best support heterogeneous programming, you need a programming language that supports the major types of heterogeneous processors from a single program. This is what OpenMP does. It of course supports multithreading for a CPU since that is the hardware context within which OpenMP was born with version 1.0 in 1997. Direct programming of SIMD vector units was added in OpenMP 4.0 in 2013. GPU programming was added in OpenMP 4.0 as well, with important enhancements added in OpenMP 4.5 in 2015 and OpenMP 5.0 in 2018. The standard continues to develop; this book is written to accompany OpenMP 5.2, the latest version of the standard released in 2021.

Not only does OpenMP address the key components of a heterogeneous system, it is also a cross-vendor solution widely supported across most commonly used compilers in high performance computing. This is important since software lasts much longer than hardware. Software should always be written so the code-base can move with minimal effort from one vendor's platform to another; or for a single vendor from one generation of hardware to another.

OpenMP is one of the only mature APIs for heterogeneous computing with true cross-vendor support. Learning it is a foundational skill required by professionals working on applications where performance is a key feature.

1.3   The Structure of This Book

In the following chapters, we will introduce the necessary concepts for programming heterogeneous systems using OpenMP. We start in Chapter 2 with an introduction to the core ideas behind OpenMP. Experienced OpenMP programmers should just skim that chapter. We provide it as a reminder for people who haven't written much OpenMP code and also to establish the jargon of OpenMP that the rest of the book depends on. We close Chapter 2 with a taste of what you can do when programming your GPU using OpenMP. In the multicore world, people think of OpenMP as finding key loops and putting a parallel loop directive before that loop, so we close the chapter with the analog to `parallel for`; a pair of directives that map a loop nest onto a GPU, which for many people will accomplish most of what they need when programming a GPU from OpenMP.

After our introductory chapters, we dive into the meat of heterogeneity with OpenMP. In Part II we introduce a "common core" for heterogeneous programming with OpenMP. This will walk through the most commonly used parts of OpenMP for programming devices such as GPUs. We cover everything you need to get started: executing on the device and managing the transfer of data between the host and device. This part alone will be sufficient in the majority of cases for learning what is required to program GPUs and other devices with OpenMP. The GPU Common Core of OpenMP showcases that writing OpenMP programs for the GPU does not have to be complicated. You can use just a few directives and clauses to get our programs running on the GPU, and in many cases this is all we'll ever need.

In Part III we introduce extra topics and additional features that you might need when writing more complicated programs. We cover programming multiple GPUs, interoperating with other parallel programming models, take a deeper dive into sharing memory between the devices and look at systems where memory can simply be shared between the host and device automatically. We close the book with a look to the future, and offer advice for continuing your journey into programming GPUs with OpenMP.

The Glossary at the end of the book is an enhanced version of the author's in [2] containing additional entries for the new concepts introduced in this book.

1.4   Supplementary Materials

This book is supported by online materials at www.ompgpu.com. The website will host an online repository containing the source code for the example programs in this book. In addition, the website includes a Fortran supplement that closely tracks the structure of the book showing Fortran versions of all code samples and figures.

2 OpenMP Overview

OpenMP is old. The first release (OpenMP 1.0 for Fortran) was in 1997. It started as the simplest way we could think of for applications programmers in high performance computing to write multithreaded code. The focus was on parallelizing loops and the full OpenMP definition took only 40 pages.

At the time we are writing this book, OpenMP is at release 5.2. The specification covers Fortran, C and C++. It includes multiple ways to parallelize loops, create explicit tasks, vectorize loops, manage complex memory hierarchies, and much more (including programming GPUs, of course).

With OpenMP 1.0, the entire language could be covered in a single day of study. Now, it takes months if not years to master the entire specification. New versions of the specification come out roughly every two years. Hence, once the language is mastered, something new comes along to expand its scope even further.

The situation with OpenMP would be unbearably frustrating, if not for one simple fact. Nobody uses the entire language. OpenMP programmers learn the foundational terminology of OpenMP and a simplified common core of the language [2]. Most of the time, that common core is all a programmer needs. When additional features of OpenMP are needed, programmers look them up in the specification. By learning and then using just those parts of OpenMP needed to solve a programming problem, the complexity of OpenMP is manageable and the inner simplicity that motivated us at the beginning shines through. The same is true for programming GPUs with OpenMP. The common core of GPU programming is the topic of Part II.

In this chapter, we will cover those core elements of OpenMP that all programmers use. We will be brief and present them through the three fundamental design patterns of multithreaded programming with OpenMP: *loop-level parallelism*, *SPMD*, and *divide-and-conquer* [8]. Then we will go back through the core elements of OpenMP and explain how they are organized around the behavior of both implied and explicit tasks. This is essential since we can't explain GPU programming in OpenMP without the low-level details of tasks. We then close the chapter with an overview of our journey into GPU programming with OpenMP.

2.1 Threads: Basic Concepts

OpenMP is fundamentally tied to the idea of *concurrent* threads that run in parallel on multiple processing elements so a program completes its work in less time. To understand how OpenMP works, we need to take a closer look at threads.

When you run a program, the program-instance is managed by the operating system as a *process*. A process contains program text, data, input/output resources, a memory space, and more. Basically everything needed to support a specific instance of a running program is included in the process. The memory space for a process is a set of addresses in memory that hold the values associated with the variables used within a program. We can think of this memory in terms of two data structures: a *heap* and a *stack*.

The heap is a hierarchical data structure for holding dynamic data. If data is allocated with a `malloc()` in C or a `new` statement in C++, then it is dynamically allocated data that is managed within the heap. There is one heap in the process's memory space, and it exists throughout the life of the program.

A stack is a linear data structure of fixed size. Any time a function is called, the parameters and variables associated with that function go on a stack. The duration of the stack is the lifetime of the function. When the function is complete and exits, the memory associated with its stack is reclaimed, and any variables on that function's stack go out of scope and no longer exist.

We talk about the stack and the heap when we explain OpenMP since the visibility of data in an OpenMP program is defined by whether it is on the stack or on the heap. We'll return to this topic later, but first, we need to consider threads. A thread executes code from the program text associated with a process. When a process begins, it starts a single thread (the *initial thread*). In C programs, this thread runs the function named `main()`. As the program executes, additional threads may be created, or *forked*, to run a specified function from the program text. When forked threads complete their work, they exit their function and resources associated with the threads are reclaimed; in essence, the thread *joins* the thread that created it (its parent thread).

This pattern of forking a team of threads to carry out a block of work and then, when done, join back together is called the *fork-join pattern*. We provide a visual representation of the fork-join pattern in Figure 2.1. This pattern is at the core of OpenMP. A program starts as a single thread (the *initial thread*). When work that can effectively run in parallel is encountered, a *team of threads* is forked. Notice that the thread that does the fork is part of the team. It is the *primary* thread of the team (with ID=0). When the parallel work completes, the threads join together, and *after all the threads join*, one thread (the parent thread that created the team) continues. This continues throughout the program execution, so we can view it as a

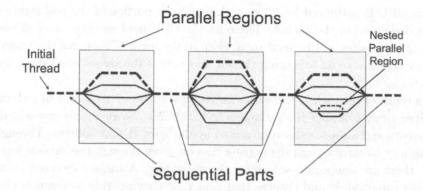

Figure 2.1: **The fork-join model** – A program starts as a single thread, the *initial thread*. It creates (or *forks*) a team of threads, each of which executes a block of code. When done, the threads *join* (i.e., they are no longer available, *as if* they were destroyed) and the single, initial thread continues. Source: [2].

sequence of parallel regions run by a team of threads connected by sequential parts that run on the original initial thread.

Now that we understand the execution of threads, let's go back to the memory space associated with a process. A thread is forked and executes a specified function. The memory associated with this function (and hence the thread) is on the stack and only visible to the thread that "owns" the stack (i.e., the variables are *private*).

A thread can, of course, work with variables that reside within its own stack, but what about the heap? The heap belongs to a process. The team of threads belongs to the process. They share the resources associated with that process, including the heap and any variables that reside in the heap. This leads to one of the fundamental rules of multithreaded programming: variables that reside in the heap are visible to all threads (i.e., they are *shared*) while variables within the stack for a thread are only visible to that thread (i.e., they are *private*).

When working with private variables alone, there really are not any new concepts for the OpenMP programmer to keep in mind. The sequence of instructions defines the order of updates to the variables, and the program order is apparent in the values the single thread sees in the variables. When shared variables are involved, however, the complications of concurrent threads can make reasoning about the state of the executing program complicated. As we discussed in Section 1.1.1, a

modern CPU is optimized for latency. A significant portion of the real estate on a
chip is dedicated to the caches. These let the CPU hold recently used values, or
values it anticipates will be used soon, close to the cores. This hides the latency of
memory accesses to an executing thread, but only if the values needed are in the
cache.

As a result of the caches, there may be multiple copies of a variable in memory at
any given time. Consider the variable γ in Figure 2.2. There is only one address in
the memory and a single value represented by the bytes at that address. Throughout
the memory hierarchy, from the register files on down through the various levels of
cache, there are temporary values for the variable γ. A cache coherence protocol
manages these values and ensures that over time they provide a common view of
memory. At any given moment, however, the values for γ may be inconsistent. In
other words, the value sitting in a register may be different from the value in the
various levels of cache, which may be different from the value in DRAM. The topic
of *memory consistency* addresses these values and how they vary with respect to
each other at a fixed point in time. When they are allowed to differ at any given
point in time, we say that the system has a *relaxed memory consistency model*.

Every practical system for multithreading, including OpenMP, assumes a relaxed
memory consistency model. When working with variables that are shared, it is
possible to write programs that return different results depending on the details
of how the threads are scheduled by the operating system. When this occurs, we
say that the program has a *race condition*. A race condition typically occurs when
threads make unordered updates to shared variables. The result is the threads race
to see which one gets to store the value that the others will see. This is called a *data
race*. When a program has a data race, the system has no way to unambiguously
define the results of a program. Hence, any program that contains a data race is
invalid. The compiler is specifically given the freedom to assume there are no data
races and that the programmer has ordered mixtures of loads and stores to shared
variables so the result is well defined. We will discuss this later in the context of
OpenMP when we discuss synchronization.

That completes our general introduction to multithreading. Any programming
model for multithreading, with few if any exceptions, share these ideas. Now we
turn our attention specifically to OpenMP.

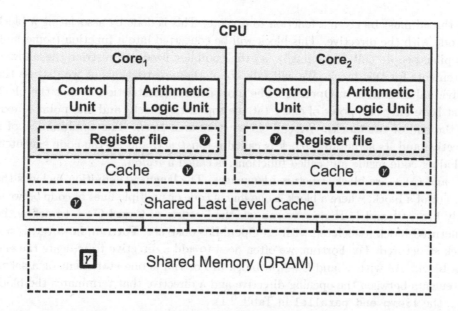

Figure 2.2: **Values of a variable across a memory hierarchy** – A simplified
view of a dual-core CPU. Elements of the memory hierarchy are shown as dashed boxes.
A variable γ represents a specific address in DRAM (shown inside a square box). At any
given time, the value associated with this address may exist at each level in the memory
as shown by the variable name in a black circle. Source: [2].

2.2   OpenMP: Basic Syntax

The design of OpenMP was driven by a foundational goal; that a programming
model should let you incrementally convert a sequential program step-by-step into a
parallel program. The parallelism in OpenMP is explicit. The programmer tells the
system what to do in order to define a parallel execution. The work of generating
the parallel code, however, is done in partnership with the compiler. Programmers
insert compiler directives into their code, and the compiler uses them to create the
parallel program. In C or C++, a compiler directive is expressed as #pragma. In
Fortran, the directive is indicated by a comment that contains a specific OpenMP
token. These forms for a directive are shown in Table 2.1.

In many cases, the directive is associated with a block of code. For example, if the
directive indicates that a team of threads should be created (the **parallel** directive),

the thread must be given a function to execute. This is done by associating a block of code with the directive. This block will be converted into a function (something compiler people call "outlining"), so the compiler needs to restrict the allowed statements for this block. We will talk about these restrictions as we discuss the individual directives in OpenMP. The most common restriction is that the block must have only one point of entry (at the top of the block) and one point of exit (at the end of the block). We call this a *structured block*. The combination of a directive and its structured block is called a *construct*, and all the code executed, including code inside any called functions, is called a *region*.

C and C++ are block structured languages. The language definition includes the concept of a block, where a block is one line of code or multiple lines of code between curly braces { and }. Hence, we can use the features of C and C++ to define the structured block associated with an OpenMP construct. Fortran, however, is not block structured. For Fortran, we often need to add a directive to indicate the end of a block. As with C and C++, a block in Fortran is one statement or a set of statements between the opening directive and a directive that terminates the block (e.g., the `!$omp end parallel` in Table 2.1).

As indicated in Table 2.1, directives can be modified by one or more clauses. The example in the table stipulates that each thread in the team created by the construct will have a private variable with the name x. This is an example of a clause that modifies the data environment seen by a thread. OpenMP includes a wide range of clauses which we will describe later as we go through the key constructs of OpenMP.

A directive fundamentally acts on the compiler to change how the program text is turned into a multithreaded program. There are issues in multithreaded programming that can only be resolved at runtime. For these, we have a library of runtime library functions and a small number of environment variables.

We'll start with the runtime library. The function prototypes from the runtime library are provided in the OpenMP include file:

```
#include <omp.h>
```

The runtime library routines have names that begin with the four characters `omp_`. As an example, we'll consider a pair of functions that interact with the system to manipulate the number of threads used in an OpenMP program. The default number of threads to create when a team of threads is forked is held internally in an opaque variable, where the term "opaque" means that a user cannot see the value of a variable or the data structure used to hold it. We call such values an

Table 2.1: **General form of directives in C/C++ and Fortran** – The combination of a directive and a structured block is called a *construct*. We provide an example of a `parallel` construct with a clause to create a private variable, `x`, for each thread in the team. Source: [2]

C/C++ directive format and an example with a structured block
`#pragma omp parallel` *[clause[[,] clause]...]*

`#pragma omp parallel` `private(x)`
`{`
`...    code executed by each thread`
`}`

Fortran directive format and an example with a structured block
`!$omp parallel` *[clause[[,] clause]...]*

`!$omp parallel` `private(x)`
`...    code executed by each thread`
`!$omp end parallel`

Internal Control Variable or ICV. Unless a programmer directs otherwise, any time a program creates a new team of threads, it will read the ICV for the default number of threads. We can set the value of this ICV with the function:

```
omp_set_num_threads(int numThreads);
```

If later, inside a parallel region, we want to know how many threads are actually in a team, we use the function:

```
int omp_get_num_threads();
```

We can use these functions to directly manipulate the number of threads, but that means the program logic, not the user, controls this important ICV. Since you usually want users of an application to control the number of threads, in practice it is far more common to *not* set the default number of threads inside a program. Instead, this value is set by the environment variable:

```
OMP_NUM_THREADS
```

There are a number of other environment variables in OpenMP, though the variable to set the default number of threads is by far the most commonly used. We will define others later.

We have presented numerous concepts without an example to help you absorb the material. We provide a simple OpenMP program with a single parallel region in Figure 2.3 and show how we would compile and run the program on a typical Linux system. The second line of the program is the OpenMP include file. Every compilation unit that contains OpenMP directives, types, or calls to functions from the OpenMP runtime library should have this include statement. In this program, we want to create a team of threads and have them print the pair of strings `"hello"` and `"world"`. We create the team of threads with `#pragma omp parallel`. Since we do not specify the size of the team of threads in the code, the program will use the default number of threads (from the associated ICV). Each thread in the team will execute the code between the curly braces. We want to distinguish between the threads, so we have each thread find its thread number with a call to `omp_get_thread_num()`. This thread number is a rank that ranges from zero to the number of threads minus one. Note that since we declare the variable `id` inside the parallel region, this variable is on the thread's stack and hence is private to each thread. The threads then print each of the pair of strings along with the value of the thread's `id`.

We compile the code using the `gcc` compiler with the `-fopenmp` compiler flag on line 14. This flag tells the compiler to interpret the OpenMP directives and to link any libraries needed to support OpenMP. The default number of threads is typically set to the number of cores as seen by the operating system (which may be different from the number of physical cores on the CPU). In this case, however, we set the default number of threads to 4 using the `OMP_NUM_THREADS` environment variable on line 15.

We run the program (`a.out`) twice: first on line 16 and then again on line 21. There are two extremely important concepts to note from the output from this program. Consider the first execution on lines 16–20. The threads do not execute their statements in a fixed order with respect to each other. Threads execute concurrently which means they are unordered with respect to each other outside of specific synchronization operations. The execution observed from a multithreaded program is "as if" any allowed way to interleave operations may occur. This is a fundamental challenge of multithreaded programming. In writing code, you need to make sure your program logic is such that the code is correct regardless of

```
1   $ cat hello.c
2   #include <stdio.h>
3   #include <omp.h>
4   int main()
5   {
6     #pragma omp parallel
7     {
8        int id = omp_get_thread_num();
9        printf("hello %d ",id);
10       printf("world %d\n",id);
11    }
12  }
13
14  $ gcc -fopenmp hello.c
15  $ export OMP_NUM_THREADS=4
16  $ ./a.out
17  hello 2 hello 3 hello 0 world 0
18  world 3
19  world 2
20  hello 1 world 1
21  $ ./a.out
22  hello 1 world 1
23  hello 0 world 0
24  hello 2 world 2
25  hello 3 world 3
```

Figure 2.3: **Hello World in parallel** – This is a simple program where each thread prints `"hello"` and then `"world"`. We compile the program, set the default number of threads with an environment variable, and then run the program twice. Note the symbol `$` is the UNIX command prompt.

how the instructions are interleaved. This is simple for a program that just prints `"hello world"` but for complex programs where the logic is spread out across many functions, this can be very difficult.

We run the program a second time on line 21. Notice that the output is completely different. This is an example of a race condition. The program does not have a data race and is therefore still a valid OpenMP program. The output, however, is dependent on how the threads are scheduled for execution by the operating system.

You now understand the syntax of OpenMP. We will now explore how the language is used to solve key problems in parallel computing by considering the fundamental design patterns used by OpenMP programmers.

2.3   The Fundamental Design Patterns of OpenMP

OpenMP is a general purpose programming language for writing multithreaded programs. With few exceptions, if you can think of an algorithm based on threads, you can express it with OpenMP. Even with this diversity of algorithmic options, however, most OpenMP programs use one of three basic patterns:

1. Single Program Multiple Data (SPMD)

2. Loop-level parallelism

3. Divide and conquer

In covering these three patterns, we will address the most commonly used items from OpenMP – that is, the common core of OpenMP. To explain these patterns we will take a single problem and express it in each of the patterns. Our problem is to estimate a definite integral by summing up the area of rectangles under a curve. We show the problem visually and mathematically in Figure 2.4: the "π program."

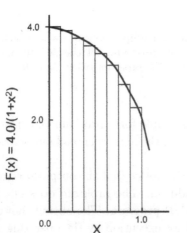

Mathematically, we know that:

$$\int_0^1 \frac{4.0}{(1+x^2)} \, dx = \pi$$

We can approximate the integral as a sum of rectangles:

$$\sum_{i=0}^{N} F(x_i)\Delta x \approx \pi$$

Where each rectangle has width Δx and height $F(x_i)$ at the middle of interval i.

Figure 2.4: **Numerical integration** – An integral can be approximated by filling in the area under a curve with rectangles and summing their areas. We choose the integrand $F(x_i)$, and the limits of integration, so the result should approximate π. Source: [2].

The C program for this problem, a program we call the "π program," is shown in Figure 2.5. We set the number of rectangles to use in our estimate of the area under the curve as a file scope variable `num_steps`. We want a large number of steps to ensure there is plenty of work to distribute between the threads. We compute the step size and then enter the loop where we accumulate the contribution to the area from each rectangle. Notice that the width of each rectangle is fixed and equal to `step`. Hence, we can pull it out of the loop and multiply `sum` by `step` just once to get π.

```
1
2    #include <stdio.h>
3    #include <omp.h>
4    static long num_steps = 1024*1024*1024;
5
6    int main()
7    {
8        double x, pi, step, sum = 0.0;
9        step = 1.0 / (double) num_steps;
10
11       for (int i = 0; i < num_steps; i++) {
12           x = (i + 0.5) * step;
13           sum += 4.0 / (1.0 + x * x);
14       }
15
16       pi = step * sum;
17       printf("pi = %lf, with %ld steps\n ", pi, num_steps);
18   }
```

Figure 2.5: **Sequential π program** – This program carries out a numerical integration of a definite integral selected such that the result should be the number π.

2.3.1   The SPMD Pattern

The SPMD pattern is by far the most common parallel design pattern in parallel computing. The idea is simple. Create a team of threads. Each thread in the team runs the same code. The thread ID (a rank running from zero to the number of threads minus one) and the number of threads in the team are used to split up the work between threads.

The SPMD pattern is ideally suited to OpenMP since basically a `parallel` directive does what the SPMD pattern says: create a team of threads, each of which runs the code in the structured block associated with the parallel construct. We show an example of the classic SPMD pattern in Figure 2.6. The threads are created with the **parallel** construct on line 11. Each thread in the team runs the code block associated with **parallel** construct on lines 13–24.

Before describing the SPMD pattern, we need to consider which data is shared and which data is private. In most cases (and the few exceptions will be discussed later), if a variable is declared prior to a parallel region, it is shared. If a variable is declared inside a parallel region, it is on the private stack associated with a thread. Hence, in Figure 2.6 the variables **numthreads**, **pi**, **step**, and **full_sum** are shared. The file scope variable on line 4 (**num_steps**) is also shared. Variables declared inside the parallel region are local to each thread (i.e., they are *private* to each thread). This includes **id**, **x**, **partial_sum**, and the loop control index **i**.

A standard feature of the SPMD pattern is that the thread ID and the number of threads are used to split up the work between threads. The thread ID is found on line 13 by a call to **omp_get_thread_num()**. Determining the number of threads is done with a call to **omp_get_num_threads()** on line 17, but there is an additional complication we need to discuss.

The number of threads is not known until one is inside a parallel region. The number of threads (in this case using the default number of threads from the relevant ICV) is requested with the **parallel** construct. This number, however, is just a request. The system may, for a number of reasons, give a program fewer threads. Hence, the actual number of threads must be determined inside the parallel region. On line 17, this number is assigned to the variable **numthreads** ,which as noted earlier, is a shared variable. All threads can read and write to the address associated with that variable.

When executing in a shared address space, if multiple threads issue a mixture of loads and stores to a single address, the value that ends up at that address is only well-defined if those loads and stores are specified to occur in a given order. If they are not ordered, the program has a data race as the threads "race" to see which one gets to set the value at that address. Even if each thread is writing the same value to an address, it is still a data race and an invalid program since, depending on the specific processor, the value at an address may be corrupted even if the same bits are being stored by each thread. Hence, we need to ensure that only one thread in the team stores a value at the address associated with **numthreads**. We do this with the **single** construct.

```
1   #include <stdio.h>
2   #include <omp.h>
3
4   static long num_steps = 1024*1024*1024;
5   int main ()
6   {
7       int numthreads;
8       double pi, step, full_sum = 0.0;
9       step = 1.0 / (double) num_steps;
10
11      #pragma omp parallel
12      {
13          int id = omp_get_thread_num ();
14          double x, partial_sum = 0.0;
15
16          #pragma omp single
17              numthreads = omp_get_num_threads ();
18
19          for (int i = id; i < num_steps; i += numthreads) {
20              x = (i + 0.5) * step;
21              partial_sum += 4.0 / (1.0 + x*x);
22          }
23          #pragma omp critical
24              full_sum += partial_sum;
25      }
26
27      pi = step * full_sum;
28      printf("\n pi is %f with %d threads \n ", pi, numthreads);
29  }
```

Figure 2.6: **OpenMP π program, SPMD pattern** – This program carries out a numerical integration of a definite integral selected such that the result should be the number π. This code uses the SPMD pattern.

The **single** construct stipulates that the code in the structured block associated with the construct will be executed by one thread in the team. The other threads wait at the end of the construct until the single thread has finished executing the code, then all the threads continue execution. This is a common synchronization construct called a *barrier*. As we will see, a barrier is implied by many constructs in OpenMP. The barrier not only synchronizes the threads (i.e., implies an ordering constraint between all the threads) it also ensures that the views of shared memory seen by all threads are consistent (an operation called a *flush*). The result is that by the loop on line 19, all threads have a value for their id and **numthreads**.

Line 19 includes a particularly common trick with SPMD programming. We need to divide iterations of the loop between threads. There are multiple ways to do this. In this case, we implement a *cyclic distribution* of loop iterations. Each thread takes as its first iteration of the loop equal to its ID. The loop control index is then incremented by the number of threads, numthreads. The result is that the loop iterations are assigned cyclically, much as one would deal a deck of cards, one card at a time.[1]

Inside the loop, we compute the contributions to the sum from each thread and accumulate the results into the variable partial_sum. This variable is private to each thread, so the loop iterations run without the need for synchronization inside the loop. This is important since placing an ordering constraint on the threads inside such a small loop would inhibit parallel execution and greatly increase the overhead associated with managing the parallelism. After the loop, however, we need to combine the partial sums and accumulate them into the single shared variable that will hold the full sum. We do this on lines 23 and 24.

As we mentioned earlier, when we introduced the concept of a data race, if writes to a single location are unordered, the final result is undefined. Synchronization fundamentally defines ordering constraints on threads. We introduced one type of synchronization earlier, the barrier. For the updates to the shared variable full_sum, we use the second major type of synchronization in the OpenMP Common Core, *mutual exclusion*. The critical directive on line 23 allows only one thread at a time to execute the code associated with the construct, which in this case is the single statement on line 24. The other threads wait at the critical directive until it is their turn to execute the block of code associated with the critical construct. In other words, the threads mutually ensure that any thread executing code inside the critical construct excludes execution by the other threads in the team. The result is that that no two threads try to assign their partial sum to the full sum at the same time, and we get the correct full sum.

On line 25, we find the curly bracket that closes the parallel region. All threads wait at this location until the full team completes the code in the parallel construct (a barrier). Then a single thread, the thread that encountered the parallel construct on line 11, continues to generate and print the final answer.

---

[1] On today's processers, this cyclic distribution is not necessarily an optimal way to share the iterations of the loop, but is sufficient to illustrate the concepts of SPMD programming in OpenMP.

That completes our description of the SPMD pattern. The core elements of the pattern are simple. It requires little of the programming environment: in this case, one directive to create the team of threads, two runtime functions to get the ID and number of threads, a directive to let one thread set a value in shared memory for all the threads to use, and one synchronization directive to accumulate the partial sum. With such simple needs, the SPMD design pattern can be implemented with most parallel programming models, which is why it is the most popular design pattern in parallel computing, particularly for distributed parallel computing.

2.3.2 The Loop-Level Parallelism Pattern

Most programmers think of OpenMP as a programming model for executing loops in parallel. As we've seen in our discussion of the SPMD pattern, OpenMP is much more than parallel loops. It is the case, however, that when work first began on OpenMP, our primary goal was to agree on how to define parallel loops. In approaching parallelization through loops, a pattern called "Loop-Level Parallelism" pattern is used:

- Create a working, well-tested version of the serial program.

- Analyze the program to find the most time-consuming loops.

- Verify that the loops can in principle execute concurrently.

- Modify the loop body to remove loop carried dependencies.

- Add OpenMP directives so the loop runs with multiple threads.

By testing at each step in the process, a serial program is transformed incrementally into a parallel program. The pattern is clear by comparing Figure 2.5 to Figure 2.7. There is one loop in the program that clearly consumes the bulk of the program runtime. We can often find these loops by inspection, but in more complex programs, one may need profiling tools to find the most time-consuming loops. In Figure 2.5 we see by inspection that the loop iterations are independent and can execute in any order other than the accumulation into sum. This is a common case called a reduction, which we will describe later. Finally, we add directives to make the loop a parallel loop.

In Figure 2.7 we use the parallel construct on line 12 to create a team of threads and a single construct on line 14 to query the number of threads. This is not too different from our SPMD version of the program. The loop is parallelized with the construct:

```
#pragma omp for
```

This construct is a worksharing loop construct. It maps loop iterations onto the team of threads (shares the work) so they execute in parallel. The loop control variable, i is made private to each thread by default. To prevent a data race on the variable x, we indicate that each thread should have its own copy of that variable. This is accomplished with the `private(x)` clause which modifies the data environment seen by each thread. For example, without the clause `private(x)` the variable x would be shared between the threads. The private clause changes the default behavior from shared to private. Alternatively, we could have declared the variable x inside the `for` loop on line 19, where it would be private as a stack variable created inside the parallel region.

There are other clauses in OpenMP to modify the data environment. We summarize the data environment clauses as follows:

private: Take a shared variable that exists before a construct (the original value) and make a copy for each thread. Other threads cannot see the value of different threads' private variables. The value of the private variable is not initialized.

firstprivate: Create a private variable and initialize it to the value of the corresponding original variable.

shared: Leave a variable that is shared on entry to the loop construct in a state where it is shared across the team.

default(none): Force the compiler to flag any variables not defined in data environment clauses.

While we only show one example of a data environment clause in Figure 2.7, we hope the other cases are clear. The last feature of OpenMP we need to describe is the `reduction(+:sum)`. Reducing values spread out among many threads into a single value (i.e., a reduction) is common in parallel programming. In OpenMP, the reduction clause changes the execution of the loop as follows:

• Make a private copy of each variable in the list (sum). The variables in the list are called *reduction variables*.

- Based on the identity for the reduction operator (+), initialize the private variable on each thread (zero for the + reduction operator).

- Carry out the computations in the body of the loop. The variable in the reduction clause can be involved in any operation. It is not restricted to the reduction operator.

- When all of the loop iterations have completed, combine the values from each thread for the reduction variable (sum) and combine them using the reduction operator (+).

- Combine the reduced value from the threads with the value of the original variable (sum = 0).

Reductions are very powerful features of OpenMP. While in Figure 2.7 it is used for a straightforward reduction over the reduction operator, the fact that in the body of the loop it can be used in any valid expressions lets us generalize it to a wide range of use cases. While we do not cover it here, it is possible within OpenMP to define user-defined reductions over user defined types.

With sum as a reduction variable and the variables i and x private to each thread, the iterations of the loop are independent and can run in parallel. The parallelization was simple and only required the addition of a few directives. Actually, it could be even simpler. In certain cases, OpenMP lets a programmer combine directives. Probably the most common *combined construct* is the combination of parallel and for. If we don't care about knowing the number of threads (which, by the way, is information that is not typically needed outside of the SPMD pattern), we can parallelize the program in Figure 2.5 by placing a single directive before the loop on line 11:

```
#pragma omp parallel for private(x) reduction(+:sum)
```

This demonstrates the power of directive-driven parallel programming. A pragma that is not recognized is skipped by the compiler. And other than its influence on the execution of the parallel version of the loop, the directive is semantically neutral. Hence, the program runs in parallel when used with an OpenMP compiler or as a sequential program when built with a C compiler that doesn't support OpenMP. You get serial and parallel execution from a single source code. From a software engineering perspective where the need to support a mix of systems from a single code-base is important, that is a powerful feature of OpenMP.

```
 1
 2   #include <stdio.h>
 3   #include <omp.h>
 4   static long num_steps = 100000000;
 5
 6   int main ()
 7   {
 8      double x, pi, step, sum = 0.0;
 9      int numthreads;
10      step = 1.0 / (double) num_steps;
11
12       #pragma omp parallel
13       {
14            #pragma omp single
15                numthreads = omp_get_num_threads();
16
17            #pragma omp for private(x) reduction(+:sum)
18               for (int i = 0; i < num_steps; i++) {
19                    x = (i + 0.5) * step;
20                    sum = sum + 4.0 / (1.0 + x*x);
21               }
22       }
23      pi = step * sum;
24      printf("\n pi is %f with %d threads\n", pi,numthreads);
25   }
```

Figure 2.7: **Parallel π program, Loop parallelism pattern** – This program carries out a numerical integration of a definite integral selected such that the result should be the number π.

There are additional features of loop-level parallelism that we can't address from our π program. Consider the matrix multiplication function in Figure 2.8. A matrix multiplication is defined as a dot product over each row of the first matrix ($A[N][P]$) with each column of the second matrix ($B[P][M]$) to fill the elements of the product matrix ($C[N][M]$). The memory access patterns are regular and predictable. A compiler can do a great deal to optimize this code and schedule it effectively. To do so, however, the compiler needs enough work to schedule to keep all the processing elements (including vector units) busy. If the matrix dimensions are small, there may not be enough work. A common technique is to combine the loops to create fewer loops but with a larger loop count. We used to do this by hand, which is tedious and error prone. OpenMP added the **collapse** clause to combine the indicated number of loops (2 in Figure 2.8) and recovers the i and j indices (which are made private

```
 1
 2   #include <omp.h>
 3   void mm_ikj_par2(int N, int M, int P, double *A, double *B, double *C)
 4   {
 5       int i, j, k;
 6
 7       #pragma omp parallel
 8       #pragma omp for collapse(2) private(k) schedule(static,10)
 9       for (i=0; i<N; i++)
10           for (j=0; j<M; j++)
11               for(k=0; k<P; k++)
12                   *(C+(i*M+j)) += *(A+(i*P+k)) * *(B+(k*M+j));
13   }
```

Figure 2.8: **Parallel matrix multiplication, Loop-level parallelism pattern** –
This function multiplies matrices A and B summing the result into matrix C. We use this
to show the use of the `collapse` and `schedule` clauses.

by default) for use inside the loop body. This only works for perfectly nested loops,
which means there can be no statements between the collapsed loops (loops over i
and j in this example). The combined loop is then ready to execute in parallel.

In parallel loops, the OpenMP compiler and runtime system will try to map loop
iterations onto threads so as to balance the load between them. The idea is that
the program isn't done until the last thread finishes, so load balancing is done so
each thread ideally carries out useful work for approximately the same amount of
time. A programmer can indicate to the OpenMP compiler how to carry out the
schedule of iterations in the parallel loop. This is done with the `schedule` clause. In
Figure 2.8 we have a stack schedule over chunks of size 10 (`schedule(static,10)`).
This means that the iterations are decomposed into chunks of size 10. Then the
chunks are dealt out to threads with a cyclic distribution (as we did "by hand" with
the SPMD program in Figure 2.6). If a `chunk` size is not given, the compiler will by
default schedule loop iterations in blocks with one block per thread.

With the static schedule, the logic for the distribution of loop iterations is mapped
onto a closed-form expression by the compiler, so much of the overhead in managing
the schedule happens at compile time. There are cases, however, when the load
is variable and unpredictable, and the scheduling decisions can only be made at
runtime. This might occur for sparse data structures, for example, or data-dependent
linked lists. In this case, the best schedule might be:

```
schedule(dynamic, 10)
```

As with the static schedule, the loop iterations are decomposed into chunks of the indicated size (10 in this case). Each thread in the team is given a chunk of work with the rest going into a queue. When a thread has finished its chunk, it goes back to the queue to get another chunk. The work, therefore is dynamic, depending on the details of the loops and the data processed by program. This shifts the overhead in managing the load to the runtime system, but for loops with unpredictable and highly variable costs per iteration, the dynamic schedule can be much better.

There is one last item we need to cover before completing our discussion of parallel loops. The `for` and `single` constructs both distribute (or share) work defined in the associated structured block across the team of threads. This type of construct is called a *worksharing* construct. After a worksharing construct, the threads in the team revert to redundantly executing the same statement(s). Assuming those statements access the variables shared between threads, the safest behavior is for the team of threads to wait until all the threads have completed the work in the worksharing construct. Hence, a barrier is implied at the end of any worksharing construct.

A barrier, however, adds considerable overhead. If it is not needed, it would be good to "turn off" the barrier. For example, the `single` statement in line 14 of Figure 2.7 saves the number of threads used in the parallel region in a shared variable. The subsequent statements in the parallel region do not use that value. Hence, there is no reason in terms of program correctness to have a barrier at the end of that single construct. We can disable that barrier using a `nowait` clause. For example, in Figure 2.7 we could put a nowait clause on the single construct:

```
#pragma omp single nowait
numthreads = omp_get_num_threads();
```

This would let the other threads go straight to the following statement (the parallel loop) while a single thread assigns the number of threads to `numthreads`.

2.3.3   The Divide-and-Conquer Pattern

Algorithms that utilize the divide-and-conquer pattern do not map directly onto a nested set of loops. The problem being solved is one that can be recursively divided into smaller subproblems. This splitting process continues leading to a tree of smaller and smaller subproblems. Eventually, the size of a subproblem becomes small enough to solve directly. We call this the *base case*. Then the base case is solved and the recursive splitting is reversed as we merge solutions to subproblems together step-by-step until we constructed the solution to the original problem. This process is represented pictorially in Figure 2.9.

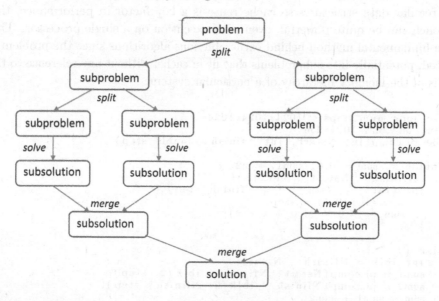

Figure 2.9: **Illustration of the divide-and-conquer pattern** – The pattern breaks down into three parts: a recursive splitting into a tree of subproblems, a direct solve, and then merging "back up the tree" to obtain the overall solution. Source: [2].

The divide-and-conquer pattern is not just for parallel programming. As a concrete example, consider the sequential divide-and-conquer solution to the π problem in Figure 2.10. We start at the top in the main program in lines 21–28. The basic parameters of the problem are defined, and a recursive function is called over the full problem domain (i.e., steps 0 to num_steps). The return value from this function will be the global solution to the problem. Moving to the recursive function in lines 3–19, we start by testing if the problem is small enough to compute directly (the base case). If the range of steps for a particular function call are below MIN_BLK, we compute over that range in the loop on lines 7–10. Otherwise, we split the problem in two with one call (for sum1) for the lower half of the range and the other (for **sum2**) for the upper half. The two results are summed and that value is returned.

This pattern is not a particularly effective way to compute the numerical integration we've been using to estimate π. If the loop in question, however, is running over regular data structures so cache reuse is a key factor in performance, this approach can be quite powerful, even with execution on a single processor. This is the fundamental method behind cache oblivious algorithms since the problem is reduced, potentially into subproblems that fit in cache, without any reference to the details of the memory hierarchy of a particular system.

```
1   static long num_steps = 1024*1024*1024;
2   #define MIN_BLK 1024*256
3   double pi_comp(int Nstart, int Nfinish, double step)
4   {
5       double x, sum = 0.0, sum1, sum2;
6       if (Nfinish − Nstart < MIN_BLK){
7           for (int i = Nstart; i < Nfinish; i++) {
8               x = (i + 0.5) * step;
9               sum += 4.0 / (1.0 + x * x);
10          }
11      }
12      else {
13          int iblk = Nfinish − Nstart;
14          sum1 = pi_comp(Nstart, Nfinish − iblk/2, step);
15          sum2 = pi_comp(Nfinish − iblk/2, Nfinish, step);
16          sum = sum1 + sum2;
17      }
18      return sum;
19  }
20
21  int main ()
22  {
23      double step, pi, sum;
24      step = 1.0 / (double) num_steps;
25
26      sum = pi_comp(0, num_steps, step);
27      pi = step * sum;
28  }
```

Figure 2.10: **Sequential π program, divide-and-conquer** – This program carries out a numerical integration of a definite integral selected such that the result should be the number π.

From what we've covered about OpenMP, there is no obvious way to parallelize the divide-and-conquer pattern. To do so, we need to introduce a new concept in OpenMP; the concept of a *task*.

2.3.3.1   Tasks in OpenMP

OpenMP is a general-purpose programming model. With constructs to support the SPMD and loop-level parallelism patterns, a wide range of problems can be addressed. Problems that do not map onto iterative control structures, so-called *irregular parallelism*, need a different approach for expressing the parallelism in a problem. This topic is best approached through an example.

Consider the code in Figure 2.11. It traverses a linked list and does some work at each node. This can be parallelized using the parallel and loop-worksharing constructs, but such solutions require multiple passes through the linked list and are cumbersome.

The solution (added in 2008 to OpenMP 3.1) was to include the concept of a *task* in OpenMP. A task is defined as code plus an associated data environment. An explicit task is defined with the task construct:

```
#pragma omp task
{
   // a structured block of code
}
```

When a thread encounters the task construct, it creates a task. A task can be executed immediately or it can be enqueued for deferred execution. We show an example of explicit tasks in Figure 2.12. We create a parallel region and then use a single construct so that one thread executes the while loop to traverse the linked list. The processing associated with each node is enqueued for deferred execution using the task construct as shown on line 7. The deferred tasks are executed by the other threads in the team waiting at the barrier implied by the single construct. Once all the tasks (including tasks created inside other tasks) complete, the computation is complete and the threads can move past the barrier.

The data environment for tasks is a natural extension of how other OpenMP constructs interact with the data environment. The clauses private, shared, firstprivate can be used on the task construct. The default behavior of shared variables with tasks is the same as with any OpenMP construct; that is, when a

```
 1
 2
 3    // definition of a node in the list
 4    struct node {
 5       int data;
 6       int result;
 7       struct node* next;
 8    };
 9
10    int main(int argc, char *argv[]) {
11        struct node *p=NULL;
12        struct node *head=NULL;
13
14
15        p = fill_list(p);  // function (not shown) to fill the list
16        head = p;
17
18        // traverse the list process work for each node
19        while (p != NULL) {
20            processwork(p); // function not provided
21            p = p->next;
22        }
23
24        return 0;
25    }
```

Figure 2.11: **Serial linked list program** – This program traverses the nodes in a linked list, carrying out some work for each node.

```
 1
 2        #pragma omp parallel
 3            #pragma omp single
 4            {
 5                    p=head;
 6                    while (p) {
 7                        #pragma omp task firstprivate(p)
 8                                processwork(p);
 9                        p = p->next;
10                    }
11            }
```

Figure 2.12: **Parallel linked list example** – This program iterates through the list, processing each list element using an OpenMP task.

variable is shared when a task is encountered, it is shared inside the task. Variables in a `firstprivate` clause are very important for tasks. When a task is enqueued for deferred execution, you need to capture the values of key parameters at the time the task is enqueued. This is done with `firstprivate`. This is the most common behavior when enqueuing a task. Hence, under the principle of making the default behavior of OpenMP constructs the safe behavior, any private variable in scope when encountering an explicit task are made `firstprivate` automatically. In essence, OpenMP captures the value of such variables and stores them in the queue with the task.

Tasks are a powerful concept and seemingly simple to work with. Adding them to OpenMP, however, was a long and arduous job. From the first prototype implementations presented to the OpenMP Language Committee [9], it took us almost eight years of hard work to add them to the OpenMP specification. Why? The problem is that in OpenMP, prior to tasks, everything was defined in terms of threads. This gave the standard a consistent execution context to define the data environment and the rules defining the behavior of OpenMP. Once tasks were added, however, there were two completely different execution contexts to manage: tasks and threads. This greatly complicates the definition of constructs inside OpenMP and makes implementing OpenMP much more difficult. The solution was to rewrite the specification to define everything in terms of tasks. A parallel region creates a team of threads, each of which uses the code in the structured block to define an *implicit task* that each thread runs. All the constructs in OpenMP are defined similarly in terms of explicit and implicit tasks.

In most cases, the OpenMP programmer doesn't need to think about such low-level details of the language. We think about threads and the code executed by threads, not the fact that a thread is tied to an implicit task. Implicit tasks, however, are a valuable addition to the OpenMP specification because they provide a consistent way to define the context for threads when they are created and when they interact with OpenMP constructs.

Hence, when we say "a thread encounters the task construct," what we really mean is "when an implicit task encounters the task construct." This implicit task creates explicit tasks that are *child tasks* of the implicit task. In many cases, we create a hierarchy of nested tasks with a top-level task creating tasks (child tasks of the top-level implicit tasks) that themselves create new tasks (which become their child tasks) and so on. We are now ready to return to the divide-and-conquer pattern and how to parallelize it using tasks.

2.3.3.2   Parallelizing Divide-and-Conquer

Converting the serial divide-and-conquer code in Figure 2.10 into a parallel program using explicit tasks is straight forward. In the main program in Figure 2.13 we create a team of threads, and then one thread starts the divide-and-conquer process inside the **single** construct on lines 33 and 34. The base case (lines 9–13) is unchanged between the serial and the parallel versions of the program. The key difference is lines 17, 19, and 21. Before each recursive function call, we add the explicit task construct. The variables **sum1** and **sum2** are declared inside the **pi_comp** function. This means they are on the function's stack and therefore private. A private variable in a parent task is made firstprivate by default for the explicit tasks it creates. Hence, the variables inside the task would not be available when the tasks are complete. Therefore, we must make **sum1** and **sum2** shared so the variables will be available on line 22 to add together to get the final sum for the pair of functions. Think of this as the parent task sharing these variables with the child tasks, with one copy of the variable for use by both the parent and child.

The addition of **sum1** and **sum2** on line 22 must wait until the tasks that define them are complete. This is done with the **taskwait** directive on line 21. The task (either implicit or explicit) that encounters the explicit tasks on lines 17 and 19 and also encounters the **taskwait** on line 21 will wait until those explicit tasks complete. The **taskwait** does not wait, however, for tasks to complete that are nested inside the child tasks. It only waits on the explicit tasks created by the same task that encountered the **taskwait**. The behavior of **taskwait** contrasts with behavior of the barrier implied by the **single** on line 33. That barrier waits for all tasks, including those nested inside other tasks.

The task construct lets OpenMP handle a wide range of dynamic control structures. It greatly expands the scope of OpenMP. Task queues are well known as a general strategy for balancing the load across a team of threads. Management of task queues, however, adds overhead as threads must synchronize updates to the queue data structure. The work inside a task should ideally be large enough to mitigate these overheads. Therefore, when practical to do so, the SPMD or loop-level parallelism should be preferred over tasks.

```
1
2  #include <omp.h>
3  static long num_steps = 1024*1024*1024;
4  #define MIN_BLK 1024*256
5
6  double pi_comp(int Nstart,int Nfinish,double step)
7  {
8      double x, sum = 0.0, sum1, sum2;
9      if (Nfinish - Nstart < MIN_BLK) {
10         for (int i = Nstart; i < Nfinish; i++){
11             x = (i + 0.5) * step;
12             sum = sum + 4.0 / (1.0 + x*x);
13         }
14     }
15     else {
16         int iblk = Nfinish - Nstart;
17         #pragma omp task shared(sum1)
18             sum1 = pi_comp(Nstart, Nfinish - iblk/2, step);
19         #pragma omp task shared(sum2)
20             sum2 = pi_comp(Nfinish - iblk/2, Nfinish, step);
21         #pragma omp taskwait
22             sum = sum1 + sum2;
23     }
24     return sum;
25 }
26
27 int main ()
28 {
29     double step, pi, sum;
30     step = 1.0 / (double) num_steps;
31
32     #pragma omp parallel
33         #pragma omp single
34             sum = pi_comp(0, num_steps, step);
35
36     pi = step * sum;
37 }
```

Figure 2.13: **Parallel π program, divide-and-conquer with tasks** – This program carries out a numerical integration of a definite integral selected such that the result should be the number π.

2.4   Task Execution

You can do a great deal of interesting work with the `task` and `taskwait` directives. They are the foundation of programming with tasks. As you dig deeper into OpenMP, however, additional details about tasks and how they execute become critical to understand. As we will see, this is definitely the case for the directives used when programming a GPU with OpenMP.

To cover what we need, let's consider the details of how tasks are created and then execute. A task (either an implicit task or an explicit task) encounters a `task` construct. We call this the *generating task*. The generating task creates a new explicit task along with its data environment. This new task is either deferred (i.e., enqueued for later execution) or executed immediately.

The option to execute the task immediately is important. If a large number of tasks are created, they could overwhelm the data structures set aside to manage tasks. Rather than overflow those data structures, the system can opt to just execute tasks as `task` constructs are encountered. When a task executes immediately, the generating task suspends, so the new task can execute.

If you suspect that a task might execute immediately, you can tell the system to let the task use the data environment of the generating task. In this case, we say the task is a *mergeable task*. This can save a great deal of memory for certain problems and reduce overheads due to excess data movement associated with establishing a new task's data environment.

Most programs that use tasks, however, treat tasks as deferred units of work. When a task encounters a task construct, it generates a task. The new task is enqueued and any other thread in the team may execute that task. This continues until all the tasks have completed. A number of complications arise, however, that require us to dig a bit deeper into task execution. It is possible that a task is blocked waiting on some resource. It may be waiting on a critical construct or some other resource that is not available. The waiting task could tie up a thread, wasting available parallelism for a program. To deal with situations of this sort, a task can be suspended so that the thread executing the task can *switch* to a new task. This is allowed to occur at distinct task scheduling points. These occur at numerous points in OpenMP, including the most common cases: when a `task` construct is encountered, when a task has completed, and at a synchronization event (such as `critical`). A programmer can also insert an explicit task scheduling point using a `taskyield` construct. This would be done, for example, if a programmer knows, based on the logic in an algorithm, that there is a significant probability that the task will be blocked waiting on a resource.

At a task scheduling point, the thread executing a task may suspend the task it is working on to shift to a different task. At some point, however, the suspended task will be picked up by a thread and execution will continue. A task is said to be *tied* if it is guaranteed that the same thread that suspended the task will later return to execute the task. This is important if a task depends on features of a particular thread (such as its ID or data environment). Alternatively, if it doesn't matter which thread executes a task, it can be designated as an untied task, which, as implied by the name, means that it is not tied to any thread and a different thread from the one that suspended it can execute the task.

There is much more to tasks in OpenMP. Most work with tasks can be addressed with what we've discussed here. In particular, we'll use the tasking features of OpenMP to run on multiple GPUs in Chapter 8. Over time, however, you'll need loops that generate tasks (the `taskloop` construct), the ability to wait for child tasks and all their descendant tasks to complete (the `taskgroup` construct), task priorities, task dependencies, and more. We do not need these additional features and frankly, it is best to wait until the constructs discussed here have been mastered before pursuing the other features of tasks in OpenMP.

2.5   Our Journey Ahead

This completes our survey of OpenMP and its use for writing multithreaded programs. We've covered a lot of ground. By organizing the discussion around the core design patterns used by OpenMP programmers, we've provided a framework around which to organize your knowledge of OpenMP. All the items from OpenMP that we discussed are summarized in Table 2.2. You can refer back to this table and use it as a reference guide as you write multithreaded code.

Many (if not most) programmers don't even use the contents of Table 2.2 to write OpenMP. They just go through their code and add this one simple pragma to their loops:

```
#pragma omp parallel for
```

It sometimes frustrates those of us close to OpenMP, eager to see people make fuller use of the language, but programmers don't (and shouldn't) care. That one pragma speeds up their programs and that's good enough.

For programming a GPU, there is an analog to *parallel for*. We show this pair of directives in Figure 2.14. These directives construct a kernel from the body of the outermost loop and then offloads execution of that kernel to a device (such as a GPU). The `target` construct offloads work from the host onto the device. The

Table 2.2: **Table summarizing the most commonly used pragmas, run-time library functions, and clauses for multithreaded programming with OpenMP** – We often refer to this OpenMP subset as the OpenMP Common Core.

OpenMP pragma, function, or clause	Concepts
#pragma omp parallel	Create a parallel region.
int omp_get_num_threads()	Number of threads (N)
int omp_get_thread_num()	Thread rank (0 to N-1)
void omp_set_num_threads()	Set default number of threads
double omp_get_wtime()	Time blocks of code
export OMP_NUM_THREADS=N	Default number of threads
#pragma omp barrier	Synchronization: explicit barrier
#pragma omp critical	Synchronization: mutual exclusion
#pragma omp for	Worksharing loops
#pragma omp parallel for	Combined parallel for
collapse(M)	Combine M nested loops
reduction(op: list)	Reduction
schedule(static [, chunk])	Static loop schedule
schedule(dynamic [,chunk])	Dynamic loop schedule
private(list)	Private variables, unintialized
firstprivate (list)	Private variables, initialized
shared(list)	Shared Variables
nowait	Disable implied barriers
#pragma omp single	Work done by a single thread
#pragma omp task	Create an explicit task
#pragma omp taskwait	Wait for sibling tasks to complete

`loop` construct directs the compiler to optimize the loop for concurrent execution. In this case, that involves creating multiple teams of threads, one for each compute unit (or the *streaming multiprocessor* using the terminology for NVIDIA® GPUs). We call these multiple teams a *league* of teams. The `loop` construct then splits up that outermost loop between teams which then run in parallel on the processing elements (i.e., the *SIMD lanes*).

For variables pulled off the stack (as opposed to storage created with a memory allocator and therefore off the heap), the data is moved onto the device (N plus the arrays A, B, and C) before the computation begins and are copied back to the host

```
1   #include<omp.h>
2   #define N 5000
3   int main()
4   {
5     float A[N][N], B[N][N], C[N][N];
6
7     init(N, A, B, C);    // a user written function to fill A, B and C
8
9     #pragma omp target
10    #pragma omp loop
11    for (int i = 0; i < N; i++) {
12      for (int j = 0; j < N; j++) {
13        for(int k = 0; k < N; k++) {
14          C[i][j] += A[i][k] * B[k][j];
15        }
16      }
17    }
18  }
```

Figure 2.14: **Matrix Multiplication program** – This program will multiply two matrices, A and B, to produce a third matrix, C, running on the target device. Notice that all three arrays have been allocated in stack memory.

at the end of the parallelized loop. That's all there is to it.

In Chapter 3, we will explain these two directives in detail. We'll stick to the default rules for data movement so we can better focus on the **target** and **loop** constructs. Then in Chapter 4, we will explore the detailed ways you can manage how data moves between the host (i.e., the CPU) and a device (typically, a GPU). This will complete what we call the *GPU Common Core*.

The rest of the book will go beyond the common core and target/loop constructs. We will describe compiler directives for optimizing how work is mapped onto a GPU and additional details that expose the full diversity of GPU programming so any program you might want to write with a proprietary language such as CUDA™ can be written with OpenMP. We suspect, however, that most people will just use the GPU Common Core with the pair of simple directives from Figure 2.14 and consider their job done.

II THE GPU COMMON CORE

A programming language (or API) must cover the full range of anticipated use cases. One person's "corner case" is another person's main concern, so this wide scope is important. The end result, however, is complexity that all too often overwhelms those working with the language.

In most cases, it turns out this complexity can be ignored. For multithreading with OpenMP, we found that of the multitude of directives and clauses defined by the OpenMP specification, only 21 are used on a regular basis (see Table 2.2). This core set of directives, clauses, and runtime library functions are common to the majority of OpenMP applications. We call this the *OpenMP Common Core*. Even if a programmer needs the less common (or even obscure) features of OpenMP, by mastering the Common Core first, those extra features are much easier to absorb.

We believe the same principle holds for the subset of OpenMP that deals with the GPU. There is a modest fraction of directives and clauses used for the GPU that are commonly used in application programming. This is the *GPU Common Core*.

In this part of the book, we present OpenMP's GPU Common Core. For most application programmers, this is all they will ever need. Even if the less commonly used items discussed later in this book are needed, by mastering the Common Core first, they will be much easier to understand.

Most of the GPU Common Core is covered in Chapter 3. This chapter breaks down into two parts. First, we describe how to offload work onto a target device with the default rules for moving data between the host and a target device. In the second part of the chapter, we describe how to run code in parallel on the device. It is a common feature of high performance computing that managing how data moves between memory and the different devices is the key to performance. We cover that topic in Chapter 4. Finally, we close Part II of the book with a recap of the GPU Common Core in Chapter 5 followed by the Eightfold Path to performance in GPU programming.

3 Running Parallel Code on a GPU

Consider our journey to this point. We've discussed heterogeneous hardware. We've reviewed OpenMP for writing multithreaded programs. These topics have given us a solid foundation to build on. In this chapter, we address this book's raison d'être: programming a GPU with OpenMP.

An OpenMP program starts as a single thread (the *initial thread*) running on a CPU. This CPU can be attached to one or more devices, typically GPUs. In addition to running multithreaded programs, the CPU also coordinates memory movement and execution for the attached devices. It serves as a *host* for each device; that is, each GPU is viewed by the CPU as a distinct *target device*.

We summarize the host/device model in Figure 3.1. Notice that the host and its devices each have their own data environments (a bit like having their own memory spaces): the host memory and device memory (for each device). If the hardware supports it, OpenMP can also operate with a unified view of memory where the whole system sees a single memory space available to all; a topic we discuss in Chapter 7. In this chapter, however, we will assume separate data environments and consider how data moves between them.

While a CPU can be a host for multiple GPUs, we typically write programs assuming one GPU in the system. We will start by specializing to that case: where there is one device that serves as the default device for the host. Later in Chapter 8 we will discuss how OpenMP handles multiple devices attached to a single host.

We explain the common core of GPU programming with OpenMP in three parts:

- How do we offload a computation onto a GPU?

- How does data move by default between a CPU (the host) and a GPU (the target device)?

- How do we specify that code should run in parallel on the GPU?

While we will end up with a simple pair of constructs programmers can use to offload computation onto a GPU, we have considerable ground to cover to explain those constructs so you can understand how they work and interact with your algorithms.

3.1 Target Construct: Offloading Execution onto a Device

OpenMP uses the `target` construct to offload execution to a target device. We define this construct in Table 3.1. It is the foundational construct on which we

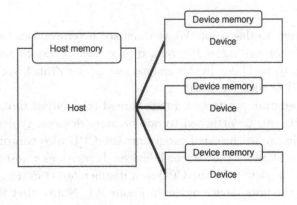

Figure 3.1: **The OpenMP host/device model** – A host device (the CPU) where execution begins and zero or more attached devices. The memories (i.e., the data environments) are distinct.

build GPU programming in OpenMP. A thread executes a task (either explicit or implicit). When that task encounters a target construct, a *device data environment* is created, and the code in the structured block associated with the **target** construct is executed by the target device instead of the host. The code within the construct plus any functions it calls defines the *target region*. By default, the task that encounters the target construct waits until the target region completes execution. This is shown in Figure 3.2. Later, in Section 8.5 we will discuss how to do useful work on the host while the code in the target region executes on the device.

Table 3.1: **A target construct in C/C++ and Fortran** – The target construct packages the code in the structured block into a kernel and offloads that kernel to a device for execution. Optional clauses will be discussed in later chapters.

C/C++ directive format
#pragma omp target *[clause[[,] clause]...]*
structured_block
Fortran directive format
!$omp target *[clause[[,] clause]...]*
structured_block
!$omp end target

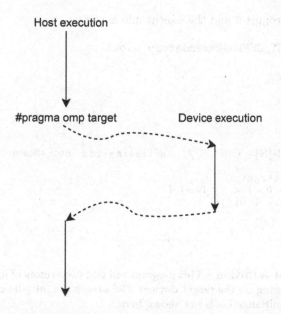

Figure 3.2: Illustration of transfer of execution from the host to the device at a target construct.

As an example, consider the "hello world" program of GPU programming: vector addition. Vector addition is defined by a simple loop. As shown in Figure 3.3, using a **target** construct, we run this loop on a device instead of the host. This is a big step. It moves execution from the host to the accelerator. The target region consists of all the code from lines 9–11 (the **for** loop). The host CPU will wait until the loop finishes executing on the device.

When you build an executable from this code (e.g., **a.out**) and run it on the command line, the program runs, but doesn't necessarily give any indication that it ran on a GPU. An implementation of OpenMP has the option to decide that a particular target directive defines work that, for whatever reason, is not suitable to offload, and it may instead silently run on the host rather than the device. Therefore, especially when working with example programs with little work for the GPU (such as the one in Figure 3.3), you need to force OpenMP to run the code on the device. You do this by setting the **OMP_TARGET_OFFLOAD** environment variable to **mandatory**. For example, we can do this on a command line when we launch an executable (e.g., from the UNIX prompt **$** and the executable **a.out**):

```
$ OMP_TARGET_OFFLOAD=mandatory a.out
```

```
1
2    #define N 4000
3
4    int main()
5    {
6        float A[N], B[N], C[N];   // initialization not shown
7
8        #pragma omp target
9        for (int i = 0; i < N; i++) {
10           C[i] = A[i] + B[i];
11       }
12   }
```

Figure 3.3: **Vector addition** – This program will add two vectors of length N to produce a third vector, running on the target device. The arrays are initialized prior to the **for** loop, though that initialization is not shown here.

The code in Figure 3.3 runs on the device, but it does so as a serial loop. We did not indicate how the work in the loop should be shared across the SIMD lanes on the GPU. We will discuss parallel execution later in Section 3.3. Before doing so, however, we will discuss the critical issue of how data moves from the host to the device.

When the **target** construct is encountered on the host, in addition to transferring execution to the device, *data* must move between the host and the device. Data transfers occur at well-defined points. We will first consider the default rules that describe how data moves at the beginning and end of a target region without use of additional clauses or other constructs from OpenMP. Explicit control of data transfer will be addressed in Chapter 4 including how to move data allocated on the heap (or, for C++, the free store).

For the vector add example in Figure 3.3, data transfer occurs at line 8 on the target construct where data moves from the host to the device, and at the end of the target region on line 11. This happens automatically using the rules for implicit data movement defined by OpenMP, which is the topic of the next section. The target construct therefore does two things: transfer execution, and transfer data at the beginning and end of the target region.

3.2   Moving Data between the Host and a Device

The target device has its own memory, distinct from the host's memory. The device memory space is called the *device data environment*. In order for the target region executing on the device to do anything useful, we must copy data from the host to the device data environment and then copy it back to the host after execution on the device completes. The `target` directive causes data movement to occur implicitly. The direction of the memory transfers in OpenMP are always from the perspective of the host; that is, data is either copied *to* the device or *from* the device. The following code snippet shows where the transfers occur for the `target` construct:

```
#pragma omp target
{ // <-- copy data to the device


} // <-- copy data from the device
```

The rules for which variables are copied implicitly are limited to scalars, arrays, and structures with complete types resident in the stack of the task that encounters the target construct. The copying of data to and from the target device is known as *mapping*. We might also say a variable is *mapped*. Data allocated on the heap (or for C++, data in the *free store*) must be explicitly copied (mapped). We will show how to work with such data in Chapter 4.

3.2.1   Scalar Variables

Memory is referenced by address. The name associated with an address is called a *variable*. A variable that references a single value is a *scalar* variable. For OpenMP programs, scalar variables are defined by the base language (C, C++ or Fortran). For a C program, for example, scalar variables typically use one of the basic data types defined by C: `char`, `int`, `float`, `double`, and so on (note that pointers are scalar variables with values that are addresses in memory. The treatment of pointers as they move between the host and a device is complicated and will be discussed later).

For scalar variables defined on the host and used within a target region, OpenMP implicitly moves them from the host to the target device when the target construct is encountered. For example, consider the program in Figure 3.4. This code multiplies entries in the array A by a scalar floating point number `alpha`. We will describe how A is mapped onto the device shortly; for now, consider the scalar variable `alpha`.

```
1
2   #define N 4000
3
4   int main()
5   {
6       float A[N];
7       float alpha = 2.0;
8
9       #pragma omp target
10      for (int i = 0; i < N; i++) {
11          A[i] = A[i] * alpha;
12      }
13  }
```

Figure 3.4: **Scaling a vector** – This program will multiply a vector of length N by a constant in place, running on the target device.

The data held in scalar variables is copied to the device on entry to the target region. OpenMP transfers them as **firstprivate** (see Section 2.3.2). This means that threads running on the target device will have their own copy of the variable with a value equal to that of the original value (**firstprivate** rather than **private**), so the value of the variable is available on the device. Hence, we know the variable **alpha** will contain the number **2.0** because this is the value of the analogous variable on the host before it encountered the target construct.

Scalar variables are implicitly mapped from the host to the target device as **firstprivate** when the target construct is encountered. The OpenMP compiler, when it compiles code with a target construct, constructs a function from the structured block within the construct. This becomes the kernel that will be executed on the GPU (see Section 1.1.3). Scalar variables mapped into a target region are passed "as if" they are "call by value" arguments to the kernels. They are available inside the kernel with the values of the original variable. As the kernel completes (i.e., we reach the end of the target region), the variables go "out of scope" and are not longer available. Hence, while OpenMP maps scalar variables into a target region when a target construct is encountered, consistent with the behavior of functions with variables passed by value, they are *not* mapped (copied) back from the device at the end of the target region.

In summary, scalar variables will be copied automatically to the target device at the start of the target region. Scalar variables have a basic type from the base language, and live on the host's stack. They will be initialized on the device with the value they held on the host prior to encountering the target construct. Any updates to the variable will not be visible on the host, consistent with the behavior of private variables in OpenMP. If the value of a scalar variable *from the device* is needed on the host, we need to explicitly map that variable. We will discuss this in Chapter 4.

3.2.2   Arrays on the Stack

In this section, we will describe the default rules for moving certain arrays and derived types to and from a device. First, we need to consider an item of "jargon" from the C programming language. An *incomplete type* in C is a variable whose size is not known at compile time. Examples are structures (and unions) where the members are not yet specified, and arrays of unknown size. For example, the integer array type `int[]` is an incomplete type. To make it *complete*, the size of the array needs to be specified (e.g., `int A[1024]`). Once a type is complete, the compiler knows how much memory to allocate on the stack for variables of that type.

A GPU is a throughput optimized device typically used for data parallel algorithms. This translates directly onto processing applied concurrently to elements of arrays. Hence, when programming a GPU with OpenMP, you often need to understand arrays and how they move between the host and a device. We will start by assuming the arrays are complete types (the compiler knows the size) and allocated on the stack of the task that encounters the `target` construct. This basically means the array is declared in the code using an array type with a known size. Later we will deal with arrays of unknown size that are allocated on the heap and accessed through pointers.

Arrays allocated on the stack are variables. They reference locations in memory. Rather than a single value at a single location, an array references a contiguous sequence of addresses. Another example of a variable that references multiple addresses in memory is a `struct`. We can use a `struct` to define a composite (aggregate) data type made up of other data types. For both structs and arrays, OpenMP will transfer the data held in these variables automatically when encountering a target directive if they are complete data types in the stack.

While scalars are mapped to the device as `firstprivate`, non-scalar types are copied to the device at the start of the target region *and* copied back to the host at the end of the target region. We can update the copy of non-scalar data inside the target region on the device, and the updated values will be copied from the device and made available on the host. The data will also be *shared* between any parallel threads that might be running inside the target region. The data is mapped into the device data environment and available to all device threads executing that target region. This is quite different from the behavior for scalar variables, where the scalar data is copied and privatized and not copied back at the end of the region.

The vector addition example we showed in Figure 3.3 utilizes this implicit behavior. The arrays A, B and C are of type `float[4000]`. They are complete data types resident in the stack of the task that encounters the target construct. N is defined as a macro (i.e., in the preprocessor), so all references to it are replaced with the value 4000 at compile time. The arrays will be copied to the device at the start of the target region. The code inside the target region updates the array C, and this array will be copied back to the host at the end of the device execution. We will also copy A and B back to the host according to the rules for copying of arrays allocated on the stack, even though they were not modified and hence copying them is a waste of bandwidth.

3.2.3 Derived Types

Structures are an aggregate data type with multiple variables grouped together under a single name. Structures that are complete (fully defined at compile time) are copied to and from the device at the start and end of a target region. In other words, a variable with a complete structure data type, along with its component parts, are mapped the same way as static arrays. The example in Figure 3.5 shows this in action.

Consider the example in Figure 3.6. This code uses a structure that holds two single-precision floating point numbers used to represent a complex number. As a slightly contrived example, we wish to use the target device to complete the absolute value of the complex number and store the result in an array stored on the stack. If the result of a computation is a scalar variable, it is implicitly mapped `firstprivate`, and the value computed inside the target region is lost. By using an array (of length one), OpenMP copies the new value back to the host automatically at the end of the target region. The `struct complex` contains two member variables (two `float`s). It is a complete type since contained variables are of a known size. As such, the variable, `data`, will be copied to the device when the target construct is encountered on line 13 and copied back at the end of the target region on line 16.

```
1   struct complex {
2     float real;
3     float imag;
4   };
5
6   struct complex data = {.real = 1.0f, .imag = 2.0f};
7
8   #pragma omp target
9   {
10     data.real *= 2.0f;
11     data.imag *= 2.0f;
12  }
13
14  // On the host, data is {.real = 2.0f, .imag = 4.0f}
```

Figure 3.5: **Mapping structures and target regions** – This structure will be copied to the device at the start of the region and back at the end of the target region.

```
1   #include <math.h>
2
3   struct complex {
4     float real;
5     float imag;
6   };
7
8   int main()
9   {
10     struct complex data = {.real = 1.0f, .imag = 2.0f};
11     float len[1];
12
13     #pragma omp target
14     {
15       len[0] = sqrtf(data.real * data.real + data.imag * data.imag);
16     }
17  }
```

Figure 3.6: **Using an array to copy results to the host** – This program shows the mapping of a C **struct** variable and the use of an array (**len[1]**) to force a scaler result of a computation on the target device to be copied back to the host.

In summary, variables of non-scalar complete types are mapped to the device at the start of the target region, and mapped back from the device at the end of the target region. These variables are structures and fixed-size arrays, allocated on the stack in the host memory. This data is shared inside the target data environment for all parallel threads that might run for the duration of the target region.

3.3   Parallel Execution on the Target Device

The target construct defines a data environment on the device and offloads a code region to the device.

As we discussed in Chapter 1, the GPU architecture is hierarchical. There are compute units, SIMD lanes, and potentially additional specialized execution units such as vector or tensor units. Mapping onto this hierarchy contributes to the ability of a GPU to sustain such high compute densities.

The execution model of a GPU is fundamentally different from that of a CPU. A good way to explain the hierarchical structure of GPU parallelism is to contrast it with that of a CPU. We do this in Figure 3.7. We start with work defined by the text of the program. For the CPU, we map this into blocks that we map onto threads. These threads execute concurrently and the Operating System (OS) schedules them fairly, so they all are able to make forward progress. The CPU threads are concurrent (i.e., unordered) outside of specific order constraints imposed by synchronization events.

The execution model of the GPU is more complicated. It is optimized for throughput, not latency. The work is decomposed in terms of an index space (an NDRange or grid). The task region defines a kernel that runs at each point in this index space. We call an instance of the kernel at each point in the index space a *work-item*. The index space is decomposed into blocks, and the work-items associated with those blocks define *work-groups*. The work-groups are enqueued for execution on the GPU. They are concurrent (i.e., unordered with respect to each other). They are managed by a queue and therefore not scheduled fairly. This means you cannot define explicit ordering constraints (i.e., synchronization) between work-groups. The queue pulls work-groups from the queue and maps them onto compute units where all the work-items in a single work-group run concurrently and are scheduled fairly. That means if the programming model supports it, you can synchronize between work-items running in a single work-group.

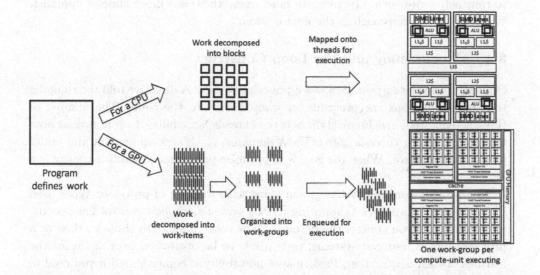

Figure 3.7: **CPU vs. GPU execution models** – The CPU has four cores with an arithmetic-logic unit (ALU), a shared L3 cache (L3$), and SIMD vector units per core. The GPU has four compute units, each with 16 SIMD lanes. For details about the GPU, see Figure 1.6. CPU threads execute concurrently with fair scheduling. Work-groups on a GPU are concurrent but scheduled through a queue without fair scheduling.

The GPU is a throughput optimized device. If the number of work-groups greatly exceeds the number of compute units, you can keep the compute units fully occupied as work-groups stream through the GPU. Any particular work-item may complete in a long time (i.e., high latency), but the collection as a whole streams through the device quickly (i.e., high throughput).

The parallelism is hierarchical. For a GPU, you offload work from the CPU to the GPU, enqueue work-groups to execute on the compute units, and then run work-items inside each compute unit. There are constructs we will cover later to control each level in the hierarchy. It leads to directives akin to the following:

```
#pragma omp target teams distribute parallel for simd \
    num_teams(4) num_threads(16)
... a loop nest ...
```

Frankly, few programmers would use OpenMP for programming a GPU if they had to routinely write such directives. In most cases, there is a much simpler approach. We describe this approach in the next section.

3.4   Concurrency and the Loop Construct

OpenMP from the earliest days was a prescriptive API. A directive told the compiler the transformations the programmer wanted done to the code. The number of threads requested, synchronization between threads, scheduling loop iterations onto threads, mapping threads onto NUMA domains, ... it was all explicit and under programmer control. When the goal is to optimize performance, explicit control is a benefit.

As hardware complexity has grown along with the mix of processor types used inside High Performance Computing (HPC) systems, explicit control has become problematic. If you control the details of how code maps onto threads, then as a program moves between systems, code needs to be optimized over again for the features of each new system. Performance portability is compromised if you need to modify code moving from one platform to another. If possible, it would be nice to have constructs that are descriptive; that is, programmers describe what is needed from OpenMP and all the details are left to the system.

Descriptive constructs are a nice idea, but if performance is key, they can be challenging. The problem is that *in general*, the compiler doesn't have enough information to figure out how to optimize code. Compilers need programmers to use their knowledge of algorithms to guide the compiler to generate optimal code. If we move away from the general case, however, and restrict the problem domain, we can sometimes circumvent these limitations and get the performance we need from descriptive constructs.

Such is the case with the `loop` construct, shown in Table 3.2. This construct is placed before a loop nest to say that the iterations of the associated loops can safely execute concurrently. There are no loop-carried dependencies, so they can execute in any order and still produce the correct result.

The loop iterations must be thread safe, race free, and truly independent. Additionally, they cannot call any OpenMP runtime library routines nor contain any OpenMP constructs, even if they occur inside functions called within loop iterations. In OpenMP jargon, we say that the programmer asserts that the loop has the *concurrent order*.

Table 3.2: **A loop construct in C/C++ and Fortran** – The loop construct notifies the system that the associated loop iterations can execute concurrently (i.e., in any order), do not contain any dependencies, and do not contain calls to OpenMP library routines or other OpenMP constructs.

C/C++ directive format
#pragma omp loop *[clause[[,] clause]...]*
loop_nest
Fortran directive format
!$omp loop *[clause[[,] clause]...]*
loop_nest
!$omp end loop

```
1
2    #define N 4000
3
4    int main()
5    {
6        float A[N]; init(A,N);
7        float alpha = 2.0;
8
9        #pragma omp target
10       #pragma omp loop
11       for (int i = 0; i < N; i++) {
12           A[i] = A[i] * alpha;
13       }
14   }
```

Figure 3.8: **Scaling a vector in parallel** – This program will multiply a vector of length N by a constant in place, running *in parallel* on the target device.

With this restriction in place, the runtime system can map a loop onto the hierarchical parallelism of a GPU without the need for any details about how the mapping should occur. We see an example in Figure 3.8. It is left to the programmer to ensure that the loop satisfies the constraints required by OpenMP. If those constraints are met, the runtime system will create work-items, work-groups of the appropriate size, and map the work-groups for execution onto the GPU.

The behavior of the loop construct takes some effort to understand based on the text in the OpenMP 5.2 specification which says that the concurrent iterations are executed by the encountering thread. We haven't gone into the low-level details, but basically the target construct starts what is called an *initial thread* on the device. This is a single thread running on the device. If there is only one thread, how can the loop construct execute with any parallelism?

There is a rule, well known in the compiler community, called the "as if" rule. It states that a compiler can apply any transformations to code during compilation as long as the transformed code makes no changes to the "observed behavior" of the program. Hence, that thread can fork other teams of threads. It can map those teams onto the compute units of a GPU. It can distribute the loop iterations between those teams of threads. In other words, the compiler can auto-parallelize the code as long as the results are the same "as if" the original sequential code was used. By using the `loop` construct, we tell the compiler that the loop iterations can execute concurrently, so it is free to schedule them however it likes, including in parallel.

The loop in Figure 3.8 is admittedly a very simple program. It's natural to ask how common the loops in a problem meet the conditions required by the concurrent order. It turns out, for data parallel problems that map onto a GPU, these conditions are met quite often. You may need to restructure code to expose the concurrency, but a wide range of problems can be parallelized for a GPU using the simple pair of a `target` construct followed by a `loop` construct. This includes many image processing problems, explicit finite difference algorithms, linear algebra routines, embarrassingly parallel algorithms and many more.

3.5   Example: Walking through Matrix Multiplication

So far, we have seen the matrix multiplication code a number of times. In this section, we'll walk through the execution of the matrix multiplication program, line by line, focusing on the data transfers. This example puts together everything in this chapter and sets the scene for later chapters where we will exploit the parallelism of the target device itself.

The program is listed in Figure 3.9. We will refer to the line numbers in this figure in the following text.

Line 2 sets the size of the arrays. N is set by the C pre-processor. Before the code is compiled, every reference to N in the program is replaced by the value 5000. We do this so that we're able to allocate our three arrays on line 5 on the stack. The arrays are of a known, fixed, size. The C compiler will allocate the memory on the stack. For an OpenMP program running on a target device, this means we're

```
1
2   #define N 5000
3   int main()
4   {
5     float A[N][N], B[N][N], C[N][N];
6
7     init(N, A, B, C);      // a user written function to fill A, B and C
8
9     #pragma omp target
10    #pragma omp loop
11    for (int i = 0; i < N; i++) {
12      for (int j = 0; j < N; j++) {
13        for (int k = 0; k < N; k++) {
14          C[i][j] += A[i][k] * B[k][j];
15        }
16      }
17    }
18  }
```

Figure 3.9: **Matrix multiplication** – This program will multiply two matrices, A and B, to produce a third, C, running on the target device. Notice that all three arrays have been allocated in stack memory.

able to use the implicit data transfer rules and we do not need to explicitly manage movement of data between the different memory spaces. OpenMP takes care of stack arrays for us. The host initializes the arrays to their starting values in the init() function on line 7.

So far we've just written a standard serial C program. On line 9, we have our first OpenMP construct: the **target** directive. The code in the structured block and the code inside any functions called within that block (none in this case) forms the target region. The target region in our matrix multiplication program is the nest of **for** loops on lines 10–17, along with the OpenMP **loop** construct. This target region executes on the target device. The outermost **for** loop (line 11) will run in *parallel* on the device. The other two **for** loops will run in sequential order, since we have not exposed any of their parallelism through the various constructs available in OpenMP for exploiting concurrency.

The target construct invokes data transfers at the beginning and the end of the construct. Variables used in the target region are made available on the device in the device data environment. There are only six variables in this example: three arrays A, B, and C, and three scalar integers i, j, and k. Note that N is replaced by a numerical literal during compilation, so is not a variable. All the scalar variables (i, j, and k) are declared inside the target region. They will, of course, be available for use on the target device, and the host has no access to or copy of these variables.

The three arrays exist on the host and reside in the stack memory of the initial thread (or if we include all the detailed OpenMP jargon, the function run by the implicit task executed by the initial thread). They are of a known size and form a complete type. OpenMP will therefore implicitly map these arrays to the device. This will happen on line 9 as part of the target construct. Space will be allocated in the device data environment (in the device memory space), and the values of these arrays will be copied from the host memory space over to these new arrays in the device memory space before the target region executes. This means both the host and device have identical copies of the three arrays just before execution is transferred from the host to the device.

Once this data is transferred, the task that encountered the target construct suspends, and execution begins with a thread (threads) on the device for lines 11–17. After the execution of the `for` loops have finished, the target region ends. The three arrays are copied back to the host. The copy of the C array on the host will now be equal to its value on the device (i.e., the result of the matrix multiplication). The other two arrays will also be copied back to the host, overwriting the values present already on the host with the same values from the device. Once the arrays have been mapped onto the host from the device, the suspended task on the host continues to execute at line 18, which simply ends the program.

As this example shows, our pair of directives are powerful thanks to the implicit rules for mapping (copying) data to and from the host and device. We now know how scalar variables are automatically mapped as `firstprivate` variables to the device data environment, and how fixed-size arrays and structures allocated on the stack are copied to and from the device automatically. We have also seen how tasks are used to transfer program execution from the host to the device and back again. We've come a long way already! There is much more to learn about the `target` directive and how it maps other types of data between the host and a target device. This is the topic of Chapter 4.

4 Memory Movement

In Chapter 3 we described how data moves by default between the host and the target device (i.e., the GPU). We define this data movement in terms of the two different ways memory is managed in a process: the heap and the stack. Memory that is managed dynamically and shared between all the threads within a process are managed as a *heap*. This is the memory you allocate with functions such as `malloc()`. The other type of memory, the *stack*, is associated with blocks (code between "curly" braces). This memory is managed by the system (i.e., the programmer does *not* allocate/free the data) and includes statically declared data associated with any block, function, or thread.

Data that is fully defined (size and type known at compile time) on the stack, is static data. This data (both scalar and array data) is copied onto the target device when a target region begins execution. Scalar variables are mapped as `firstprivate` variables. This means the target region has a copy of the data, but that data won't be copied back to the host at the end of the target region. Arrays declared on the stack are copied to device memory at the start of the target region and copied back to host memory when the target region finishes. There will just be a single copy of the array, stored in device memory, and that array will be available to all threads launched on the device. Structures of a known size declared on the stack behave just like static arrays.

This chapter focuses on explicit data movement. It is mostly concerned with the different ways data from the heap is managed. This data is dynamic (not fully defined at compile time) and accessed via a pointer. These pointers behave differently than scalar variables. The actual value of a pointer, which resolves to a location in memory, has no meaning with respect to device memory. Hence, pointers are mapped from an address in host memory to an address in device memory. This happens at the start of the target region. The data pointed to by a pointer, however, is not copied by default onto a device. That copy must be done explicitly (as we'll show in this chapter).

To show where we are heading, we present the matrix multiplication program we use to track our progress through the book in Figure 4.1. We've updated the code so the arrays are allocated on the heap. The matrices are passed as pointers. As such, the data they point to will not be implicitly transferred, and we must specify the movement through `map` clauses. This chapter introduces the `map` clause and then describes how to optimize memory movement by managing the memory on a device. Before we can talk about the `map` clause, however, we need to digress and talk about the way we specify subsections of arrays in OpenMP.

```
1   void matmul(int Ndim, int Mdim, int Pdim,
2                float *A, float *B, float *C) {
3
4     A = (float *) malloc(Ndim*Pdim*sizeof(float));
5     B = (float *) malloc(Pdim*Mdim*sizeof(float));
6     C = (float *) malloc(Ndim*Mdim*sizeof(float));
7
8     init(A,B,C); // initialize the matrices ... code not shown
9
10    #pragma omp target map(tofrom: A[0:Ndim*Pdim], B[0:Pdim*Mdim], C[0:
         Ndim*Mdim])
11    #pragma omp loop collapse(2)
12    for (int i = 0; i < Ndim; i++) {
13      for (int j = 0; j < Mdim; j++) {
14        for(int k = 0; k < Pdim; k++) {
15          C[i*Mdim+j] += A[i*Pdim+k] * B[k*Mdim+j];
16        }
17      }
18    }
19  }
```

Figure 4.1: **Matrix multiplication** – This program will execute a target region on a device to multiply two matrices, A and B, to produce a third, C. All arrays are allocated in heap memory on the host. Mapping between the host and the device is explicit and managed through `map` clauses.

4.1   OpenMP Array Syntax

OpenMP supports array sections to specify a subset of the elements from an array. In the C programming language, arrays allocated from the heap are pointer-based. The familiar index in square brackets used to access elements of the array does two things. First, it defines the offset from the pointer-address to specify a particular location in memory. Second, it dereferences that pointer to return the value at that location in memory. An array section defines a contiguous subset of the memory referenced by a pointer. Array sections in OpenMP are used in clauses to define how data moves between host and target data regions.

For a pointer to an array, `var`, an array section is defined as follows:

```
var[lower_bound : length]
```

The `lower_bound` is the offset to where the array section begins. The `length` defines the number of elements, beginning at the lower bound, that are included in the array section. For example, if `var` is a pointer to an array of length `N=100`, the array syntax `var[0:N]` refers to the entire array. The array syntax `var[5:3]` specifies three elements starting a location 5 (i.e., `var[5]`, `var[6]`, and `var[7]`).

In the Fortran programming language (and therefore in OpenMP for Fortran), an array section is defined differently. The Fortran array section defines a range. For example, `var(2:4)` would be the elements from 2 to 4 (i.e., `var(2)`, `var(3)`, `var(4)`). We mention this point here since the difference between the OpenMP C/C++ definition of an array section and the Fortran definition is a point of confusion for many programmers.

It is important to remember, for C and C++, the array section defines a lower bound (initial offset) and the number of elements, and *not* a range.

The lower bound parameter is optional, and if omitted, defaults to the start of the array. As such, an array sections may just specify the length, `var[:N]`. Note that we must still include the colon character. The length is usually included, but is optional if the size of the array is already known. The offsets defined by the array sections are in units of the data type of the elements of the array. Hence, in defining array sections, you do not need to take the data type into account.[1]

OpenMP defines a zero-length array section. This takes the form `var[:0]`. The length parameter is set to zero. Pointers in OpenMP are implicitly mapped as zero-length arrays.[2] As the array has zero length, the associated section of the array has no length, so if this was used to copy data between the host and target device, no data would move. Zero-length arrays give OpenMP the information it needs about the start of an array (i.e., the pointer value) so that it can translate between the host and GPU address spaces. Zero length arrays are an important

---

[1]OpenMP also supports a third parameter: a stride. We omit it here because array sections using strides are not supported by the `map()` clause.

[2]Note that if an array section appears in a `map()` clause, the topic of the next section, the pointer associated with that variable (known as the *base pointer*) is mapped as a `firstprivate` variable. If the pointer also explicitly appears in a `map()` clause, in addition to the array section, the pointer becomes an *attached* pointer. An attached pointer cannot be modified in the target region. The implicit behavior for pointers that don't appear in a `map()` clause is to map them as zero-length arrays.

concept when reasoning about mapping of data in OpenMP, but are usually not used explicitly in code.

4.2   Sharing Data Explicitly with the Map Clause

For data allocated on the heap (accessed via a pointer), programmers must tell OpenMP what to do with such data when encountering a target region. We do this with a `map()` clause placed on the `target` directive. This clause defines how data is mapped between the host and the device and when any associated data movement occurs.

Consider the simple sketch of a program in Figure 4.2, where we allocate some memory on the heap and then offload execution to a target device. Following the implicit rules, all the scalar variables are mapped `firstprivate`. The pointers are mapped as zero-length arrays, so while the pointer itself is copied, the data it points to is not. The data that we allocated and accessed via the `A` pointer is not copied—it remains on the host inaccessible to the device.

```
1   int N = 1024;
2   int* A = malloc(sizeof(int) * N);
3
4   #pragma omp target
5   {
6       // N and the pointer A exist here
7       // The data pointed to by A _does NOT_ exist here
8   }
```

Figure 4.2: **Pointer variables are implicitly mapped as zero-length arrays** The pointer variable `A` is implicitly mapped as a zero-length array, while `N` is implicitly mapped as `firstprivate`.

In order to make the data that `A` points to available on the target device, we add the `map()` clause to the `target` directive, as shown in Figure 4.3. We must use the OpenMP array syntax (recall Section 4.1) to describe which data is copied. By default, data in a map clause is copied to the target device at the start of the target region and from the device back to the host at the end of the target region.

As we will see, the `map()` clause gives us a lot of power and flexibility for controlling how data is copied between the host data environment and the target data environment.

```
1   int N = 1024;
2   int* A = malloc(sizeof(int) * N);
3
4   #pragma omp target map(A[0:N])
5   {
6     // N and the pointer A exist here, as firstprivate variables.
7     // The data pointed to by A _does_ exist here as well!
8   }
```

Figure 4.3: **Mapping an array into the device data environment** – The `map()` clause is used to map all of the array `A` into the device data environment.

4.2.1   The Map Clause

The movement of data between the host and device in OpenMP is always defined from the perspective of the host. It is the host that encounters the `target` directive, and the data to be moved is described with the host's perspective in mind. We will always talk of "copying data to the device" and "copying data from the device." We will try to refrain from using phrases such as "copying data from the host to the device" as this can become confusing with the OpenMP syntax.

The `map()` clause takes a list of variables to copy between the host and device, in one or both directions. The list of variables is a comma-separated list of variable names, with much in common with the familiar data-sharing clauses such as `private`, `firstprivate`, etc.

We can specify the directions data moves using one of the map types: `to`, `from` and `tofrom`. There are other modifiers (`alloc`, `release` and `delete`) that we use less often and will discuss later in Section 7.1.1.

A map type of `to` will copy data that exists on the host to the device data environment on entry to the target region. The variables are made available on the device, and they are populated with the same values as on the host. This is a copy of data to the device.

A map type of `from` will copy data from the device data environment back to the host at the end of the target region. Those device variables are copied back to their original locations on the host—the location that is used is what was given in the `map()` clause. Note that with this map type, the mapped variables exist in the device data environment but are uninitialized.

A map type of `tofrom` has the same effect as a map type of both `to` and `from`. Data is copied to the device at the start of a target region, and copied from the device to the host at the end of the target region. This means that the device will contain a copy of the host data, ready for use in the target region, and will return these (updated) values back to the host when the region ends. This is the default behavior if a map type is not specified.

It is worth noting that the copying of data occurs when the target region is executed. So far, this is when the `target` directive is encountered by the host. Later, in Chapter 8 we will introduce the mechanisms for launching target regions *asynchronously*, so that the host can continue doing useful work while a target region executes on a device. As we will see in Chapter 8, this distinction of when the mapping occurs is important when working with asynchrony.

4.2.2   Example: Vector Add on the Heap

To see the `map` clause in action, consider the vector addition program we first encountered in Chapter 3. In this version of the program, we will allocate arrays on the heap before adding them in parallel on the target device. The program is shown in Figure 4.4. The execution of the program proceeds similarly to that in Section 3.1, but in this version of the program, the data movement is explicit.

On line 12, the host encounters the target directive. The scalar variable N is mapped into the device data environment.[3] The pointers A, B, and C appear in `map()` clauses. We have used the OpenMP array section syntax to show the extent of those arrays. For example, `A[0:N]` describes the full extent of the array A (i.e., N elements starting from the beginning of the array). The map types define when data is copied between the host and device. On line 12, at the start of the target region, the `map(to:...)` clause is invoked causing the arrays A and B to be copied at the start of the target region.

We use a different map type for the array C: `map(from:...)`. This ensures that memory is allocated for the array C on the device, but it will be uninitialized. This is perfect for our loop where we write to this array, but do not read from it inside the target data region. The `map(from:...)` clause therefore does not copy anything from the host to the device. It will later, however, copy the array from the device back to the host. This will occur at the end of the target region, at line 16. Once

---

[3]The pointers to the arrays A, B, and C would be mapped as zero-length arrays if they did not appear in the `map()` clauses.

```
1   int N = 4000;
2
3   int main()
4   {
5
6       float * A = malloc(sizeof(float) * N);
7       float * B = malloc(sizeof(float) * N);
8       float * C = malloc(sizeof(float) * N);
9
10      init(A,B,C); // Set initial values
11
12      #pragma omp target map(to: A[0:N], B[0:N]) map(from: C[0:N])
13      #pragma omp loop
14      for (int i = 0; i < N; i++) {
15          C[i] = A[i] + B[i];
16      }
17  }
```

Figure 4.4: **Vector addition** – This program will run on the target device to add two vectors of length N to produce a third vector.

the array C has been copied back to the host, the target region ends and execution returns back to the host.

Consider our earlier vector addition program from Figure 3.3. The arrays reside on the stack, and the OpenMP runtime automatically copied the arrays A, B, and C between the host and the device at the beginning and the end of the target construct. In Figure 4.4, however, the arrays are on the heap and we use map() clauses to explicitly manage the mapping of the arrays A, B, and C. By using a map(to:...) clause for A and B, we eliminated the unnecessary data movements of A and B at the end of the target region. By using map(from:...) for C, we eliminated an excess copy at the beginning of the target construct. As we consider more complicated examples and problems with larger arrays, explicit control over data movement will become increasingly important as we optimize data movement, going well beyond what can be done with the implicit rules for moving stack arrays.

4.2.3   Example: Mapping Arrays in Matrix Multiplication

We now discuss the matrix multiplication example in Figure 4.1 that we used to introduce this chapter. We will use the OpenMP array section syntax to show the extents of each of the three arrays. In this case, they are all different sizes, and note how we can use integer expressions in the clause. The following clause on the `target` directive describes how the arrays are mapped:

```
map(tofrom: A[0:Ndim*Pdim], B[0:Pdim*Mdim], C[0:Ndim*Mdim])
```

Since we used the `tofrom` map type, all three arrays are copied to the device at the start of the target region and then from the device back to the host at the end of the target region. As with the vector addition program in Figure 4.4, the matrix multiplication program only updates one of the arrays. The other two arrays are only read. As an optimization, therefore, we can map the `A` and `B` arrays with the `to` map type and avoid the unnecessary copy from the device at the end of the target region.

We must ensure, however, that the `C` array is initialized on the device. It would not be enough to use a `from` map type because we use the `+=` operator inside the target region. The original value of `C` is updated inside the target region. We must copy it from the device at the end of the target region, so the host can use the result of the matrix multiplication. We ensure this behavior by using a `tofrom` map type on the map clause. Hence, to optimize data movement in the matrix multiply code from Figure 4.1 we should use the map clauses:

```
map(to: A[0:Ndim*Pdim], B[0:Pdim*Mdim]) map(tofrom: C[0:Ndim*Mdim])
```

4.3   Reductions and Mapping the Result from the Device

Reductions are an important operation in parallel computing. In OpenMP, we support reductions by placing a reduction clause on a worksharing loop construct,

```
reduction(op:list)
```

where `list` is a comma-separated list of reduction variables, and `op` is a binary operation such as `+`. While array sections are allowed in a reduction clause, the most common case by far is to use scalars for the reduction variables.

A scalar variable by default is mapped to the target device as a `firstprivate`; each thread on the device gets its own private copy of the scalar variables, and those copies are initialized according to the value of the original variable. A `firstprivate` variable is a type of `private` variable, so it goes "out of scope" at the end of the region. For a reduction to be of any value, the reduction variable must be mapped from the device. Therefore, when we put a reduction clause on a `loop` construct, we must ensure that the reduction variables appear in a `map` clause with the `tofrom` map type.

As an example, consider the program we used to compute π on a CPU (Figure 2.7). Figure 4.5 shows the analogous program for computing π on a target device. To offload work to the target device (i.e., the GPU), we use a `target` construct on line 8. The `loop` construct on line 9 causes the `for` loop on line 10 to run in parallel on the GPU. Consider how variables are mapped between the host and the device. The scalar variables mapped to the target region are `step`, `num_steps`, and `sum`. The variables `step` and `num_steps` are scalar variables on the stack. They are mapped `firstprivate` according to the implicit data mapping rules from Section 4.1. The `sum` variable is a reduction variable listed in the `reduction` clause on line 9. It must be initialized (on the host at line 5), and then, since it's the result we care about from this computation, it must be mapped from the device after the computation is done. Hence, it must appear in a map clause on the `target` construct on line 8 using the `tofrom` map type:

```
map(tofrom: sum)
```

```
1   #include <omp.h>
2   #include <stdio.h>
3   static long num_steps = 100000000;
4   int main() {
5     double sum = 0.0;
6     double step = 1.0 / (double)num_steps;
7
8     #pragma omp target map(tofrom:sum)
9     #pragma omp loop reduction(+:sum)
10    for (int i = 0; i < num_steps; i++) {
11      double x = (i + 0.5) * step;
12      sum += 4.0 / (1.0 + x * x);
13    }
14
15    double pi = step * sum;
16    printf(" pi with %ld steps is %lf\n", num_steps, pi);
17  }
```

Figure 4.5: **Pi program** – This program will compute π on the target device. Note how the reduction variable must appear in a map clause with a `tofrom` map type in order to make the result available on the host.

Later, in Section 6.4.2, we will discuss combined constructs where `target`, `loop`, and other constructs are combined into a single directive. The details won't make sense until we get to Chapter 6, but the most common case is the combination of `target`, `teams`, and `loop`. The behavior of this combined construct is essentially the same as the pair of directives we've been using (`target` followed by `loop`). With this combined construct, we could parallelize the `for` loop in Figure 4.5 by replacing the pair of directives on lines 8 and 9 with the single directive:

```
#pragma omp target teams loop reduction(+:sum)
```

In order for the `reduction` clause to work with this directive, OpenMP changed the implicit mapping rules for a scalar variable when it is used as a reduction variable in combined constructs that include `target`. Instead of the normal rule for scalar variables (mapped as `firstprivate`), scalar reduction variables are now implicitly mapped using the map-type `tofrom`. Hence, when using this combined construct, you get the expected behavior with the `reduction()` clause alone and do not need an additional `map()` clause; that is, the reduction variable is mapped *to* the device so its initialized value is available in the target region and *from* the device after the target region has ended, so the result of the reduction is available on the host.

4.4   Optimizing Data Movement

In all our examples so far, we've looked at how data is transferred between the host and the device (and back again) when target regions are encountered. We've only considered programs with a single target region. The program starts on the host, transfers data and execution to the device, and then returns execution and some data back from the device. Most applications are far more complicated and will have multiple target regions. How do we optimize data movement across multiple target constructs?

For example, consider the iterative algorithm in Figure 4.6, where for every iteration we have a target region. The array, `A`, will be copied to and from the device *every* iteration. The host doesn't need the data until all the iterations (the `for`-loop over `it`) have completed. The array is copied to the device at the start of each iteration, and copied back the host at the end, only for it to be copied to the device again unchanged at the start of the next iteration. This wasted memory movement is expensive (as we said back in Chapter 1). Moving data unnecessarily is clearly not optimal.

```
1   for (int it = 0; it < num_iters; ++it) {
2     #pragma omp target map(A[0:N])
3     {
4       // Iterative_Update the data stored
5       // in A on the target device
6       Iterative_Update(A, it);
7     }
8   }
9
10  // Then, use A on the host
11  use(A);
```

Figure 4.6: **Multiple target regions** – This program fragment shows the basic structure of an iterative algorithm and the data movement complications specific to such algorithms.

We can solve this problem by explicitly managing the *device data environment*. OpenMP defines a *data environment* as all the variables associated with a particular region. For example, the device data environment is the memory to hold all the variables available to a device. It is created implicitly when a program begins its execution. When we map variables to and from the device (using **map** clauses) at the beginning and end of target regions, they are placed into this device data environment where they are available for use inside the target region.

OpenMP defines constructs to map variables into the device data environment *without* also transferring execution to the device (as it would for the **target** directive). This means that we handle the mapping of data separately from the transfer of execution. In the following sections, we will cover the constructs used to manage the device data environment. In each case, we will present these constructs with all their various clauses. We will only discuss in this chapter, however, the most commonly used clauses. This is important since we don't want to inhibit understanding of the core functionality by diverting attention to rarely used low-level details.

4.4.1 Target Data Construct

The simplest way to keep data resident on the device between target regions is with the **target data** directive in Table 4.1. This construct is associated with a structured block. The device data environment starts on entry to the structured block and ends upon exit from the structured block. We show an example of this construct in Figure 4.7. This program uses three target regions: two to initialize the A and B arrays, and a third to add them together.

Table 4.1: **The target data construct in C/C++ and Fortran** – The target data construct maps data to the device data environment for the duration of the structured block. In this chapter we only discuss the map clause without the *map-type-modifier*. The other clauses will be discussed in Chapter 7.

C/C++ directive format
#pragma omp target data *[clause[[,] clause]...]*   structured_block
Fortran directive format
!$omp target data *[clause[[,] clause]...]*   structured_block **!$omp end target data**

device *([device-modifier:] integer-expression)* **if** *(scalar-expression)* **map** *([[[map-type-modifier[,]] map-type:] list])* **use_device_addr** *(list)* **use_device_ptr** *(list)*

The program first allocates memory and initializes the A and B arrays in the host memory space (on the heap) on lines 2–3. On line 5, we have the **target data** construct. The map clauses behave as we discussed before when we described the **target** construct. In particular, the arrays A and B are mapped to the device on entry to the target data construct. We then have three target regions inside the structured block associated with the target data construct:

1. Lines 9–10, updates the A array.

2. Lines 14–15, updates the B array.

3. Lines 19–20, element wise addition of array B to array A.

Each of these target regions are performed in turn with the host waiting for each target region to complete. We then arrive at the end of the structured block on line 21, at which point the arrays A and B are mapped from the device data environment into the host data environment.

```
1   const int N = 1024;
2   int *A = malloc(sizeof(int)*N);  initA(A,N);
3   int *B = malloc(sizeof(int)*N);  initB(B,N);
4
5   #pragma omp target data map(tofrom: A[0:N], B[0:N])
6   {
7     #pragma omp target
8     #pragma omp loop
9     for (int i = 0; i < N; ++i)
10      A[i] += 1;
11
12    #pragma omp target
13    #pragma omp loop
14    for (int i = 0; i < N; ++i)
15      B[i] += 2;
16
17    #pragma omp target
18    #pragma omp loop
19    for (int i = 0; i < N; ++i)
20      A[i] += B[i];
21  }
22
23  // Continue using A and B on the host
24  use(A, B);
```

Figure 4.7: **Target data region** – The arrays are kept resident on the device between target regions, and mapped from/to the host once.

Notice that there are no `map` clauses on any of these target directives. The only data mapping for new target regions happens because of the implicit mapping rules (e.g., scalars as `firstprivate`, etc.). Mapping for the arrays A and B is defined with the **target data** construct on line 5. The arrays are copied to the device at the start of the target data region on line 5, and copied back to the host at the end of the target data region on line 21. Inside the structured block associated with the target data construct, those arrays are present in the device data environment and available for any target region.

If there was any code between target regions in the program from Figure 4.7 and that code modified the arrays A or B, those changes would be overwritten at the end of the target data region. These updates to shared memory would be unordered, and hence this pattern would constitute a data race. The program behavior would be undefined. We'll show you how to access data on the host whilst inside a target data region in Section 4.4.2.

4.4.2   Target Update Directive

Using target data regions to keep data resident on the device between target regions
is crucial for good performance. In some applications, the host needs access to some
of the data on the device in between those target regions. In other words, we need
a way for the host to access data that was mapped by a `target data` construct in
the middle of the target data region.

A simple way to do this using only the mechanisms we've explained so far is to
end the target data region. This would bring everything back (according to the `map`
clauses). The application would then need to create a new target data region and
setup the device data environment again. This is clearly not a good approach; we
want to keep the device data environment with the data resident on the device, and
initiate a data transfer between the host and device only for the data we want to
access.

OpenMP provides the `target update` directive to move data between the host
and device on demand. The syntax is shown in Table 4.2. Of the six clauses available
for this directive, we'll only use two of them in this chapter: `from` and `to`. The other
clauses are described in Part III where we consider the more advanced features of
OpenMP for GPU programming.

Table 4.2: **The target update construct in C/C++ and Fortran** – The target
update construct copies data between the host and device data environment.

C/C++ directive format
#pragma omp target update *[clause[[,] clause]...]*
Fortran directive format
!$omp target update *[clause[[,] clause]...]*

depend *(dependence-type: list)*
device *([device-modifier:] integer-expression)*
from *(list)*
if *(scalar-expression)*
to *(list)*
nowait

Update is a stand-alone directive. It performs the task of copying data between
a device and the host with the direction of the data movement established by the

```
1   const int N = 1024;
2   int *A = malloc(sizeof(int)*N);  initA(A,N);
3   int *B = malloc(sizeof(int)*N);  initB(B,N);
4   int *C = malloc(sizeof(int)*N);  initC(C,N);
5
6   #pragma omp target data map(tofrom: A[0:N], B[0:N], C[0:N])
7   {
8     #pragma omp target
9     use_A_B_C_on_device(A,B,C);
10
11    // Copy A to the host
12    #pragma omp target update from(A[0:N])
13
14    // Reinitialize the array
15    initA(A,N);
16
17    // Copy A back to the device
18    #pragma omp target update to(A[0:N])
19
20    #pragma omp target
21    use_A_C_on_device(A,C);
22  }
```

Figure 4.8: **Target update** – The host needs the A array between target regions, so it copies the data from and back to the device using update directives.

clauses on the update directive. These data movement clauses are very similar to the map clauses, though the syntax is slightly different.

The code in Figure 4.8 shows how the **target update** directive is used. The three arrays A, B, and C are allocated and initialized on the host. We define a target data region to map these arrays into the target data environment. Inside that region are two target regions. We want to keep the data resident on the device across both target regions. However, in this example, the host needs to update the A array between target regions. A **target update** directive is used with a **from** clause. This has a similar effect to a **map(from:)** clause on a **target** region, bringing the data back from the device. The A array is mapped (copied) from the device, back to the host, so the host copy of A contains the latest data that was updated in the first target region on lines 8–9.

The host is then free to modify the array, but those changes won't be seen on the device unless we remap (copy) the data back into the device data environment. To do this, the **to** clause is used on the **target update** directive. This has a similar effect to a `map(to:   )` clause on a `target` region, brining the host data over to the device. The `A` array is mapped (copied) to the device, from the host, so that the device contains the latest data ready for use in future target regions (lines 20–21).

4.4.3   Target Enter/Exit Data

We've seen how important it is to keep data resident on a device by minimizing transfers between the host and the device through a `target data` construct. This construct is convenient for small programs that fit inside a single structured block. For larger programs however, forcing our target regions to fit inside a single structured block is not practical.

To resolve this limitation, OpenMP provides two stand-alone directives for mapping variables to and from the device data environment. The result is the same as with the more structured `target data` directive. With two directives, one for entry to the target data environment and the other on exit from the target data environment, the programmer has much more flexibility when writing code with multiple target regions. We show these directives in Table 4.3. These directives manipulate the device data environment which is then available to subsequent target regions.

Table 4.3: **The target enter data and target exit data constructs in C/C++ and Fortran** – The `target enter data` and `target exit data` constructs map data between the host and device data environments. In this chapter, we will only discuss the map clause without the `map-type-modifier`. The other clauses will be discussed in later chapters.

C/C++ directive format
#pragma omp target enter data *[clause[[,] clause]. . .]*
#pragma omp target exit data *[clause[[,] clause]. . .]*
Fortran directive format
!$omp target enter data *[clause[[,] clause]. . .]*
!$omp target exit data *[clause[[,] clause]. . .]*

depend *(dependence-type: list)*
device *([device-modifier:] integer-expression)*
if *(scalar-expression)*
map *([[map-type-modifier[,]] map-type:] list])*
nowait

The `target enter data` directive maps data *to* the device and keeps it there for future target regions. While the directive can be placed where a `target data` directive might occur, the `target enter data` supports a more flexible coding style that doesn't require all associated `target` constructs to occur inside a single structured block. The `target exit data` directive maps data from the device, removes it from the target data environment and copies it back to the host. While the directive could replace the closing curly bracket of a `target data` region, we are not restricted to a structured block and can use the `target exit data` directive where it best fits into a program.

We provide two examples to help compare and contrast these different approaches to managing data across multiple target regions. Figure 4.7 showed how the `target data` directive keeps data resident on the device between three target regions. The code in Figure 4.9 shows the same example but instead uses the `target enter data` and `target exit data` directives to achieve exactly the same behavior.

The directives should be used as a pair, just as we would ensure memory allocation and deallocation routines are used as a pair (i.e., every `malloc()` should have a matching `free()`). As with memory allocators, we are free to call them on the host in more convenient locations in the code. Consider the program fragment in Figure 4.10. This program has a routine that initializes the data. We could make that data available on the target device, mapping (copying) it into the target data environment by adding the `target enter data` directive straight into that routine, on line 5. When we later use the data in our main routine on lines 16–18, notice that we do not need to map the pointer again. The A array is already mapped to the device, and does not need copying again. A similar pattern could be used in C++ programs, with `target enter data` directives being used in class constructors, and `target exit data` directives being used in class destructors.

4.4.4   Pointer Swapping

Keeping data resident on the device is crucial for performance. Memory movement limits performance, so avoiding unnecessary data transfers between the host and the device is one of the first things you should look at when optimizing performance (a topic we will discuss at length in Chapter 5). We've seen how we can use the `target update` directive to update copies of data between target regions executing within a shared device data environment. There are cases, however, where we do not need to copy data between target regions. We just need to change the pointers

```
1   const int N = 1024;
2   int *A = malloc(sizeof(int)*N); initA(A,N);
3   int *B = malloc(sizeof(int)*N); initB(B,N);
4
5   #pragma omp target enter data map(to: A[0:N], B[0:N])
6
7   #pragma omp target
8   #pragma omp loop
9   for (int i = 0; i < N; ++i)
10    A[i] += 1;
11
12  #pragma omp target
13  #pragma omp loop
14  for (int i = 0; i < N; ++i)
15    B[i] += 2;
16
17  #pragma omp target
18  #pragma omp loop
19  for (int i = 0; i < N; ++i)
20    A[i] += B[i];
21
22  #pragma omp target exit data map(from: A[0:N], B[0:N])
23
24  // Continue using A and B on the host
25  use(A, B);
```

Figure 4.9: **Target enter/exit data example** – The arrays are kept resident on the device between target regions, and mapped from/to the host once using target enter/exit data directives.

we use to reference data already resident in a device data environment. This occurs in a wide range of iterative algorithms using a technique known as *pointer swapping*.

Consider an algorithm where in each iteration, we store new values in one array using the data computed from a second array. At the end of the iteration, we need to swap the arrays in advance of the next iteration, where the updated values will be used as the input array used to compute a new set of values. We could simply copy everything over, but that results in wasteful data movement. A much more efficient approach is simply to swap the *names* of those arrays or, equivalently, swap the pointers to the arrays.

In Figure 4.11 we provide a simple program that uses pointer swapping. This is a class of algorithm known as a *relaxation method*. The problem starts with data in an initial state (the function called on line 9) and then iteratively applies an

```
1    void init_array(int *A, int N) {
2      for (int i = 0; i < N; ++i)
3        A[i] = i;
4
5      #pragma omp target enter data map(to: A[0:N])
6    }
7
8    int main(void) {
9
10     int N = 1024;
11     int *A = malloc(sizeof(int) * N);
12     init_array(A, N);
13
14   #pragma omp target
15   #pragma omp loop
16     for (int i = 0; i < N; ++i) {
17       A[i] = A[i] * A[i];
18     }
19
20     #pragma omp target exit data map(from: A[0:N])
21
22   }
```

Figure 4.10: **Initializing data with target enter data** – The `target enter data` directive is used to set up the device data environment so that data is initialized for later use in a target task.

operation until the solution "relaxes" into a final state. In this case, our operation is a three-point stencil with the end points of the array fixed at their initial state (since the loop on line 17 runs from 1 to N-2). This particular three-point stencil corresponds to replacing the central point in the stencil with the average of that point and its two nearest neighbors (line 18).

A particularly simple way to handle relaxation methods is to allocate two arrays; one to receive the updated values in the current iteration (`A_new`) and the other to hold the results from the prior iteration (`A_old`). One array is read-only (`A_old`) while the other array is write-only (`A_new`). We parallelize this program for a CPU using OpenMP with a **parallel for** construct on line 16. Since we are using the two arrays and are not mixing reads and writes into any single array, we can run this loop in parallel without the need for any synchronization.

The key is to swap the roles for the two arrays prior to each iteration. We do this with the pointer swap in lines 22–24. After this code executes, the `A_new` pointer

```
1
2   #define N 100000
3   #define niters 100
4   int main(void) {
5
6      float *A_old = malloc(sizeof(float)*N);
7      float *A_new = malloc(sizeof(float)*N);
8
9      init_A(A_old, A_new); // Initialize the data
10
11     // Loop over a fixed number of iterations
12     for (int it = 0; it < niters; ++it) {
13
14        // Loop over the array, computing the average of
15        // the neighbouring elements of the array
16        #pragma omp parallel for
17        for (int i = 1; i < N-1; ++i) {
18           A_new[i] = (A_old[i-1] + A_old[i] + A_old[i+1]) / 3.0f;
19        }
20
21        // Swap pointers!
22        float *temp = A_new;
23        A_new = A_old;
24        A_old = temp;
25
26     } // End of iteration it loop
27
28     print_results(A_old, A_new);
29  }
```

Figure 4.11: **Swapping pointers** – The pointers to the arrays are swapped each iteration so the updated values are used as input to the current iteration.

will point to the data that `A_old` used to point to, and vice versa. So now, `A_old` points to the data just updated in the current iteration, `it`, ready for its use in the next iteration, `it + 1`. Notice how this just swaps the pointers; none of the actual data is moved.

We want to use a similar procedure to swap data arrays stored on the device by simply swapping pointers. The good news is pointer swapping in general just works, as shown in Figure 4.12. A target data region is established on the device and populated with the two arrays, shown in line 11. We use the `target` and `loop` constructs for the computation loop on lines 18–19. Notice that we do not add `map` clauses as the arrays are already present on the device. We then swap the pointers on the host on lines 25–27, just as in the example in Figure 4.11. Crucially, we are swapping the pointers on the host, and not on the device, but the device *will* see the pointers swapped correctly. How can this be? We will have to use our knowledge of both the implicit and explicit mapping of data between the host and device to explain.

```
1
2   #define N 100000
3   #define niters 100
4   int main(void) {
5
6     float *A_old = malloc(sizeof(float)*N);
7     float *A_new = malloc(sizeof(float)*N);
8
9     init_A(A_old, A_new); // Initialize the data
10
11    #pragma omp target enter data map(to: A_old[0:N], A_new[0:N])
12
13    // Loop over a fixed number of iterations
14    for (int it = 0; it < niters; ++it) {
15
16      // Loop over the array, computing the average of
17      // the neighbouring elements of the array
18      #pragma omp target
19      #pragma omp loop
20      for (int i = 1; i < N-1; ++i) {
21        A_new[i] = (A_old[i-1] + A_old[i] + A_old[i+1]) / 3.0f;
22      }
23
24      // Swap pointers on the host
25      float *temp = A_new;
26      A_new = A_old;
27      A_old = temp;
28
29    } // End of iteration it loop
30
31    #pragma omp target exit data map(from: A_old[0:N], A_new[0:N])
32
33    print_results(A_old, A_new);
34  }
```

Figure 4.12: **Swapping pointers of device data** – The pointers to the arrays are swapped each iteration so the updated values are used as input to the current iteration.

These pointers refer to arrays on the host that were mapped onto corresponding arrays in the target device data environment through the use of one of the target data constructs. This mapping creates an association between the pointer into the host address space and the analogous pointer into the address space associated with the target device data environment. That association is fixed by `map` clauses on the target data constructs.

When a `target` construct is encountered, all of the implicit data mapping rules apply. Scalar variables are mapped `firstprivate`, and fixed-size stack arrays are mapped `tofrom` and copied to the device data environment at the start of the target region. The fixed-size stack arrays are copied back onto the host from the target device at the end of the target region. In addition, as we mentioned in Section 4.1, pointers are mapped as zero-length arrays. This means that the pointer itself will be mapped into the device data environment, but there will be no copying of data as the array has no (zero) length. So pointers are mapped on entry to every target region.

This means that each target region will see new values for pointers if they have been changed on the host, just as they had in our example in Figure 4.12. The `A_new` and `A_old` pointers will be mapped as zero-length arrays on entry to the target region on line 18, and the target device will use the updated pointers inside the target region.

There is a subtle but important point to appreciate concerning pointers and how they are mapped onto the host when the target device data environment is managed with a `target data` construct. Consider the code in Figure 4.13, where the pointer is set to NULL inside the `target data` region. This code is correct, and the data movement implied by the `map(from:A[0:N])` will proceed. The data will be copied back to the data referenced by the original value of the pointer A (i.e., the one saved in the `orig_A` pointer). This is because the destination of the data to be copied back to the host at the end of this target region is fixed by the map clause on the target data directive on line 8. We are free to change the pointer value on the host inside the target data region, as on line 17. That assignment of the pointer to NULL will not affect where the array originally at A will be stored after the target data region ends. The pointer on the host was set to NULL on line 17, so we can't use it on the host anymore. The copy from the target device back onto the host, however, will still place the data in the memory pointed to by the old value of A since that destination in memory was fixed by the map clause on line 8.

```
1   int main(void) {
2     int N = 1024;
3     int *A = malloc(sizeof(int)*N);
4
5     // Take a copy of the A pointer
6     int *orig_A = A;
7
8     #pragma omp target data map(from: A[0:N])
9     {
10      #pragma omp target
11      #pragma omp loop
12      for (int i = 0; i < N; ++i) {
13        A[i] = i;
14      }
15
16      // Set A to NULL before end of target data region
17      A = NULL;
18    }
19
20  }
```

Figure 4.13: **The destination of the map(from) is set when the target data construct is encountered** – Although the pointer, A, is set to NULL inside the target data region, the destination of the copy from the device has already been set when the **target data** directive was encountered on line 8—the device data will be copied from the device to the host at the original location of A.

This can have have implications when the number of pointer swaps in the data region is not known in advance. In particular, if the number of pointer swaps is even (or zero), then the pointers point to their original targets (i.e., they swap and swap back). If the number of pointer swaps is odd, the targets are switched. For a code such as that shown in Figure 4.12 where the number of pointer swaps is determined on the number of iterations of a loop, we must ensure that we collect the final result from the correct location. This issue is not caused as a result of mapping data to and from the device, but is an inherent wrinkle when pointer swapping occurs inside a target region. To make this easier to keep track of, it is convenient to collect the result from the final location with a **target update** directive, instead of relying on the mapping placed on the **target data** region. This will evaluate to the current value of the pointer when the **target update** directive is encountered and perform the mapping directly.

Likewise, if the data is mapped back using a `target exit data` directive, the
current value of the pointer is again used. It is worth restating the difference
between these two cases with the following code fragments. In this first case, shown
in Figure 4.14, we use a `target data` construct. The data that `A_old` points to is
fixed by the `map` clause on the `target data` construct. Data copied from the device
onto the host will always be mapped back to that same location at the end of the
region, no matter how many times the pointers are swapped.

When `target exit data` is used instead, as shown in Figure 4.15, the data that
`A_old` points to will be mapped back to wherever address `A_old` is pointing to when
the `target exit data` construct is encountered. In this case, the pointers following
the `target exit data` directive will point to the data as defined by the values of
the pointers after the final swap.

```
1  #pragma omp target data map(tofrom: A_old[0:N], A_new[0:N])
2  {
3      // Swap pointers N times
4  }
```

Figure 4.14: **Pointer swapping with a target data directive** – The target data
directive will map from the device at the end of the region using the value of the pointer
when the target data directive was encountered at the start of the region. This may not
correspond to the latest values of the pointers, depending on the number of times they
were swapped.

```
1  #pragma omp target enter data map(to: A_old[0:N], A_new[0:N])
2
3  // Swap pointers N times
4
5  #pragma omp target exit data map(from: A_old[0:N], A_new[0:N])
```

Figure 4.15: **Pointer swapping with target enter data and target exit data
constructs** – Using the `target enter data` and `target exit data` constructs ensures
the map from the device at the end will use the latest values of the pointers.

4.5   Summary

This chapter completes our discussion of the most commonly used elements from OpenMP for programming a GPU. We refer to this as the OpenMP GPU Common Core. We can offload work to a target device (the GPU) and map loop iterations onto the processing elements of the GPU. Data movement is implicit (for data on the stack) or, as we covered in this chapter, explicit (for data on the heap). For most programmers, the OpenMP GPU Common Core is all that is needed.

In Chapter 5, the final chapter of Part II of the book, we will recap our progress up to this point and then talk about how to use the common core to write code that performs well. This is an essential point since the only reason to offload work to a GPU is to achieve better performance. That means you should be willing to work a bit to make your code run correctly while exploiting a large fraction of the performance available from a GPU.

5 Using the GPU Common Core

We have completed our journey through OpenMP's GPU Common Core and have established a foundation to build on as we explore the more advanced features of GPU programming in the rest of the book. We summarize the GPU Common Core in Table 5.1. With only 10 items to consider, mastering the GPU Common Core is straightforward. Using these items effectively, however, requires an understanding of the fundamentals of performance programming for GPUs.

We start this chapter with a review of the items that make up the GPU common core. Then we move on to discuss the fundamental principles that guide effective use of OpenMP to produce efficient, high-quality code. In other words, a solid foundation is not just a set of constructs and clauses. A good foundation also includes the concepts needed to take an idea from algorithm to code to optimized application. To that end, we will explore (often through concrete examples) the fundamentals of performance-programming for a GPU using OpenMP. We will refer to these performance principles often as we move through the rest of the book.

5.1 Recap of the GPU Common Core

To summarize the OpenMP GPU common core, we will explore a simple application and its parallelization. Consider a Jacobi method for solving a system of linear equations.[1] This is the famous $Ax = b$ problem; find the vector x such that the matrix A times x equals the vector b. A and b are the inputs to the problem. The vector x is the solution we aim to find.

The Jacobi solver works by first rewriting the matrix A as a sum of its diagonal, upper triangular, and lower triangular parts. Those triangular parts are just the matrix entries above and below the diagonal. We rewrite the matrix $A = L + D + U$, where L is the lower triangular entries, U is the upper triangular entries, and D is

---

[1] Relaxation methods are usually used for solving partial differential equations. They only work for the $Ax = b$ problem when A is close to a unit matrix. We use the Jacobi solver when teaching OpenMP, however, since it's easy to test for correctness by comparing the product Ax to the input vector b.

Table 5.1: **The GPU Common Core.**

OpenMP pragma, clause, or environment variable	Description
`#pragma omp target`	Offload execution to a target device (a GPU)
`#pragma omp loop`	Follows a target construct to run the following loop(s) in parallel on a target device
`reduction(op: list)`	Reduction using *op* for variables in *list*
`collapse(n)`	Combine *n* nested loops into one logical loop
`map([to | from | tofrom :] list)`	Map variables in *list* between the host and a device
`#pragma omp target data`	Manage data on a device for a structured block
`#pragma omp target update to(list)` `#pragma omp target update from(list)`	Update data *to* or *from* a device
`#pragma omp target enter data`	Move data into a target device data region
`#pragma omp target exit data`	Move data from a target device data region
`OMP_TARGET_OFFLOAD=mandatory`	Force target region to execute on a target device

the entries on the diagonal. We can then rearrange the equation $Ax = b$ as follows:

$$Ax = b$$
$$(L + D + U)x = b$$
$$(L + U)x + Dx = b$$
$$Dx = b - (L + U)x$$
$$x = D^{-1}(b - (L + U)x)$$

where D^{-1} is the inverse of the diagonal entries of A. This is easy to compute as it is a diagonal matrix where the entries are one divided by the corresponding entries in D.

With x on both sides of the equation, we approximate x through an iterative relaxation scheme. We guess the value of x on the right-hand side and use it to produce a better guess on the left-hand side. We then use this guess on the right-hand side to produce an even better guess. This process continues until x stops changing significantly, typically within a defined tolerance. We can write the update as follows:

$$x_{\text{new}} = D^{-1}(b - (L+U)x_{\text{old}}) \tag{5.1}$$

The associated code for the Jacobi solver parallelized to run on a GPU using OpenMP is shown in Figure 5.1.

We will now walk through this code and, in doing so, discuss the items in Table 5.1. When thinking of parallel code in terms of loop-level parallelism, you always start with the time-consuming loops at the heart of the computation. This loop is found on lines 21–26. These nested loops over i and j implement a matrix-vector multiplication of $(L+U)$ times the current "guess" for the solution vector, xold. This is followed on line 25 with the difference of the b vector and the diagonal elements of the matrix-vector product followed by the division by the diagonal elements of the A matrix.

The body of the innermost loop on line 23 defines too little work to justify running on a GPU. Hence, we map the loop over i onto the GPU and each work-item on the GPU includes the loop over j. In GPU parlance, we say that that loop over i defines the index space onto which we map instances of the kernel defined by lines 22–25. The following pair of pragmas launches the work onto the GPU:

```
#pragma omp target
#pragma omp loop
```

Now that we've identified the work that we'll run on the GPU, we review the data environment required to support that work. Looking at the code in lines 21–26, the matrix A and the vectors b, xnew, and xold are accessed. Since all of this work happens as part of an iterative algorithm (as seen by the while loop on line 16), the target construct on line 19 will be encountered repeatedly. Hence, it is important that we pull data movement outside the target regions associated with computation. We do this with the pragma on line 14:

```
#pragma omp target enter data \
    map(to: xold[0:N], xnew[0:N], A[0:N*N], b[0:N])
```

```
1   #include <omp.h>
2   #define TOLERANCE 0.001
3   #define MAX_ITERS 100000
4
5   int main() {
6     int iters = 0,   N = 1000; // A[N][N]
7     double conv=100000.0, err, *A, *b, *xold, *xnew;
8     A = (double *)malloc(N * N * sizeof(double));
9     b = (double *)malloc(N * sizeof(double));
10    xold = (double *)malloc(N * sizeof(double));
11    xnew = (double *)malloc(N * sizeof(double));
12    initializeProblem(N,A,b,xold,xnew);
13
14  #pragma omp target enter data map(to: xold[0:N], xnew[0:N], A[0:N*N], b[0:N])
15
16    while ((conv > TOLERANCE) && (iters < MAX_ITERS)) {
17      iters++;
18
19      #pragma omp target
20      #pragma omp loop
21      for (int i = 0; i < N; i++) {
22        xnew[i] = (double)0.0;
23        for (j = 0; j < N; j++)
24          if (i != j)    xnew[i] += A[i * N + j] * xold[j];
25        xnew[i] = (b[i] - xnew[i]) / A[i * N + i];
26      }
27      // test convergence
28      conv = 0.0;
29
30    #pragma omp target map(tofrom:conv)
31    #pragma omp loop reduction(+ : conv)
32      for (int i = 0; i < N; i++) {
33        double tmp = xnew[i] - xold[i];
34        conv += tmp * tmp;
35      }
36      conv = sqrt(conv);
37
38      // pointer swap
39      double* tmp = xold;
40      xold = xnew;
41      xnew = tmp;
42    }
43    #pragma omp target exit data map(from: xnew[0:N])
44  }
```

Figure 5.1: **Jacobi linear equation solver** – This program finds the vector x for input matrix A and input vector b. We only show the code for the iterative solution. The full program and other details about this program are available online (www.ompgpu.com).

The arrays A, b, xnew, and xold are all represented as pointers into dynamically allocated memory (memory associated with a process's heap), so we must specify the range of values from the arrays that must be moved to the device using the OpenMP array section syntax (e.g., $xold[0:N]$). We are moving them from the host to the target device, so we represent the array mapping with the to map type in the map clause.

We then go to the next loop in lines 32–35. This loop computes an element-wise difference between xnew and xold which we square and then sum to produce a measure of how close the two arrays are to each other. There is very little work inside this loop, but since the data is already resident on the GPU (due to the earlier target data enter construct), it is reasonable to do this on the GPU. The pragma that accomplishes this is on lines 30–31:

```
#pragma target map(tofrom:conv)
#pragma loop reduction(+:conv)
```

At the end of this target region, the map clause stipulates that the reduction variable is mapped back onto the host where we take the square root (i.e., complete computation of the L2 norm) and produce the value used to assess convergence of this iterative process (i.e., the while loop on line 16).

Once the computation has converged and we have our final approximation to the solution vector, xnew, we copy that value back with the pragma on line 43:

```
#pragma omp target exit data map(from: xnew[0:N])
```

Remember that a map clause is expressed in terms of the host. You use map with to when mapping data on the host device *to* the target device. Similarly, to move data *from* the target device onto the host, you use map with the from map type.

With this Jacobi solver example from Figure 5.1, we have covered most of the items listed in Table 5.1. All that remains is the collapse clause, the update directive, and the construct to create a target data region.

The collapse clause is discussed later in Section 5.2.4. It is used to combine loops in a loop-nest to create more work-items for the GPU scheduler to map onto the GPU. The goal is to keep all the processing elements inside the GPU fully occupied. This amount of work needs to be at least equal to the number of processing elements (i.e., the *SIMD lanes*) inside the GPU. Ideally, you actually want much more work than the number of SIMD lanes to give the scheduler room to overlap computing with higher latency operations such as memory movement.

```
1   #include <omp.h>
2   #define TOLERANCE 0.001
3   #define MAX_ITERS 100000
4
5   int main() {
6     int iters = 0,    N = 1000; // A[N][N]
7     double conv=100000.0, err, *A, *b, *xold, *xnew;
8     A = (double *)malloc(N * N * sizeof(double));
9     b = (double *)malloc(N * sizeof(double));
10    xold = (double *)malloc(N * sizeof(double));
11    xnew = (double *)malloc(N * sizeof(double));
12    initializeProblem(N,A,b,xold,xnew);
13
14  #pragma omp target data map(to: xold[0:N], A[0:N*N], b[0:N]) \
15                                              map(to:xnew[0:N])
16  {
17    while ((conv > TOLERANCE) && (iters < MAX_ITERS)) {
18      iters++;
19
20      #pragma omp target
21      #pragma omp loop
22      for (int i = 0; i < N; i++) {
23        xnew[i] = (double)0.0;
24        for (j = 0; j < N; j++)
25          if (i != j)   xnew[i] += A[i * N + j] * xold[j];
26        xnew[i] = (b[i] - xnew[i]) / A[i * N + i];
27      }
28      // test convergence
29      conv = 0.0;
30
31    #pragma omp target map(tofrom: conv)
32    #pragma omp loop reduction(+ : conv)
33      for (int i = 0; i < N; i++) {
34        double tmp = xnew[i] - xold[i];
35        conv += tmp * tmp;
36      }
37      conv = sqrt(conv);
38
39      // pointer swap
40      double* tmp = xold;
41      xold = xnew;
42      xnew = tmp;
43    }
44    #pragma omp target update from(xnew[0:N])
45  } // end of target data region
46  }
```

Figure 5.2: **Target data region** –This program is a variation of the program from Figure 5.1. In this version of the Jacobi solver, we use a **target data region** to manage the memory movement.

The next item we need to cover from Table 5.1 is the directive to create a target data region. This is best understood through an example. In Figure 5.2 we show the Jacobi solver from Figure 5.1, but this time we use a target data region to manage the data movement. Instead of two stand-alone directives to define data movement, `target enter data` and `target exit data`, we have a single region that defines data movement:

```
#pragma omp target data \
    map(to: xold[0:N], A[0:N*N], b[0:N]) \
    map(tofrom:xnew[0:N])
```

This is an OpenMP construct which means there is an associated structured block (i.e., the code between the curly braces on lines 16 and 45). The behavior is similar to placing a `target data enter` at line 16 and a `target data exit` at line 45. Since all the data movement is defined in a single directive, we might be tempted to use the `tofrom` map type. A `tofrom` mapping is equivalent to a mapping from the host *to* the target device at the beginning of the target data region and a mapping *from* the target device to the host at the end of the target data region. However, depending on the number of iterations, the original location for `xnew` may not contain the final result (recall Section 4.4.4 on pointer swapping).

In order to ensure that the latest data, contained in `xnew` is copied back to the host at this possibly updated address, the `update` directive is used instead. The `from` clause is used to update the value on the host, copying the data back:

```
#pragma omp update from(xnew[0:N])
```

As with the `map` clauses, the perspective for `update` is the host's. You use `from` to move *from* the target device onto the host and `to` for mapping data on the host *to* the target device.

Finally, in Table 5.1, the last row is an environment variable, used to control whether offloading if required: `OMP_TARGET_OFFLOAD`. If this variable is set to the value `mandatory`, then the OpenMP programs that reference a device are forced to actually use that device. In other words, the OpenMP runtime is not allowed to decide that the program might be better served by running on the host alone. It must launch a kernel corresponding to target construct on the device. In practice, this is used as shown in the following line:

```
$  OMP_TARGET_OFFLOAD=mandatory   ./a.out
```

In this command line, $ is the UNIX command prompt and a.out is the program executable.

   That completes our summary of the items that make up the GPU common core. There is much more yet to cover in programming a GPU with OpenMP. This includes asynchronous execution, multiple target devices, explicit control of how work maps onto the hierarchical parallelism of the GPU and more. Before we *go there*, however, we need to pause and discuss the general principles of performance programming on a GPU.

5.2   The Eightfold Path to Performance

Programming is a journey. You start with a problem and move to an algorithm that solves the problem. This algorithm is crafted into a program which hopefully produces "useful" results. Programmers have found "four noble truths"[2] of GPU programming to guide them in this journey.

The essence of GPU programming is performance: The only reason to write code for a GPU is to achieve high performance—to get answers to your problem in less time.

Programmers rarely achieve the performance they hope for: Sometimes we get lucky. The state of our existence as programmers, however, is to struggle with programs that do not deliver the performance we hope for. They often are good enough, but it is rare that we achieve the performance we want compared to the maximum available performance of the system we are using.

We attain performance by working around limitations in the hardware: The hardware in a system, that is, the host (CPU) and the target devices (GPU), presents the programmer with a range of resource constraints. Memory bandwidth, interconnects between hosts and devices, latencies across the memory hierarchy— these and other aspects of a system present a wide range of challenges a programmer must overcome to produce performant code.

---

[2]With apologies to Siddhārtha Gautama.

The path to performant code: Programmers working over the years have found an eightfold path to performance.

1. Only write portable code. Use portable programming models and test execution on diverse devices.

2. Only write the code you need to write; use libraries.

3. Pick the right algorithm for the job.

4. Have enough work to keep the GPU fully occupied. Write code for high *occupancy*.

5. Converged execution flow.

6. Minimize data movement.

7. Memory Coalescence.

8. The slowest task sets the pace; balance the load.

Follow this path as you write GPU code and you will achieve performance-bliss.

5.2.1 Portability

Software lasts longer than hardware. Today's amazingly fast processor is history after a few years whereas a good piece of software is useful for decades. Therefore, when you write software, it is essential that you think beyond current hardware and consider how that software will move between systems over time.

This is why it is so important to use a programming language or API that is not tied to a single processor or "owned" by a single vendor. You need to write software using a portable programming environment that is "cross vendor" in reality, not in theory. Programming models evolve as hardware changes, so it is also important to use programming technologies that are controlled in a vendor-neutral manner. This is why OpenMP is going so strong even though it is over 25 years old.

A more subtle point is to test software with multiple processors from different vendors. Memory models vary in subtle ways between processors. Internal data formats for floating point computations may change how numbers are rounded. Compilers, believe it or not, like all software, have bugs. There are a host of potential challenges that may cause subtle differences in the results of a program as you move between processors. Hence, a robust testing strategy should include running a validation test suite on multiple processors from multiple vendors.

Performance is critical. We turn to GPUs and write parallel code all in the name of achieving good performance. Do not forget, however, the old adage that "premature optimization is the root of all evil" [10]. Write code for portability. Let the compiler and supporting runtime systems handle performance, when possible with descriptive constructs such as the `loop` construct.

You will often hear of performance portability, that is, code that you write once and it runs near its peak performance on all systems of interest [11]. This is a goal those who implement our programming environments dream of but rarely achieve. The fact we often fail to achieve performance portability is not a serious problem. The essential feature is *maintainability*, which we define as the ability to support an application across heterogeneous systems from a single code-base. Even if you must sometimes write specific functions differently to optimize for different processors, it is still cost effective as long as you can use a single code-base across systems. That being said, it is indeed very much possible to write code in OpenMP that runs near its peak performance on multiple different systems [12].

5.2.2 Libraries

If you are a programmer, you probably (hopefully?) like to write code. If you enjoy math and numerical analysis, you like to dive into the details of a platform and understand how your code maps onto the low-level features of a system. Even if you are a "performance" or "math obsessed" programmer, the code you write is code you understand, and you avoid unpleasant surprises.

However, experienced programmers eventually learn (often the hard way) that you should only write code when someone else (often a professional) hasn't done so and provided a library from which you can pull the function you need. It is truly surprising how often this seemingly simple principle is ignored.

As a good example, consider matrix multiplication. This is one of our favorite examples pedagogically. With computations that scale as $O(N^3)$ and communication that scales as $O(N^2)$, it is possible for large N to run in a compute bound mode and achieve high performance. Using the OpenMP code we've discussed earlier in this book (e.g., Figure 4.1) for multiplication of order 10,000 matrices of double precision numbers (a *DGEMM*), we achieved 136 GFLOPS on an NVIDIA® GeForce® RTX 2080 Ti GPU. On that same GPU, however, calling the DGEMM function from the cuBLAS library (the details of which are described in Chapter 9), the program ran at 423 GFLOPS (billions of Floating Point Operations Per Second). This latter result is close to the peak performance of 480 double precision GFLOPS available from that GPU.

The fact is that while our triply nested loop version of matrix multiplication is easy to understand and even easier to write, that program bears no resemblance to the code a professional library writer would produce. A professional would tile the loops using local memory to hold intermediate results. Tile sizes are selected based on the properties of the memory hierarchy, tuned to specific devices, and matrix sizes. Loop orders lead to different algorithms that are mathematically quite different from the dot products our simple algorithms use.

It is worth noting that this holds for a simple problem such as multiplying two matrices. When you consider more complex problems such as fast Fourier transforms or generating pseudorandom numbers in parallel, it is even more important to use a library.

5.2.3   The Right Algorithm

In a Particle-Particle N-body method, we can use a direct sum to compute the force vector on each particle due to the individual force, $\overrightarrow{f(i,j)}$ of particle j on particle i. These sorts of computations appear often in physics problems. Perhaps the simplest case to understand is the force on a particle i due to pairwise force with all the other particles due to gravity:

$$\overrightarrow{F_i} = \sum_{j=0}^{N-1} \frac{Gm_i m_j}{r_{i,j}^3} \overrightarrow{r_{i,j}}$$

where $\overrightarrow{r_{i,j}}$ is a vector from particle i to particle j and $r_{i,j}$ is the length of that vector (i.e. the distance between i and j). Computer scientists love this problem. It is simple to code (a pair of nested loops over i and j around a trio of loops over the three spatial dimensions x, y, and z) and scales as $O(N^2/2)$, so there is plenty of work to execute in parallel. The problem is this is a bad algorithm. It's easy to parallelize and speeds up nicely as the number of processing elements grows, but it is not particularly stable numerically. Particles range from very close to very far, so the dynamic range of force values is huge across the full set of particles. This results in a substantial loss of precision as values are summed.

A better algorithm is the Barnes-Hut algorithm [13]. The spatial domain is hierarchically subdivided into boxes. The outermost box (the whole problem domain) is split in each of the three spatial dimensions to create eight boxes of roughly equal numbers of particles. This continues recursively to build an *oct-tree* until the boxes at the leaves have few enough particles to sum directly (and correctly) with the $O(N^2/2)$. The final forces on each particle is then computed as the sum of forces from nearest neighbors (i.e., the particles inside a particle's innermost box) and the force due to the center of gravity to all the other, more distant boxes. This is $O(NlnN)$, so it is much less work, but it is also more accurate.

The Barnes-Hut algorithm, however, is much harder to parallelize effectively, so in computer science books (such as this book) it is usually not shown. They use the "bad" algorithm. We are better than that and won't show either. We'll just caution you that when approaching a problem, pick the algorithm that gives the best answer with the best performance Spend the time up front to find and then implement the right algorithm.

5.2.4 Occupancy

Our goal is high performance. We want our programs to use the full resources of a processor effectively. If resources such as processing elements are unused, they consume power without doing any useful work. That is inefficient from a power point of view, but more directly, it results in performance well short of what a processor is capable of delivering.

Hence, when designing a GPU program, you must make sure there is enough work to keep all the processing elements fully occupied. The term *occupancy*[3] is used to refer to this situation with full occupancy meaning all the processing elements available for a computation are busy.

Consider matrix multiplication. The key loop nest for this computation follows:

```
for (int i=0; i<Ndim; i++)
    for (int j=0; j<Mdim; j++)
        for(int k=0; k<Pdim; k++)
            *(C+(i*Mdim+j)) += *(A+(i*Pdim+k)) *  *(B+(k*Mdim+j));
```

---

[3]NVIDIA® expresses occupancy as the ratio of active warps to the maximum number of warps a streaming multiprocessor can support. There are differences between this definition and the one we are using, but they are ultimately measuring the same thing—namely, how close to fully occupied are the resources of a GPU as a program runs.

We can parallelize this loop for a GPU with a simple pair of OpenMP directives placed before the nested loops:

```
#pragma omp target
#pragma omp loop
```

Running this code on a GPU[4] to multiply three (relatively small) double precision matrices of order 1000, the program runs at 6.6 GFLOPS. This is a far cry from the expected peak performance of the GPU (480 GFLOPS in this case). For the GeForce® RTX 2080 Ti GPU, there are 68 compute units (i.e., streaming multiprocessors) with 64 processing elements (i.e., CUDA™ cores) per compute unit for a total of 4352 processing elements. Our above loop parallelizes over the columns of the product matrix and only generates 1000 work-items that execute in parallel. That is nowhere near enough to keep the full GPU occupied.

   The solution is simple. Since the loops are independent, we can collapse the loops over i and j into a single larger loop so that the parallelization is over the dot products associated with the computation of each element of the product matrix. This creates 1000^2 work-items which is more than enough to keep the GPU's processing elements fully occupied. We do this with the collapse(2) clause in the following pair of directives placed right before the matrix multiplication loop nest:

```
#pragma omp target
#pragma omp loop collapse(2)
```

For multiplication of order 1000 matrices, the program now runs at 173 GFLOPS. Is this good enough? If the peak performance from the GPU is 480 GFLOPS, should we be satisfied with 173 GFLOPS? This is a question that comes up often when analyzing the performance of parallel code. There is so much going on when a processor executes code, unless an analytic cost model is available for the program, a general answer is not available. In this case, however, we can answer the question. If you consider a library version of a program produced by performance professionals experienced in writing code to the low-level details of a system, we can compare to that code's performance to get an idea of the best that can be expected given the size and structure of a problem. In this case, we consider the DGEMM function from the cuBLAS library which runs this order 1000 matrix multiplication at 213 GFLOPS.

---

[4]NVIDIA® GeForce®· RTX 2080 Ti GPU

Given the simplicity of using a declarative constructs such as `loop` and that we left all the hard optimization work to the compiler, getting within 20 percent of expert optimized code with such a simple (*and* portable) construct is impressive. For larger matrices, the library will likely perform better, and so following the path with libraries in Section 5.2.2 remains important.

5.2.5   Converged Execution Flow

A GPU is a hierarchical parallel system. The GPU appears to the OpenMP programmer as a target device connected to the host. The GPU further breaks down into a number of distinct compute units (streaming multiprocessors) that are composed of a large number of processing elements which, depending on the target device, may include vector units. At the lowest level in this hierarchy are SIMD lanes.[5] The SIMD lanes are driven by a single stream of instructions. For example, given a sequence of instructions A, B, C, D each SIMD lane in a compute unit involved in a computation executes A then B then C and finally D. We call this a *converged execution flow*.

Logic that introduces a branch of any kind, breaks this converged flow; that is, the execution flow diverges. For example, consider the Jacobi solver from Figure 5.1. The code in the major, compute-intensive loop contains an `if` statement.

```
#pragma omp loop
for (int i = 0; i < N; i++) {
  xnew[i] = (double)0.0;
  for (int j = 0; j < N; j++)
    if (i != j)   xnew[i] += A[i * N + j] * xold[j];
  xnew[i] = (b[i] - xnew[i]) / A[i * N + i];
}
```

This `if` statement separates the matrix-vector multiplication using the off-diagonal elements from the subsequent vector operations along the diagonal. This breaks up the convergent execution flow.

To avoid this problem, we remove the `if` statement so all SIMD lanes working on the innermost loop execute the same instructions.

---

[5]In some modern GPUs, the processing elements at the bottom of the hierarchy execute as loosely coupled processors rather than "lock-step" SIMD lanes. GPU programming languages, however, continue to assume SIMD-lane behavior, so this continues to be the right abstraction for GPU programming.

```
#pragma omp loop
for (int i = 0; i < N; i++) {
  xnew[i] = (double)0.0;
  for (int j = 0; j < N; j++) {
    xnew[i] += A[j * N + i] * xold[j] * (double)(i != j);
  }
  xnew[i] = (b[i] - xnew[i]) / A[i * N + i];
}
```

The term `(double)(i!=j)` is equal to one when `i` is not equal to `j` and zero when they are equal. This accomplishes the same result as the `if` statement in the earlier code block. More work is being done, but since the work is the same across all the SIMD lanes, the performance can be much better. How much better? For the Jacobi solver with the if statement running on an older GPU[6] and for $N = 4096$, the program ran in 18.4 seconds. When we used the logical expression `(i!=j)` to execute with converged execution flow, the runtime dropped to 13.8 seconds, even though additional work was carried out per instruction.

The penalty for diverged execution flow has been shrinking over time. Newer GPUs and compiler innovations have allowed the SIMD lanes at the bottom of the parallelism hierarchy to act more like loosely coupled processors and less like "lock-step" lanes in a SIMD unit. However, some penalty still remains for divergent execution flow in modern GPUs. Given the need to write code that runs well on the full range of GPUs, including older GPUs, it is still good practice to write code that maximizes converged execution flow.

5.2.6 Data Movement

A program defines a set of operations that act on data. When you think of an algorithm, it's natural to focus on the operations that implement an algorithm. That is where the math is and, for many programmers, that's the fun stuff. We often overlook, however, the implications of the data the operations act upon. This data needs to move across the memory hierarchy from the file system (often on a disk) to DRAM across multiple levels of cache to finally land in the register file where a processing element applies the operations to it. This data movement can be a significant part of a program's runtime.

---

[6]NVIDIA® K20X™ GPU.

As an example, in this section (and the next) we will consider the partial differential equation that represents how heat diffuses through a system over time. In two spatial dimensions (i.e., diffusion of heat across a very thin homogeneous plate) this equation is:

$$\frac{\partial u}{\partial t} - \alpha\left(\frac{\partial^2 u}{\partial x^2} + \frac{\partial^2 u}{\partial y^2}\right) = 0$$

We explain all the math elsewhere[7] and provide just a high-level summary here. We decompose our continuous temporal and spatial coordinates into a discrete set dividing time into fixed points separated by Δt and, in both spatial coordinates (x and y), fixed points separated by $\Delta x = \Delta y$ (i.e., evenly spaced in x and y). Using central difference formulas for the derivatives, we end up with the following finite difference expression:

$$u_{i,j}^{k+1} = u_{i,j}^k + \frac{\alpha \Delta t}{\Delta x^2}(u_{i+1,j}^k + u_{i-1,j}^k + u_{i,j+1}^k + u_{i,j-1}^k - 4u_{i,j}^k)$$

where the superscript k represents points in time, and subscripts i and j are the spatial coordinates. Code to implement the core of this simulation (i.e., omitting initialization, testing, etc.) is shown in Figure 5.3. We parallelized this program by focusing on the pair of loops over the spatial domain. We need to map the two arrays over the spatial domain onto the GPU, which we want to access on the host as well so we use `map` with `tofrom`.

In the body of the loop, we handle the boundary conditions with a ternary statement for each term in the difference equation:

```
((i < n-1) ? u[i+1+j*n] : 0.0)
```

This is an easy way to specify that at the boundaries of the thin plate, the temperature is fixed at a value of zero. Every work-item executes this same conditional logic; therefore, as discussed in Section 5.2.5, the work-items do not diverge. The result is simplicity of the code with the high performance we expect from a converged execution flow.

Speaking of performance, how well does the code from Figure 5.3 perform? When we run this code on our GPU[8] and the NVIDIA® nvc compiler version 22.5 for 10 time steps and $N = 10,000$ steps in x and y, the program in Figure 5.3 ran in

---

[8]NVIDIA® GeForce® RTX 2080 Ti GPU

```
1
2    #include <stdlib.h>
3    #include <math.h>
4    #include <omp.h>
5
6    int main(int argc, char *argv[]) {
7      int n = 1000;           // Problem size, forms an nxn grid
8      int nsteps = 10;        // Number of timesteps
9      double alpha = 0.1;     // heat equation coefficient
10     double length = 10000;// physical size of domain: length x length square
11     double dx = length/(n+1);// physical size of each cell
12     double dt = 0.5 / nsteps;      // time interval (total time of 0.5s)
13     double r = alpha * dt / (dx * dx); // Stability
14     // Allocate two nxn grids
15     double *u   = malloc(sizeof(double)*n*n);
16     double *u_tmp = malloc(sizeof(double)*n*n);
17     double *tmp;
18
19     initial_values(n, dx, length, u);
20     zero(n, u_tmp);
21
22     const double r2 = 1.0 - 4.0*r;
23     for (int t = 0; t < nsteps; ++t) {
24
25   #pragma omp target map(tofrom: u[0:n*n], u_tmp[0:n*n])
26   #pragma omp loop collapse(2)
27       for (int i = 0; i < n; ++i) {
28         for (int j = 0; j < n; ++j) {
29           u_tmp[i+j*n] =  r2 * u[i+j*n] +
30           r * ((i < n-1) ? u[i+1+j*n] :  0.0) +
31           r * ((i > 0)   ? u[i-1+j*n] :  0.0) +
32           r * ((j < n-1) ? u[i+(j+1)*n] :  0.0) +
33           r * ((j > 0)   ? u[i+(j-1)*n] :  0.0);
34         }
35       }
36       // Pointer swap
37       tmp = u;
38       u = u_tmp;
39       u_tmp = tmp;
40     }
41   }
```

Figure 5.3: **Five-point stencil code** – This program advances the temperature profile across an n by n thin square plate over a range of time steps. The time interval is dt, and the spatial interval is dx. alpha is a constant, capturing the thermal properties of the plate.

113.9 seconds. Ideally, what time would we expect for this computation? If we look
at the heat diffusion equation expressed in terms of finite differences, we see that
for each point in the spatial domain, each update in time requires five adds and one
multiplication. There are N^2 spatial points and six floating point operations per
point. For our GPU, we should be limited by the bandwidth to the device memory;
our GPU has a peak performance of 616 GB/s (gigabytes per second). With the
problem size of $N = 10,000$ and 10 time steps, the loops on lines 27–35 move 16 GB
of data. If we ignore everything other than this data movement, the computation
should run in approximately 0.03 seconds. Hence, we see that our runtime of 113.9
seconds is well off from our ideal projections, assuming the kernel should be bound
by the throughput of main memory on this processor.

```
1   #pragma omp target enter data map(to: u[0:n*n], u_tmp[0:n*n])
2   for (int t = 0; t < nsteps; ++t) {
3
4     #pragma omp target
5     #pragma omp loop collapse(2)
6     for (int i = 0; i < n; ++i) {
7         for (int j = 0; j < n; ++j) {
8
9         u_tmp[i+j*n] =  r2 * u[i+j*n] +
10        r * ((i < n-1) ? u[i+1+j*n] : 0.0) +
11        r * ((i > 0)   ? u[i-1+j*n] : 0.0) +
12        r * ((j < n-1) ? u[i+(j+1)*n] : 0.0) +
13        r * ((j > 0)   ? u[i+(j-1)*n] : 0.0);
14      }
15    }
16    // Pointer swap
17    tmp = u;
18    u = u_tmp;
19    u_tmp = tmp;
20  }
21  #pragma omp target exit data map(from: u[0:n*n])
```

Figure 5.4: **Five-point stencil code: target data regions** – The core loops
from our heat diffusion example parallelized to execute on a GPU. To reduce excess data
movement, we use a target data region, so we map arrays onto the loop only once.

Clearly, just focussing on writing a parallel program does not always get us a high
performing program. The problem is that by putting the **map** clauses on the target
construct, the data movement between the host and the GPU happens at each time
step. We can reduce this by explicitly mapping data into the target data region

before the loop over time and then map data back from the data region on exit after the time loops are complete. The code to accomplish this is shown in Figure 5.4. This code ran on our system (using the same parameters as before) in 2.7 seconds. This is a significant speedup; the program now runs over 42 times faster! We are still far from the ideal number, but we are getting closer. This brings to bear one of the most fundamental principles of performance programming. Data movement is the key to performance. If data movement is done poorly, anything else you do to optimize a program won't matter very much.

5.2.7 Memory Coalescence

Memory movement between the host and the GPU is the most critical factor to address when optimizing code. Once data is on the GPU, however, you still need to consider data movement on the GPU. The key is to think about how memory is used across the work-items in a work-group. If work-item w_i uses memory at location m_i, then ideally you want work-item w_{i+1} to use memory at location m_{i+1}. This brings memory references across work-items together, that is, the memory accesses *coalesced*.

Consider the heat diffusion example in Figure 5.4. The loop block at the core of the computation is:

```
#pragma omp target
#pragma omp loop collapse(2)
for (int i = 0; i < n; ++i) {
    for (int j = 0; j < n; ++j) {

    u_tmp[i+j*n] =  r2 * u[i+j*n] +
    r * ((i < n-1) ? u[i+1+j*n] : 0.0) +
    r * ((i > 0)   ? u[i-1+j*n] : 0.0) +
    r * ((j < n-1) ? u[i+(j+1)*n] : 0.0) +
    r * ((j > 0)   ? u[i+(j-1)*n] : 0.0);
    }
}
```

As we move through adjacent work-items in the combined loop, since the innermost loop is over j and offsets used with the pointers u_tmp and u are expressions in which j is multiplied by n, adjacent work-items' memory accesses are spaced by a fixed

```
1    const double r2 = 1.0 - 4.0*r;
2    #pragma omp target enter data map(to: u[0:n*n], u_tmp[0:n*n])
3    for (int t = 0; t < nsteps; ++t) {
4
5      #pragma omp target
6      #pragma omp loop collapse(2)
7      for (int j = 0; j < n; ++j) {
8          for (int i = 0; i < n; ++i) {
9
10             u_tmp[i+j*n] =   r2 * u[i+j*n] +
11             r * ((i < n-1) ? u[i+1+j*n] :  0.0) +
12             r * ((i > 0)   ? u[i-1+j*n] :  0.0) +
13             r * ((j < n-1) ? u[i+(j+1)*n] :  0.0) +
14             r * ((j > 0)   ? u[i+(j-1)*n] :  0.0);
15         }
16     }
17     // Pointer swap
18     tmp = u;
19     u = u_tmp;
20     u_tmp = tmp;
21   }
22   #pragma omp target exit data map(from: u[0:n*n])
```

Figure 5.5: **Five-point stencil code: memory coalescence** – In this version of the program, the order of the two loops have been swapped.

stride of n. This is better than random locations from one work-item to another, but the result is still far from adjacent work-items accessing adjacent memory locations. If we want memory accesses to be adjacent, we can switch the loop order to make the loop over j the outermost loop. The result is the code in Figure 5.5. With this order, the i loop is the innermost loop, and the indices inside the expressions for u and u_tmp reference adjacent memory locations. For the same GPU and calculation parameters as before, our performance is now 1.7 seconds.

Reviewing our progress, ideally performance should be under one second. We started at 113.9 seconds running on a GPU. Optimizing memory movement between the host and the GPU, this number dropped to 2.7 seconds. Changing loop orders so the fastest changing index references adjacent memory locations, our memory was coalesced and performance fell to 1.7 seconds. While still well above our overly optimistic performance projections, we are now off by factors of 10 instead of the factors of 1000 we started with, and the program is 67 times faster.

5.2.8 Load Balance

When you submit work to a GPU, the work is not done until the last work-item is finished. In other words, the slowest work-item determines the runtime for the program. Your goal as a programmer, therefore, is to adjust the amount of work done by each work-item so they all finish at the same time. We call this balancing the load between the work-items.

In the GPU Common Core, we defined the `loop` construct, which converts a loop-nest into a collection of work-items running on a GPU. We have not discussed, however, how the loop iterations map onto the GPU. In the GPU common core, there is no way to influence the mapping of loop iterations onto a GPU and therefore there are few ways to influence how you achieve a good load balance.

This is why, in our discussion of the Eightfold Path, we've put load balancing at the end. It is important. In designing a good parallel algorithm, it is essential that you achieve a good load balance across the work-items. In most cases, however, to do this, you need to go beyond the OpenMP GPU Common Core. And to do that, you need to read the rest of this book.

5.3 Concluding the GPU Common Core

We have completed our coverage of the OpenMP GPU Common Core and the general principles guiding the writing of efficient GPU code. This brief subset of OpenMP is useful for a large portion of the GPU programming you are likely to do. This core subset of OpenMP, however, also defines a foundation you can build on as you learn the rest of OpenMP relevant for GPU programming.

Let's review that foundation. GPU programming languages are based on a host/device model. The program begins its execution on the host. Work is defined on the host and enqueued for execution on one or more target devices that, in our case, are GPUs. The host and each GPU have their own data environments. Clauses on OpenMP directives are used to map data between the host and GPU data environments.

Work for execution on a GPU is defined by a set of one or more nested loops combined into one logical-loop with a `collapse` clause. The loop iterations of the logical-loop defines an index space, and the body of the logical-loop defines a function (called a kernel), an instance of which runs at each point in the index space.

These instances (called work-items) are collected into groups (called work-groups) that are queued for execution on a GPU.

Of course, OpenMP defines an abstraction that hides many of these low-level details. We encourage programmers whenever possible to work at the level of the high-level abstractions in OpenMP. This is done with a pair of directives placed before the loops mapped onto the GPU index space. The first is the `target` directive, which transfers execution to the GPU while the host waits for the work in the target region to complete. The second is a `loop` directive (possibly with a `collapse` clause) to create the work for the GPU. The key point of the codeloop directive is to leave it to the OpenMP compiler and runtime to decide how to map work onto the GPU. This is a declarative directive that stipulates what the programmer desires (map this loop nest onto the SIMD lanes of a GPU) but says *nothing* about how to achieve that desire. This works quite well in many cases, but more importantly, the resulting code is portable.

As you consider a wider range of GPU algorithms, however, cases will arise where the `loop` directive is not enough. We mentioned the case of load balancing. There are other cases where work must be managed explicitly across a memory hierarchy. In other cases, a program needs to run asynchronously between the host and the GPU so that useful work can take place on the host in parallel to work on the GPU. In these and other cases, the GPU common core is not enough. A programmer needs to go beyond the common core – which of course, is the topic pursued in the rest of the book.

III BEYOND THE COMMON CORE

As you write more complicated programs and target more diverse hardware, it is likely you will need to move beyond the GPU Common Core. That is the topic of Part III of this book.

We start with Chapter 6, where we return to the topic of the parallelism available inside a device. This time, rather than hiding behind the declarative `loop` construct, we focus on detailed control of the hierarchical parallelism within a GPU.

We then address more advanced features of the memory subsystem. The goal is detailed, dynamic control of memory. An important trend in system architectures, however, is to simplify memory management by providing a shared address space between the host and the device, something called *Unified Shared Memory* (USM). This dramatically simplifies porting an application to a heterogeneous system. At the same time, it gives you the flexibility needed to dynamically balance the load between GPUs. USM and advanced topics in memory management are the topics of Chapter 7.

We often think of one or two CPUs and a single GPU as the canonical heterogeneous platform. There are times, however, when a node contains several GPUs. In Chapter 8 we discuss the multi-GPU problem. To really benefit from multiple GPUs on a node, you need them (and the host) to run at the same time. This is the problem of asynchronous execution, which we also cover in Chapter 8.

Programs today are often composed of modules from many sources. When the programmer has access to the source code and all the modules use the same parallel programming language, composition across modules doesn't present any insurmountable problems. Reality, however, isn't that nice. Often you have to compose modules written in different programming languages or modules offered as libraries where you do not have access to source code. The complex topic of interoperability across software modules plus a few remaining advanced topics are covered in Chapter 9.

With Chapter 9 we finish our presentation of the subset of OpenMP used for GPU programming. We close the book with two final chapters. In Chapter 10, we share our thoughts on the importance of heterogeneous computing and offer some advice on how to keep up with OpenMP as it continues to evolve. Then, in the Appendix we summarize all the items from OpenMP covered in this book. This gives you one place to refer to as you write code.

6   Managing a GPU's Hierarchical Parallelism

The GPU Common Core described in Part II is simple but powerful. With just 10 items from OpenMP, we map parallel loops onto a GPU and control how data moves between the GPU and the CPU. Most programmers will rarely (if ever) need to go beyond the Common Core.

What happens, however, when algorithms are complex and require explicit control over how the concurrency in an algorithm maps onto a GPU? What happens when the compiler working with our basic `loop` construct is unable to optimally map work and data onto the GPU? We will discuss such cases in this chapter, where we learn how to use directives beyond `loop` to express *hierarchical parallelism*.

Hierarchical parallelism, as we learned in Chapter 1, is a fundamental aspect of both CPUs and GPUs. For the GPU, we have a number of Compute Units (Streaming Multiprocessors), each of which is composed of multiple Processing Elements (SIMD lanes). Using the `loop` construct, we express our algorithms at a high level, leaving it to the runtime system and compiler to map the program's work onto the hierarchical parallelism of a GPU. By representing the parallelism at such an abstract level, the resulting code is portable (and hopefully performant) across a wide range of GPUs. For those times when the `loop` construct alone is not enough, OpenMP includes directives and clauses that let a programmer explicitly control execution of a program at each level of the parallelism hierarchy.

The challenge for the programmer is that the nature of the concurrency you can exploit changes as you move across the parallelism hierarchy. There are levels inside the parallelism hierarchy where individual units of work (or work-items) run on threads that can synchronize with each other. There are others where the concurrently executing items are managed in work-queues, meaning they are not *fairly scheduled* and hence cannot synchronize. There may be other levels in the hierarchy that execute in parallel "in lock-step." OpenMP includes what is needed to manage all of these cases, but it can get complicated.

In this chapter, we describe how OpenMP can be used to manage concurrency across the hierarchical parallelism of a GPU. There are two broad themes as we move through this material. First, how the GPU threads are organized for hierarchical parallelism. Second, how the work, defined by loops in a program, is distributed about these threads.

6.1 Parallel Threads

We are already familiar with a key part of OpenMP's parallelism hierarchy: threads executing in a shared address space. This is the realm of traditional OpenMP programming with CPUs. Refer back to Section 2.3.1 for an in-depth recap of threads.

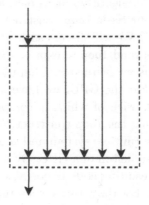

Figure 6.1: **An OpenMP parallel construct creates threads within a single team** – Threads must be able to synchronize at any time within the parallel region.

The **parallel** construct creates threads. The threads all belong to a single team. We show this pictorially in Figure 6.1. The **parallel** construct creates a team of threads, with the thread that encountered the construct joining the team as well. The threads are concurrent and scheduled for execution such that we can define ordering constraints (synchronization events) at any point within the region. While any OpenMP synchronization construct can occur within a parallel region, as we learned with the Eightfold Path to performance (Section 5.2), the need for *high occupancy* and a *converged execution flow* means that on a GPU, you should only use synchronization events that involve all the threads together (i.e., collective synchronization), the classic example of which is a **barrier**. At the end of the parallel region, there is a barrier where threads join together again, after which the thread that encountered the construct continues on its own.

We can share the work of a loop between threads in a team using the `for` worksharing construct. We can put `for` and `parallel` into a combined construct:

```
#pragma omp parallel for
```

The iterations of the loop are divided into chunks and scheduled onto each of the threads for parallel execution. We saw how to do this in Section 2.3.2. On a GPU, we can express this same sort of thread-level parallelism inside a target region by using the `parallel` and `parallel for` constructs. You might think we can use this to spread out the work from a large parallel loop across all the Processing Elements in a GPU, just as we did with the `loop` construct. To find out why this is not the case, we need to delve into how the parallel threads in a single team are mapped onto a GPU.

A GPU Compute Unit schedules work for all of its Processing Elements. In order to do this efficiently and to allow the GPU to be throughput-optimized, each Compute Unit is very quick at context switching, allowing those Processing Elements to stop working on their current task and start working on a completely unrelated one. This is very useful when those Processing Elements need to wait for something for a long time, such as a load from memory or a barrier. In order to keep the Processing Elements fully engaged as we swap work in and out, the Compute Unit is over subscribed with batches of parallel work from which to choose instructions to schedule for execution. These batches of parallel work are not scheduled fairly for execution on the Compute Units. The unit schedules them for execution without any guarantees that the threads make forward progress. It is able to just switch out to other threads and execute those instructions, so a waiting thread might wait a long time before making progress.

What does all this mean for OpenMP? It means that if our OpenMP threads within a team run on Processing Elements in different Compute Units, when we want to synchronize between these threads, we might wait forever (deadlock). The hardware gives us no strong guarantees of when those threads will be scheduled. This means it is very difficult for our threads in the team to synchronize if they are scheduled across different Compute Units. GPUs guarantee that threads (work-items) running on a single Compute Unit are scheduled to execute together (fair scheduling), so by mapping the threads in a team onto a single Compute Unit, we support the synchronization features we expect (and require) with a parallel team of threads.

As such, OpenMP implementations map a team of threads (a work-group) onto a single Compute Unit so that the *hardware* can provide the guarantees required to synchronize between the threads in the team. This means that when we write `target parallel for`, we will only generate one team, which means we will only be utilizing one Compute Unit on the GPU, leaving all others idle!

Using the parallel threads within a team can still be very useful. However, threads are only one level of the OpenMP parallel hierarchy. Notice that the threads all run within a team. In the next section, we'll see how having multiple teams of threads, giving us a second layer to our hierarchy, enables us to run across multiple Compute Units on the GPU.

6.2   League of Teams of Threads

When we launch threads with a parallel construct, they all live within a single team. But OpenMP allows us, in certain specific locations, to launch multiple teams. These teams form a league. For those familiar with sports, this term for multiple teams is probably intuitive! When we have multiple teams, each with multiple threads, we greatly increase the amount of parallel work that can be scheduled to run on our GPU. It also gives us the control we need to write hierarchical algorithms, where our programs use parallelism across teams combined with the parallelism of the threads within each team.

A league of teams can be created immediately within a target region using the `teams` construct, presented in Table 6.1. In Figure 6.2, we show how the `teams` construct is typically used. There must not be any statements between the `target` and `teams` constructs. In other words, the `#pragma omp teams` must occur directly after the `#pragma omp target`.[1] We can of course still use any clauses on the `target` construct, such as `map()`, but we cannot have any code in between the constructs.

As mentioned previously when discussing synchronization of threads within a team in Section 6.1, there is no synchronization of threads existing in different teams. This flexibility of scheduling of teams means that the hardware can schedule multiple teams to each Compute Unit, and the GPU hardware can handle scheduling them on the device efficiently.

---

[1] A league of teams can also be launched as the first statement in the entire OpenMP program. In this book we only focus on the case where a league of teams is created in a target task.

Table 6.1: **The teams construct in C/C++ and Fortran** – The `teams` construct creates a league of teams. It must be directly nested inside a target region.

C/C++ directive format
#pragma omp teams *[clause[[,] clause]...]*   structured_block
Fortran directive format
!$omp teams *[clause[[,] clause]...]*   structured_block   **!$omp end teams**

allocate *(alloc-nam: list)*   **default(shared | none)**   **firstprivate** *(list)*   **num_teams** *(integer-expression)*   **private** *(list)*   **reduction** *(reduction-identifier : list)*   **shared** *(list)*   **thread_limit** *(integer-expression)*

```
1  #pragma omp target
2  #pragma omp teams
3  {
4      // Target region executed by threads in multiple teams
5  }
```

Figure 6.2: **Creating a league of teams in a target region** – The `teams` construct is used to create a league of teams.

The only way to synchronize the teams themselves is by ending the target task in which they were generated. Recall that the `target` construct generates a task containing the code in a target region. Although we don't know in what order the teams will be scheduled on the hardware—limiting the synchronization between them—we do know that all teams in the league will finish executing when the target task has ended.

The code in Figure 6.2 launches a league of teams on the target device. We show this pictorially in Figure 6.3. The thread launches a target task (shown as

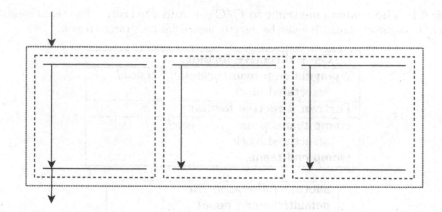

Figure 6.3: **An OpenMP teams construct creates a league of teams** – Each team has one thread. The league of teams must be the first thing that's created at the start of the target region.

a box with a solid line), which executes on the device. The target initial thread then launches a league of teams, each containing just a single thread. The code in the target region will be executed by each of these threads; the one thread in each team will do exactly the same work. These teams will be executed on the device concurrently: some will be executed in parallel on different Compute Units, and some will be executed concurrently on the same Compute Unit, as determined by the hardware at runtime.

6.2.1 Controlling the Number of Teams and Threads

We can control the number of teams created with the `num_teams()` clause. We do not generally recommend specifying the number of teams for performance portability reasons, as the optimal number of teams can vary significantly for different devices and problem sizes. However, in the cases where we need to control this, we can specify the number of teams we would like to create using this clause. When we specify a single number, such as `num_teams(8)`, we will get eight teams. Unlike the `num_threads()` clause, the `num_teams()` clause gives us strictly the number of teams requested. When we specify two numbers, such as `num_teams(8,16)`, we can get a number of teams anywhere between the two numbers (8 and 16) inclusive.

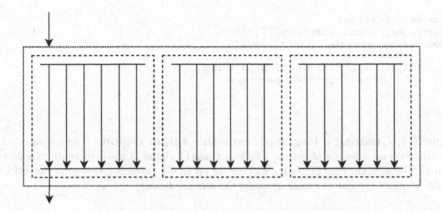

Figure 6.4: **The team initial thread can spawn extra threads within the team with the parallel construct** – Threads in the same team are able to synchronize, but threads in different teams cannot.

We can combine the **teams** construct with the **parallel** construct to expand the teams to run with more than one thread per team. We can see how this looks in Figure 6.4. The single thread in each team encounters the parallel region and launches some number of threads within that team, following the usual behavior. The number of threads launched is implementation defined but can be controlled with the **num_threads()** clause. Figure 6.4 shows three teams, each with six threads,[2] and we would write this in our code as shown in Figure 6.5.

Once again, each thread in each team executes the target region, as we are not sharing any work. We can use the SPMD-pattern (recall Section 2.3.1) and use functions from the OpenMP API to manually distribute the work. The function signatures from the API are summarized in Table 6.2. Using these functions, we can manually share the work of loops, following the two-level hierarchy of teams and threads.

It is much easier to use the worksharing constructs in OpenMP. We already know about the **for** construct for sharing iterations of a loop between threads in a team. In the next section, we will show how to distribute work between teams as well.

---

[2]In practice, you usually want a number of teams equal to the number of Compute Units (streaming multiprocessors) and a number of threads equal to the subgroup size (for NVIDIA® GPUs, the size of a warp or 32).

```
1  #pragma omp target
2  #pragma omp teams num_teams(3)
3  #pragma omp parallel num_threads(6)
4  {
5     // Target region executed by 3 teams,
6     // with up to 6 threads per team
7  }
```

Figure 6.5: **Creating a league of teams in a target region** – The `teams` construct is used to create a league of teams. The `num_teams()` clause is used to create exactly three teams. The `num_threads()` clause will create up to six threads per team. For GPUs, it would be more typical to create 32 or 64 threads per team.

Table 6.2: **OpenMP functions for SPMD-style programming of threads and teams in a target region** – These functions are used to query the runtime for thread and team IDs from inside the appropriate region.

OpenMP API	Description
`int omp_get_num_teams(void)`	Returns the number of teams in the league
`int omp_get_team_num(void)`	Returns the team ID of the team containing the calling thread
`int omp_get_num_threads(void)`	Returns the number of threads in the team
`int omp_get_thread_num(void)`	Returns the thread ID within the current team of the calling thread
`#pragma omp teams`	Create a league of teams (the number of teams is implementation defined)
`#pragma omp teams num_teams(N)`	Create a league of N teams
`#pragma omp parallel`	Create threads within the current team (the number of threads is implementation defined)
`#pragma omp parallel num_threads(N)`	Create up to N threads within the current team

6.2.2 Distributing Work between Teams

Using the `teams` and `parallel` constructs, we can launch a league of teams, each with multiple threads, to create a large amount of concurrent threads for the GPU. This is important since a GPU needs a large amount of work to be fully occupied—at least the number of Compute Units times the number of processing elements per Compute Unit (a number that can easily reach up into the thousands). We still need, however, a way to distribute the work defined by the loops in a program among these parallel resources. Otherwise, each of the threads will process exactly the same sequence of instructions. We can use the SPMD style of manually partitioning our work, but it is far simpler to use a worksharing construct.

We already saw how the `for` construct works in Section 2.3.2. This construct schedules the iterations of a loop across the threads in the team. With a static schedule (with no chunk size), the loop extent is divided as equally as possible across threads in the team. This is often desirable so that each thread has a balanced amount of work to do.

We need to go further, however, to share the iterations of a loop between different teams. For this, OpenMP provides the `distribute` construct defined in Table 6.3. As with the `for` construct, `distribute` must appear directly before a loop (or before multiple loops using the `collapse` clause).

Consider our vector addition example in Figure 6.6. This code will execute the target region (the for loop) on the target device, and the arrays will be copied automatically by the implicit mapping behavior. Notice that we have included a `teams` construct to launch a league of teams inside the target region. Each of these teams consists of a single thread. The `distribute` construct will share the loop iterations evenly across the *teams*, according to a static schedule. Our vector addition will now execute like the picture in Figure 6.3, with the thread in each team processing a portion of the N loop iterations.

Unlike the `for` construct, the `distribute` construct can only share the work statically. If you recall how teams are mapped to the GPU hardware, this is a perfectly natural restriction. We can specify the chunk size of the static schedule using the `dist_schedule()` clause; for example, to set a chunk size of 16 iterations per team, we would use the follow clause: `dist_schedule(static:16)`.

With `teams` and `parallel`, we can launch work across a large number of parallel resources. With `distribute` we can share loop iterations across teams, and with `for` we can share loop iterations across threads in a team. When we combine these,

Table 6.3: **The distribute construct in C/C++ and Fortran** – The `distribute` construct workshares loop iterations between teams in a league of teams.

C/C++ directive format
#pragma omp distribute *[clause[[,] clause]...]*   for-loop
Fortran directive format
!$omp distribute *[clause[[,] clause]...]*   do-loop   **!$omp end distribute**

allocate *(alloc-nam: list)*   **collapse** *(n)*   **dist_schedule** *(kind[, chunk_size])*   **firstprivate** *(list)*   **lastprivate** *(list)*   **order** *(concurrent)*   **private** *(list)*

we are able to share those loop iterations across all the threads in each of the teams: `teams distribute parallel for`.

For our vector addition example, we can use this combined construct as in Figure 6.7. We are now sharing those N iterations across the teams, according to a static schedule, and then the iterations assigned to each team are shared across the threads in that team.

To see how the loop iterations are assigned, consider a small example. We will set the number of threads and number of teams, so we have some concrete numbers to work with. The code in Figure 6.8 launches four teams, each with (up to) eight threads, as specified by the clauses. In total, there will be at most 32 threads. The `distribute` and `for` clauses work together to share the 64 iterations of the loop across those 32 threads.

First, `distribute` will divide the iterations between teams. With 64 iterations, and four teams, each team will get $64/4 = 16$ iterations. Because a static schedule is used, the iterations will represent a chunk of adjacent iterations in the loop. See Table 6.4 for the iterations assigned to each team. These iterations will be assigned to the initial thread of each team.

```
1   #define N 4000
2
3   int main()
4   {
5
6       float A[N], B[N], C[N];  // initialization not shown
7
8       #pragma omp target
9       #pragma omp teams distribute
10      for (int i = 0; i < N; i++) {
11          C[i] = A[i] + B[i];
12      }
13  }
```

Figure 6.6: Vector Add across teams – This program will add two vectors of length
N to produce a third vector, running in parallel on the target device with the loop iterations
shared across teams.

```
1   #define N 4000
2
3   int main()
4   {
5
6       float A[N], B[N], C[N];  // initialization not shown
7
8       #pragma omp target
9       #pragma omp teams distribute parallel for
10      for (int i = 0; i < N; i++) {
11          C[i] = A[i] + B[i];
12      }
13  }
```

Figure 6.7: Vector Add across teams and threads – This program will add two
vectors of length N to produce a third vector, running in parallel on the target device with
the loop iterations shared across teams and threads.

Second, eight threads are launched in each team, and the iterations that were
assigned to the initial thread of each team by the **distribute** construct will be
further shared between threads in the team. Although a static schedule will be used,
most implementations set a chunk size of 1 when the **for** worksharing construct
is used in a target region (i.e., like **schedule(static:1)**). This is to ensure that

```
1  #pragma target
2  #pragma omp teams distribute parallel for num_teams(4) num_threads(8)
3  for (int i = 0; i < 64; ++i) {
4     // loop body
5  }
```

Figure 6.8: **Scheduling of iterations across teams and threads** – Four teams, each with up to eight threads, will share the 64 iterations of the for loop. Assuming each team contains eight threads, each thread will process two iterations.

Table 6.4: **Example of the scheduling of a distribute construct** – The 64 iterations are shared across four teams.

Team ID	i Iterations
0	0, 1, ..., 15
1	16, 17, ..., 31
2	32, 33, ..., 47
3	48, 49, ..., 63

threads with adjacent thread IDs will compute adjacent loop iterations, an important optimization we discussed in Section 5.2.7. For these reasons, in real application codes, it's important to let the runtime and implementation set the number of teams and number of threads per team along with the schedules appropriate for the specific target device. See Table 6.5 for the final distribution of iterations across the 64 threads; notice how threads with consecutive IDs work on adjacent iterations in the loop.

We sometimes combine this with simd construct on the end of the combined construct to indicate that those threads can also use the SIMD instructions of the processor. This results in a directive such as the following:

`#pragma omp teams distribute parallel for simd`

Most compilers map these three levels of hierarchical parallelism (teams, threads, vectors) onto the two levels of parallelism on a GPU (Compute Units and Processing Elements). These compilers typically ignore the simd clause, but there are compilers that benefit from its inclusion, so it is important to be aware of it.

For large loops (by *large* we mean there is enough work to keep the GPU fully occupied), the iterations of which execute correctly in any order (they are concurrent)

Table 6.5: **Example of the scheduling of the distribute and for constructs** –
The 64 iterations are shared across four teams and eight threads, assuming a static schedule
with a chunk size of one.

Team ID	Thread ID	i Iterations
0	0	0, 8
0	1	1, 9
	...	
0	7	7, 15
1	0	16, 24
1	1	17, 25
	...	
1	7	23, 31
2	0	32, 40
2	1	33, 41
	...	
2	7	39, 47
3	0	48, 56
3	1	49, 57
	...	
3	7	55, 63

and the body of the loop does not include any additional OpenMP constructs or
functions from the OpenMP API, we can replace the long directive listed above
with:

```
#pragma omp loop
```

The `loop` construct is convenient and supports the good practice of leaving the
details of mapping work onto a GPU to the runtime system. For algorithms that
need to directly work around the parallelism hierarchy and the synchronization
guarantees offered by each level of the hierarchy, the constructs to control and share
work between each level can be critical.

6.3   Hierarchical Parallelism in Practice

We have now shown how to write code that explicitly exploits the hierarchical
parallelism of a GPU using OpenMP. The example we've shown so far, vector

addition, is convenient for showing what the directives are, but it is too simple to help you understand how to use hierarchical parallelism in OpenMP. Frankly, for vector addition, there is no reason to go beyond the simple `loop` construct. To showcase the hierarchical parallelism and explain how it is used in practice, we need a more complicated example that can take advantage of it.

6.3.1   Example: Batched Matrix Multiplication

Matrix multiplication is a common building block of many simulation codes. While many simulations require multiplications of very large (and often sparse) matrices, there are other cases where enormous numbers of multiplications over small matrices are needed. This occurs, for example, in finite element codes where the meshes defining the problem domain lead to large block-sparse arrays. Each matrix multiplication is independent, yielding plenty of concurrency, but each matrix multiplication is small. Using a function from the standard BLAS[3] API for each multiplication is problematic since these routines are usually optimized for multiplication of large matrices. This situation motivates the need for *batched* matrix multiplication functions that can apply a BLAS-like function to multiple independent matrices [14].

We will explore how to implement such a routine using OpenMP. Obviously, you are encouraged to use vendor-supplied linear algebra libraries for these routines in your actual application codes, as we do not optimize our implementation for optimal performance. We use a batched DGEMM operation simply as an illustrative example of writing an algorithm that exploits hierarchical parallelism.

A batched DGEMM routine solves the following set of L matrix multiplications:

$$C_l = A_l B_l, \quad l \in [0, L) \tag{6.1}$$

Each of the matrices A_l, B_l, and C_l are relatively small. As such, there is not much work to do for each matrix multiplication, but as there are many matrices in the batch, there is plenty of concurrent work if we do each matrix multiplication in parallel.

The Compute Units in a GPU often contain caches, and so the threads (assigned to Processing Elements on one Compute Unit) should benefit from reusing matrix data that will reside in the caches due to its small footprint. Our hierarchical

---

[3]BLAS stands for Basic Linear Algebra Subprograms. The most famous function from the BLAS is DGEMM, which stands for Double Precision General Matrix Multiply.

parallelism scheme is therefore as follows: solve one matrix per team, using the threads in that team to compute the multiplication.

The input and output matrices are stored in arrays containing all L matrices. The data for each matrix is stored contiguously, so in memory the rows and columns for matrix $l = 0$ are stored, followed by matrix $l = 1$, and so on. This maintains coalesced memory access for the threads in the team (as far as is possible with this kernel).

Figure 6.9 shows an implementation of the batched DGEMM routine. There are L matrices in the batch, where each C is an $N \times M$ matrix, each A is an $N \times P$ matrix, and each B is a $P \times M$ matrix. The routine is very similar to our previous matrix multiplication examples, but we have now included the loop over the matrices in the batch. For this loop, we use the combined construct to launch teams and distribute the batch between the teams. That is:

`teams distribute`

We use the familiar combined construct on the regular DGEMM loop nest. That is:

`parallel for collapse(2)`

Each team will use its threads to cooperatively compute the matrix multiplications for its batch of matrices.

```
1   #pragma omp target
2   #pragma omp teams distribute
3   for (int l = 0; l < L; ++l) { // loop over batch
4
5     // Compute C_l = A_l x B_l
6     #pragma omp parallel for collapse(2)
7     for (int i = 0; i < N; ++i) {
8       for (int j = 0; j < M; ++j) {
9         for (int k = 0; k < P; ++k) {
10          C[l*N*M + i*M + j] +=
11            A[l*N*P + i*P + k] * B[l*P*M + k*N + j];
12        }
13      }
14    }
15  }
```

Figure 6.9: **Batched DGEMM** – Hierarchical parallelism to solve a large batch of small matrix multiplication operations.

In the code, we have not specified the number of teams or the number of threads in each team. We could include the `num_teams(L)` clause on line 2 to ensure that each team solves a single matrix. Adding a `num_threads(N*M)` clause on line 6 would ensure that we launch up to that many threads; however, we must take care because the hardware often has a limit to the number of threads per team. This limit is a fundamental detail of the specific target architecture, so it is hard to give concrete advice, however a typical limit is around 1024. Hence, it is easier to hit this ceiling that you might expect—if our matrix C were larger than 32-by-32, then explicitly setting the number of threads could well fail. Without specifying this limit, the compiler and hardware will automatically tile (strip mine) our collapsed loop, choosing a number of threads per team that is suitable for the target hardware. Indeed, this can happen in any case as the `num_threads()` clause defines an upper limit on the number of threads per team.

6.3.2   Example: Batched Gaussian Elimination

Another fundamental building block in many finite element codes is a direct linear solver of small dense matrices. A linear solver takes the equation $Ax = b$ and solves for the vector x, where A is a square matrix and b is a vector of known values. Gaussian elimination is the standard algorithm used for this problem. The algorithm operates over rows of the system, updating them in order to compute an upper triangular matrix, which is then used to find the solution vector x using backwards substitution. This algorithm updates rows concurrently but requires synchronization between each of these row updates. For large matrices, there are much better algorithms to solve the system (remember to use the right algorithm—Section 5.2.3), but when the matrix is small, Gaussian elimination is sufficient. Furthermore, as for batched matrix multiply, for a finite element code we would expect a large batch of small systems to solve.

An implementation of a batched Gaussian elimination program (adapted from a mini-app by Deakin et al [15]) using OpenMP is shown in Figure 6.10. As with our previous example in Section 6.3.1, the matrices and vectors are stored in a shared array, with the data for each matrix and vector stored together. For the algorithm to work, the matrices must be square (N-by-N), and non-singular.[4] We launch the batch in a target region and use the `teams distribute` construct to solve each system in different teams (i.e., each team will have a batch of systems to process).

---

[4]For our case, *non-singular* means the diagonal elements of A are non-zero.

The matrix and right-hand side vector b are updated with row-operations. Working from top to bottom, multiples of a row are subtracted from subsequent rows to eliminate entries below diagonals of the A matrix. This results in an upper triangular matrix. This loop, shown on line 6, must be serial, with each iteration happening in order. The update to the elements on each row can happen concurrently, so the loop on line 12 uses the OpenMP threads in a team to do this work in parallel. The parallel region ends on line 14, with an implicit barrier, ensuring all threads finish updating the row before continuing with the next. This also guarantees that the loop over rows on line 6 occurs in order.

Backwards substitution occurs after the upper triangular factorization of A. It works in much the same manner, with a concurrent loop inside a serial loop. Notice the concurrent loop on line 24 is not of a fixed size. The number of iterations in this loop increases with each iteration of the outer loop.

The complexity of this code comes from the need to synchronize between serial steps in the algorithm. OpenMP threads inside a team can synchronize with each other, so we share the work of the parallel loops between these threads. Threads from different teams, however, cannot synchronize directly with each other. By mapping batches onto distinct teams, however, we avoid the need for cross-team synchronization, making it straightforward to manage these solvers as independent batches mapped onto teams.

6.4   Hierarchical Parallelism and the Loop Directive

This chapter has focused on explicit control of the hierarchical parallelism fundamental to a GPU. The programmer tells the system precisely how to map the concurrency in an algorithm onto the various levels in the parallelism hierarchy. This is known as *prescriptive* programming.

Up until this chapter, we have focused on an alternative approach where a programmer describes *what* is to be executed on the GPU but very little about how the various features of a GPU are to be used in that parallel execution. This is called *descriptive* programming.

Descriptive programming gives the system flexibility to adapt to differences between GPUs and hopefully generate code that is both performant and portable. Prescriptive programming emphasizes control and lets a programmer maximize performance for a particular GPU.

```
1   #pragma omp target
2   #pragma omp teams distribute
3   for (int l = 0; l < L; ++l) { // loop over batch
4       // Triangulation step
5       // Subtract multiples of rows from top to bottom
6       for (int j = 0; j < N; ++j) { // Loop over rows
7           const double Ajj = A[N*N*l + N*j + j]; // Diagonal value
8           if (Ajj != 0.0) {
9               for (int i = j+1; i < N; ++i) { // Loop over rows beneath jth row
10                  const double c = A[N*N*l + N*i + j] / Ajj;
11                  #pragma omp parallel for
12                  for (int k = 0; k < N; ++k) { // Loop over entries in row
13                      A[N*N*l + N*i + k] -= c * A[N*N*l + N*j + k];
14                  } // implicit barrier
15                  b[N*l + i] -= c * b[N*l + j];
16              }
17          }
18      }
19
20      // Backwards substitution
21      for (int j = N-1; j >= 0; --j) {
22          x[N*l + j] = b[N*l + j] / A[N*N+l + N*j + j];
23          #pragma omp parallel for
24          for (int i = 0; i < j; ++i) {
25              b[N*l + i] -= x[N*l + j] * A[N*N*l + N*i + j];
26              A[N*N*l + N*i + j] = 0.0;
27          } // implicit barrier
28      }
29  } // end of batch loop
```

Figure 6.10: **Batched Gaussian elimination program** – Hierarchical parallelism is used to solve a large batch of small linear systems using Gaussian elimination. Each system is solved by a team, with parallel threads in the team working together and synchronizing appropriately to solve for the vector x.

OpenMP traditionally emphasizes prescriptive programming. As we move to heterogeneous hardware (such as a combination of a CPU with one or more GPUs), the advantages of a descriptive approach grows. This is why we put so much emphasis on the `loop` construct. When it delivers a reasonable fraction of the performance available from a GPU, the `loop` construct with its potential for performance portability should be used. Start there, and when it fails to deliver, then shift to the prescriptive techniques from this chapter.

While we can think of a prescriptive versus descriptive dichotomy, OpenMP supports a middle ground where the levels of the parallelism hierarchy are exposed, but the specific details of how loops map onto the hierarchy remain descriptive. This *middle ground* is the topic of this section. We start with a description of the combined constructs in OpenMP that include the `loop` construct. Then we close by describing a clause to the `loop` construct that specifies the level in the parallelism hierarchy upon which loop iterations are to be bound.

6.4.1   Combined Constructs that Include Loop

A *combined construct* is a shortcut for writing one construct that is tightly nested inside another. For example, a `teams` construct must occur right after a `target` construct. That's what it means to say the two must be *tightly nested*.

The functionality of a combined construct is precisely the same as if the pair of constructs were separate, the second right after the first. There are three combined constructs that include the `loop` construct:

- `target teams loop`

- `target parallel loop`

- `teams loop`

Throughout the book we have written the pair of directives:

```
#pragma omp target
#pragma omp loop
```

OpenMP does not define a combined construct with `target` and `loop`. When working with a GPU, however, there is always a level of concurrency around Compute Units associated with the `teams` construct. Hence, we can replace the pair above with the single directive:

```
#pragma target teams loop
```

With the split constructs, we specify that the loop iterations are all independent and can execute concurrently, and so OpenMP can map them however it likes to the device. Here, with the combined construct, we also say the loop iterations are independent and can execute concurrently, so a good OpenMP implementation will share the work across the whole device, perhaps by creating many teams each with a single thread, which can be aggregated together and run on Compute Units and Processing Elements in any manner, thanks to the guarantee that the loop iterations are concurrent.

When there is a complex set of map clauses, common practice is to leave them on the `target` clause and use the combined `teams loop` construct, for example:

```
#pragma omp target map(to:A[0:N]) \
    map(tofrom:B[0:N*N]) \
    map(from:C[0:N*N])
#pragma omp teams loop collapse(2)
```

It is legal OpenMP code to put them all onto one long construct, but stylistically it is easier to read the program if data mapping is kept separate from how the parallelism is described for the loops.

6.4.2 Reductions and Combined Constructs

In Section 4.3, we saw that when using the usual pair of `target` and `loop` constructs, we needed to explicitly map the reduction variable with a `map(tofrom)` clause. If we forget this, the variable will instead be mapped as `firstprivate`, and the reduction result will be lost.

There is different implicit behavior for the combined constructs. For all target combined constructs (constructs that start `target...`) that can accept a `reduction` clause, the reduction variable will be automatically mapped `tofrom` and no programmer intervention is required. When using the pair `target` and `loop`, as this is not a combined construct, we must include the `map` clause. Table 6.6 shows a summary of what happens for the various combined constructs.

6.4.3 The Bind Clause

We are now ready to explore how to strike a balance between prescriptive and descriptive programming. We can control the parallelism hierarchy by generating teams and parallel threads with the `teams` and `parallel` constructs, but remain *descriptive* in how concurrent loops map onto the hierarchy by using the `loop` construct. This unburdens implementations by allowing them to share the work between the resources however they like.

The `loop` construct can be explicitly bound to other constructs to specify the parts of the GPU's parallel hierarchy onto which the loop's concurrent iterations

Table 6.6: **Mapping behavior of reduction variables with different target constructs** – For all target combined constructs, the reduction variable is mapped implicitly. But for the pair of `target` and `loop` constructs, it is not, and we must use a `map(tofrom)` clause.

OpenMP constructs	Mapping behavior
`#pragma omp target` `#pragma omp loop`	*Not* mapped, use `map(tofrom)`
`target teams loop`	Implicitly mapped `tofrom`
`target parallel loop`	Implicitly mapped `tofrom`
`target teams distribute`	Implicitly mapped `tofrom`
`target parallel for`	Implicitly mapped `tofrom`
`target teams distribute parallel for`	Implicitly mapped `tofrom`
`target teams distribute parallel for simd`	Implicitly mapped `tofrom`

will be mapped. Specifically, we can bind the `loop` region to a `teams` region or a `parallel` region. We can also leave this undefined and allow the implementation to choose which parts of the hierarchy are used.

The code in Figure 6.11 shows how the `bind()` clause is used to map the two for loops to teams and parallel threads. The iterations of the outer loop on line 3 are executed concurrently by each team. We could specify `num_teams()` to control the number of teams, but we leave that up to the runtime to decide in this example. We would get the same behavior if the construct on line 2 also included a `bind(teams)` clause, as the `loop` construct will bind to the construct it is tightly nested with.

Note, however, that the `loop` construct gives the implementation the freedom to create extra parallel sources, as long as they do not change the semantics of the code in any observable way (recall Section 3.4). This gives the team the option to spawn more threads beyond just the initial thread (again, this is why an OpenMP implementation is free to schedule a loop using the `teams loop` combined construct across an entire device when no inner parallel regions appear in the program text). We can explicitly share the iterations of the inner loop on line 7 between threads in the team. We've used the `bind(parallel)` clause to associate the construct with the parallel region that exists within each team. Normally, we just use the initial thread and use the `parallel` construct to explicitly create a parallel region. By binding the inner `loop` construct to the parallel region with the `bind()` clause, we can use all (multiple) threads in the team to work together.

In practice, the code in Figure 6.11 is very similar to that in Figure 6.12. In the latter example, we use the standard worksharing constructs rather than the `loop` construct with appropriate bindings. However, this second example does not assume the iterations of the loop are concurrent unless we also add the `order(concurrent)` clause, something which is implied by `loop`. In practice, as we write this book it is mostly a matter of preference in which constructs we use, but we are giving the OpenMP implementations more freedom to transform our code with the `loop` approach.

```
1  #pragma omp target
2  #pragma omp teams loop
3  for (int i = 0; i < N; ++i) {
4    // code here is executed by each team
5
6    #pragma omp loop bind(parallel)
7    for (int j = 0; j < M; ++j) {
8      // code here is executed by the threads in the team
9    }
10 }
```

Figure 6.11: **Binding the loop construct** – The `loop` construct is bound to teams and threads in the team with the `bind()` clause.

```
1  #pragma omp target
2  #pragma omp teams distribute
3  for (int i = 0; i < N; ++i) {
4    // code here is executed by the team's initial thread
5
6    #pragma omp parallel for
7    for (int j = 0; j < M; ++j) {
8      // code here is executed by the threads in the team
9    }
10 }
```

Figure 6.12: **Binding worksharing loops** – This example has the same binding to the code in Figure 6.11, where the outer loop is shared across the initial threads in the teams, and the inner loop is shared across the threads in each team.

6.5   Summary

This chapter explored ways to use OpenMP to exploit the hierarchical parallelism inside a modern GPU. A target task enqueues a large amount of concurrent work that can execute on the GPU. This concurrent work is organized into teams that run on the Compute Units inside a GPU. Inside the Compute Units are Processing Elements that execute parallel threads (work-items). OpenMP supports an additional level of hierarchical parallelism with SIMD execution on each processing element, though in practice, this is rarely available in modern GPUs.

To keep the processing elements across the hierarchy fully occupied, a programmer needs much more work than one might expect, given the number of Compute Units. Basically, you want so much work that if any given team of threads is blocked waiting on some resource, a new block of work is ready to be swapped in. This lets the GPU overlap delays in memory accesses and other overheads with useful work, delivering the high throughput a GPU is famous for. This has consequences for synchronization on a GPU. Parallel threads inside a team are all active and making forward progress inside a Compute Unit. Hence, they can synchronize with each other. Threads belonging to different teams, however, do not generally make forward progress at the same time and therefore cannot synchronize with each other. This is a key factor in designing algorithms that exploit hierarchical parallelism on a GPU.

The OpenMP constructs for working with hierarchical parallelism include the familiar `parallel` and `for` constructs for defining work inside a team. The set of constructs for hierarchical parallelism also includes a new construct that distributes work called, not surprisingly, `distribute`. It schedules iterations from one-or-more nested loops across the teams. We can even mix the explicit constructs for hierarchical parallelism with the `loop` construct to maintain the flexibility the system needs to adapt to different GPUs.

Working with hierarchical parallelism is important. It supports detailed tuning for specific GPUs which, depending on the situation, can be very important. It also is more general than use of the `loop` construct. Remember, the `loop` construct requires that the iterations of a loop are concurrent and can therefore run in any order. Additionally, the `loop` construct does not support loops with iterations that contain OpenMP directives or calls to OpenMP library routines. When such limitations are inherent to an algorithm, it may not be possible to use the `loop` directive. In such cases, the explicit hierarchical parallelism constructs presented in this chapter become critical.

7 Revisiting Data Movement

We have already covered many of the concepts in OpenMP for managing the memory hierarchy of a heterogeneous system. OpenMP migrates some data between the host and device data environments automatically. For explicit data movement (required for data allocated on the heap), the `map()` clause provides control of data transfers. Other constructs explicitly transfer data on demand, keeping it on the GPU between target regions, so data does not have to move when it doesn't need to. Minimizing data movement is a very important concept in the Eightfold Path to performance (Section 5.2).

Many OpenMP programs will only need the memory management constructs from the GPU Common Core (Chapter 4). There are situations, however, where we need memory management beyond the Common Core, which is the topic of this chapter. We start by introducing some of the finer details for how data is mapped between the host and the device and how it can be controlled further. We cover how to get OpenMP to map more complex data structures. We also cover some of the routines in the OpenMP API for allocating device memory directly. Finally, we explore other aspects of the memory hierarchy: team-only memory and systems where host and device memory are shared thereby eliminating the need for mapping.

7.1 Manipulating the Device Data Environment

The movement of data between host and device data environments is a crucial part of writing efficient programs that use the GPU. The `map()` clauses along with the `target update` directive can be used to transfer data between the host and the device. An important concept that makes OpenMP programming easier is the idea of a *corresponding variable*. These have appeared in our examples so far, but we haven't pointed them out. A variable has a name. That name is used to access the data stored in the memory associated with the variable. The data is mapped between the (possibly distinct) host and device data environments, but we use the same variable name in both data environments. Before we map the data to the device, the variable is stored on the host. After mapping, the same variable name gives us access to the data in the device data environment. This is convenient, as we don't need to write programs that are aware of these two copies of the variables. OpenMP calls the host variable the *original variable*, while the copy on the device is the *corresponding variable*. In this case, we have a *mapped variable*—there is an original and corresponding variable pair. The mapped variables are allowed to share storage; this might be the case on systems that enable Unified Shared Memory (we'll discuss this further in Section 7.6) or where the device is the host device.

The `target update` construct makes mapped variable pairs consistent. This means data will be copied to or from the original and corresponding variables. The direction of the copy is determined by the data motion clause on the `target update` directive. When the `to` clause is used, the corresponding variable (on the device) will take on the value of the original variable (on the host): a *host-to-device* transfer. When the `from` clause is used, the original variable (on the host) will take on the value of the corresponding variable (on the device): a *device-to-host* transfer.

When the `map` clause is used on the `target` directives (other than `target update`), OpenMP can sometimes elide memory transfers to remove redundant copies. In other words, while `target update` will always cause a data transfer, the `map` clause sometimes doesn't!

To support data transfer elision, OpenMP uses a technique called *reference counting*. To understand reference counting, consider its use with recursive functions. Each time we call the function, we enter a lower level of recursion and maintain a count of the level we're on. If we query this reference count inside the function, we can find out how many times the function call has occurred. Eventually we hit a base case and then start unwinding the recursive stack, decreasing the reference count at each of the recursive function returns. Eventually the reference count returns to zero, and the function call stack is empty.

This same approach is used with reference counting of variables in the device data environment. OpenMP uses reference counting when mapping variables into and from the device data environment using the `map` clause. Each block of memory (a variable) that can be mapped to the device is given a counter that tracks the number of times that block is used. For example, `target map(tofrom: var)` maps the variable `var` from the host to the device when the target region starts executing and maps it back when the target region finishes. The reference count for the variable is updated at both of these places: when the map clause is evaluated on entry to a region (such as a target region) and on exit from the region.

On entry to a construct, if the variable does not have a corresponding variable (it does not yet exist in the device data environment), some storage is allocated for it, and it is given a reference count of zero. If the corresponding variable already exists, it will already have a reference count. Then, the reference count is incremented by one as there is a new reference to that variable in the data environment. For all variables listed in the `map` clause, if the reference count is exactly equal to one, and we have used a `to` or `tofrom` map type, then the data in the original variable will be copied to the corresponding variable in the device data environment. Otherwise, no transfer occurs!

Consider the example in Figure 7.1. Let's track the reference count of the variable A. On line 5, a `target data` construct is used to set up the device data environment. This is the first time the data environment has heard about the variable, so it creates the storage, setting a reference count of zero. The reference count is then incremented to one. Finally, because there is a `to` map type (from `tofrom`) *and* the reference count equals one, the data is copied from the host to the device.

The `target` construct on line 7 is another entry to a mapping construct. Notice that the `map` clause again lists the variable A. However, the variable already exists in the device data environment, so no new storage is created. After incrementing the reference count because the variable has been referenced in a `map` clause, the reference count equals two. As two does not equal one, no transfer occurs this time. The reference count needs to be exactly one for a transfer to occur, along with an appropriate map type. Notice that this data copy would have been redundant in the example as the original variable was not changed between these two constructs. Do not forget that accessing the original variable needs careful synchronization: they might share storage, so any unsynchronized access can result in data races. This means that even though the `map` clause on line 7 suggests a memory transfer, no transfer should occur, and it is safe to have ignored that transfer.

```
1   int N = 10000;
2   double *A = malloc(sizeof(double) * N);
3   init(A, N);
4
5   #pragma omp target data map(tofrom: A[0:N])
6   {
7     #pragma omp target map(to: A[0:N])
8     {
9       // Use A
10    }
11  }
```

Figure 7.1: **OpenMP will elide redundant memory transfers between the host and device** – Reference counting memory objects in OpenMP means that `map` clauses do not always cause a memory transfer to occur. The clauses on the target constructs within the target data region do not cause a transfer.

A similar procedure occurs when the region exits for map types **from** and **tofrom**. If the map clause refers to a variable that is not in the device data environment, then it is ignored. Where the variable does exist, the reference count is checked, and if it is exactly equal to one, and when a **from** (or **tofrom**) map type is used, the data is copied back to the host. Then the reference count is decremented by one, for all map types.[1] If the reference count is now zero, the storage associated with the variable is deallocated.

Returning to our example in Figure 7.1, we exit the target region on line 10. Because the **A** variable is in the **map** clause on exit, it is still processed by this reference counting algorithm. The map clause only refers to the variable **A** with a map type of **to**, so there is no checking of the count to determine transfer (which in this case only applies for **from** and **tofrom**). The reference count decrements, now being equal to one. This is not zero, so the data remains on the device. This makes sense since the target region is nested inside a target data region that referred to the same variable, so the reference in the outer scope is still "active." On line 11, the target data region ends, and we follow the algorithm again. This time, the variable is used with a **tofrom** clause, and the reference count is one, so that data is copied back to the host. The reference count is decremented, so it is now zero and is deallocated from the device.

This can be complicated. We do not have a mechanism to inspect the reference count of the current variable. We can, however, inspect whether the variable exists in the device data environment by querying the host address of the variable with the **omp_target_is_present()** function from the OpenMP API, as shown in Table 7.1. The code in Figure 7.2 shows how we use this function on the host to query whether variables have been mapped. The code will print **N: 1, M: 0**, indicating that the mapped variable **N** *is* present in the device data environment while the variable, **M**, is not.

Table 7.1: **OpenMP C/C++ API for querying if a pointer is present in the data environment of the indicated device** – You can use the function **omp_get_default_device()** to find the **device_num** of the default device (as discussed in Section 8.2).

> **int omp_target_is_present(const void *`ptr`, int `device_num`)**

---

[1] The reference count will instead be set to zero at this stage if we use the **delete** map type, but we defer this discussion until Section 7.1.1.

```
1    int N = 10;
2    int M = 11;
3    #pragma omp target data map(tofrom: N)
4    {
5      int dev = omp_get_default_device();
6      int N_here = omp_target_is_present(&N, dev);
7      int M_here = omp_target_is_present(&M, dev);
8      printf("N: %d, M: %d\n", N_here, M_here);
9    }
```

Figure 7.2: **Example of using an OpenMP API to query if a variable is mapped to the device** – The device data environment can be queried using the address of the original variable.

Maintaining the reference count is the responsibility of the OpenMP implementation associated with your compiler. We usually do not have to worry about it. It is important, however, to understand how the mapping rules work in OpenMP and that they do not always result in a data transfer. This can sometimes surprise us when variables have not been copied to or from the host. When in doubt, we can use the `target update` directive to explicitly initiate a transfer. Alternatively, we can use the `always` map type modifier, which we'll discuss in Section 7.1.2.

7.1.1   Allocating and Deleting Variables

In all the `map()` clauses so far, we've used them to copy data in the original (host) variables to the corresponding (device) variables or vice versa. But when we allocated those original variables on the host, usually on the heap using an allocator such as `malloc()`, the data was not initialized. In fact, on CPUs, it is often important to initialize data in parallel as well as processing it in parallel for the best performance, particularly on systems with strong NUMA behavior.

When we create variables in the device data environment, we do not necessarily want to first initialize them on the host, particularly if they are large. Nor do we want to waste time copying uninitialized data when we could simply allocate the storage for it directly in the device data environment.

OpenMP provides additional map types to allocate and free device memory without copying it to or from the host. We already know three map types: `to`, `from`, and `tofrom`. There are three more used for allocation: `alloc`, `release`, and `delete`. Table 7.2 shows which map types we can use in the `map` clauses for the various target constructs in OpenMP.

The `alloc` and `release` map types can be used wherever the `to` and `from` map types, respectively, can be used.[2] However, they do not cause a transfer to occur. They follow the same reference counting behavior as the map types we already know, allocating storage if it does not exist on entry to the construct. Data will only be copied, however, based on the reference count and for the map types `to`, `from`, or the combined `tofrom`.

Table 7.2: **Allowable map types in map clauses for the target constructs** – These map types can appear in a `map` clause on the respective target constructs.

Target construct	Allowable map types
target	to, from, tofrom, alloc, release, delete
target data	to, from, tofrom, alloc
target enter data	to, tofrom, alloc
target exit data	from, tofrom, release, delete

In some sense, the `alloc` and `release` do not really prescribe the behavior they suggest. They are terms we use to relax the behavior of `to` and `from`. The `to` and `alloc` map types will both allocate storage if it is not yet present in the data environment, but unlike `to`, the `alloc` map type will not cause a copy from the original variable to this new storage. If the variable is already present, then the reference count ensures no extra storage is allocated and no copy occurs. The `from` and `release` clauses are similar, both following the reference counting algorithm when target mapping region exits, but only `from` might invoke a data copy.

This is extremely useful for cases where we do not wish to start a copy. The example in Figure 7.3 shows how we can use the `alloc` map type in the `map` clause on a `target enter data` construct. In this case, the three arrays will be allocated storage in the device data environment and associated with the original variables, creating mapped variables. But the uninitialized data in the original host allocation will not be copied to the device, and the corresponding variable will also be uninitialized on the device. We can then initialize the corresponding variables in parallel on the device as usual. The example then uses the `release` map type in

---

[2]The `target data` construct is an exception and only allows map types `to`, `from`, `tofrom`, and `alloc`.

```
1   int N = 10000;
2   double * A = malloc(sizeof(double)*N);
3   double * B = malloc(sizeof(double)*N);
4   double * C = malloc(sizeof(double)*N);
5
6   #pragma omp target enter data map(alloc: A[0:N], B[0:N], C[0:N])
7
8   #pragma omp target
9   #pragma omp loop
10  for (int i = 0; i < N; ++i) {
11    A[i] = initA(i);
12    B[i] = initB(i);
13    C[i] = 0.0;
14  }
15
16  #pragma omp target
17  #pragma omp loop
18  for (int i = 0; i < N; ++i)
19    C[i] = A[i] + B[i];
20
21  #pragma omp target update from(C[0:N])
22
23  #pragma omp target exit data map(release: A[0:N], B[0:N], C[0:N])
```

Figure 7.3: **Vector addition program with device initialization** – The arrays are allocated on the host and mapped to the device using the `alloc` map type. This allocates storage for them in the device data environment but does not copy the (uninitialized) data in the original host variables. A target region is used to initialize the data directly on the device. Note: We will discuss how to define functions for use inside a target region in Section 7.2.

the `target exit data` construct to reduce the reference count, perhaps freeing the data if it is not referenced elsewhere.

The `delete` map type will deallocate the device storage for the variable. For this map type, the reference count will be set to zero, and the storage will always be deallocated. This will happen no matter the value of the reference count before it was set to zero, so any future references to the variable in `map` clauses may create new allocations.

The behavior of the map types that map without copying are not aligned with our usual use of memory allocation and deallocation. We usually allocate and deallocate in pairs, but that is not strictly necessary with certain map types. The `alloc` and `release` types assert that access to a variable is required or will no longer be required on entry or exit (respectively) from the target region. Whether the storage is allocated or released depends on the reference count. The `delete` map type is the exception and will always deallocate the storage. These map types, however, help programmers reduce the places where data copies might occur between the host and device. By using these map types, we can ensure that those potentially expensive transfers do not take place when the situation does not require them.

7.1.2 Map Type Modifiers

With OpenMP reference counting to reduce unnecessary transfers of data between the host and device, sometimes we need to provide additional information to ensure that transfers occur when the algorithm demands them.

The `map` clause can be modified with a map type modifier. There are three modifiers: `always`, `present`, and `close`. They are placed before the list of items using the usual modifier syntax; for example, `map(always, tofrom:  A[:N])`.

The `always` modifier ensures that data will be transferred, irrespective of the reference count. In the previous section we showed that by default, data is only copied between the host and device when the reference count is equal to one for an appropriate map type. With the `always` modifier, the data will always be copied between the host and the device when using an appropriate map type, irrespective of the reference count. The `always` modifier itself does not update the reference count. This means we can use the `always` modifier on an existing `map` clause and avoid an additional `target update` directive in our program.

To show how the `always` modifier works in practice, consider the code in Figure 7.4. The target data construct allocates storage on the device for the variable N. According to the reference counting algorithm, the `map` clauses on the two `target` constructs nested within the target data scope would ordinarily not result in a data transfer between the host and device. It is easy to get caught out here because at first glance the `map` clauses might suggest otherwise, although now we are aware of reference counting we know better. By including the `always` modifier in the `map` clause on lines 4 and 11, the latest copy of N will be copied back to the host after each target region, ensuring the program correctly outputs N=2 followed by N=3. Note that without the `always` modifier, we cannot be sure what will be printed as it is unknown if the original and corresponding variables share storage.

```
1   int N = 1;
2   #pragma omp target data map( alloc : N)
3   {
4     #pragma omp target map( always , tofrom : N)
5     {
6        N += 1;
7     }
8
9      printf("%d\n" , N);
10
11    #pragma omp target map( always , from : N)
12    {
13       N += 1;
14    }
15  }
16   printf("%d\n" , N);
```

Figure 7.4: **Program using the always map type modifier** – Without the `always` map type modifier, there will be no data transfers between the target regions inside the target data region because the variable already exists on the device. The `always` modifier will ensure the program correctly copies the data so it can be consumed on the host in the print statement.

The `present` modifier is used to check that the data exists in the device data environment. If it does not exist when the region starts executing, the program will terminate with an error.

An example of its use is where one part of a large program is delegated responsibility for allocating the memory, including on the device, and another is a consumer of that data. This is a common software design pattern, where for performance purposes we want to ensure that the data is preallocated in the right place before using it for a long time during an iterative computation. For the consumer function, it may wish to check that the data already exists on the device. The `present` modifier will ensure the program terminates safely rather than perhaps crashing if the allocator function forgot to allocate the data.

An example of using the `present` modifier is shown in Figure 7.5. The `target` construct uses the `present` modifier to ensure that the `A` array is already mapped to the device data environment. If it was not, the clause would cause it to be copied to and from the device with each iteration of the loop. The `allocate()` function was supposed to allocate the data in both the host and device data environments, but the developer of this function forgot to use the `target enter data` directive

```
1   void allocate(double **A, int N) {
2     *A = malloc(sizeof(double) * N);
3     // BUG! Forgotten to allocate in device data environment too
4     // #pragma omp target enter data map(alloc: (*A)[0:N])
5   }
6
7   int main(void) {
8
9      double *A; int N = 10000;
10     allocate(&A, N);
11
12     for (int t = 0; t < 100000; ++t) {
13       #pragma omp target map(present, tofrom:A[0:N])
14       {
15         // target region using A
16       }
17     }
18
19     check_solution(A,N);
20  }
```

Figure 7.5: **The present clause is used to ensure data is on the device** – The memory allocator routine has forgotten to map the data into the device data environment, so the target region will terminate the program instead of accidentally copying large amounts of data.

shown as a comment. With the **present** modifier on the map clause, the program will terminate when the target region is executed for the first time; without it, the program would run, copying the data to and from the host every iteration of the loop, resulting in unexpected low performance.

Finally, consider the **close** modifier. The modifier stipulates that the storage allocated for the corresponding variable must be "close" to the device. Given trends in heterogeneous architectures, where different memory spaces in the system are accessible by all devices but with different performance characteristics, providing hints to OpenMP to allocate memory close to where it will be accessed may become important.

7.1.3   Changing the Default Mapping

OpenMP combines implicit and explicit transfers of data between the host and device. When **target** constructs are encountered and the target region executed, variables can be copied to and from the device data environment either by the rules outlined in Section 3.2 or mapped via a `map` clause. The `map` clause lets us control the setup of variables in the device data environment. We can also use the `firstprivate` clause to create private copies of variables for the device threads to use, which of course go out of scope and are lost when the target region ends. With these clauses, we can detail the behavior we need for each variable in the scope of the target region. However, this can become verbose when there is a particular class of variables for which we want to change the default behavior.

The `target` construct can take a `defaultmap` clause to change the default mapping behavior for a class of variables. OpenMP treats scalars, pointers, structures, and stack arrays with different implicit mapping rules. We can override the normal rules for variables in these categories for a specific target region with the `defaultmap` clause.

There are a number of variable types in a C/C++ program for which default mapping behavior can be chosen: `scalar`, `pointer`, `aggregate`, and `all`. For each category we can set the default mapping to be one of `alloc`, `default`, `firstprivate`, `from`, `none`, `present`, `to`, or `tofrom`.

Consider the clause `defaultmap(none)`, equivalent to `defaultmap(none: all)`. In this case, no implicit mapping will occur, and we need to explicitly map all variables. Note that if we do not choose a category, it is implied to be `all`. If the category is indeed `all`, then there can only be one `defaultmap` clause.

A similar base case is the `default` behavior, which uses the implicit mapping rules from the GPU common core that we discussed in Section 3.2.

The other `defaultmap` cases are straightforward and most likely give the behavior one would expect. Choosing `defaultmap(tofrom)` will map all variables `tofrom`, instead of following the usual distinctions. In this case, scalars will no longer be mapped `firstprivate` and instead will be mapped `tofrom`. Any heap allocated arrays would still need explicit map clauses as usual, using the OpenMP array syntax so that the full extent of the array would be mapped.

We can override just a single category of variable by adding one of the modifiers listed at the start of this section. A `scalar` variable is a non-pointer variable of one of the standard C types. A `pointer` variable is a pointer to a range of addresses in memory, and an `aggregate` variable is one that contains multiple variables, which includes stack arrays and defined types (structures).

The example in Figure 7.6 defines a data structure to store a coordinate in two-dimensional space: a `point`. By default, these are mapped `tofrom`, but we want to instead treat it, along with all other aggregate variables (structures and stack arrays), as a `firstprivate` variable in the target region. The `defaultmap(firstprivate:` `aggregate)` clause was added to the `target` construct on line 7 to override the default behavior.

```
1   struct point {
2     double real, imag;
3   };
4
5   struct point p = {.real = 0.0, .imag = 0.0};
6
7   #pragma omp target defaultmap(firstprivate: aggregate)
8   {
9     // p is a firstprivate variable
10  }
```

Figure 7.6: **Changing the implicit mapping behavior for all aggregate variables** – The `defaultmap` clause can be used on the `target` construct to change the default mapping rules for different classes of variables.

7.2 Compiling External Functions and Static Variables for the Device

Programs are often written in a modular fashion, with functions and subroutines created to better describe the structure of the code. When we call the functions inside a target region, we need the compiler to produce a version of that function that can execute on the device. Luckily, since OpenMP 5.0, the compiler will automatically build device-compatible versions of any function we use inside a target region. This might mean a compiler has to create multiple versions of each function, one that can run on the host and another that can run on the device.

There is one catch, however, and for that we must consider what is visible to the compiler as it is building an OpenMP program. A compiler will process *compilation units* independently. A compilation unit in C/C++, also known as a *translation unit*, is a source file after it has been preprocessed. In simple terms, the compiler can only have visibility into what is in the *current* file. In order for a compiler to build functions for our OpenMP device, it must see the *function definition*: the body of the function.[3]

For functions called inside a target region, if the compiler can see its definition in the current compilation unit, it will automatically build a device version that can execute on the supported device. For example, the `identity(float)` function in Figure 7.7 is defined in the same file as the target region in which it is used; therefore, the compiler will ensure a version of the `identity(float)` function is compiled for the target device.

```
1   float identity(float x) { return x;}
2
3   int N = 1024;
4   float * A = malloc(sizeof(float) * N);
5   initalize(A, N); // Some external routine run on the host
6
7   #pragma omp target map(tofrom: A[:N])
8   #pragma omp loop
9   for (int i = 0; i < N; ++i)
10    A[i] = identity(A[i]);
```

Figure 7.7: **Functions used in a target region that are defined in same compilation unit** – The function is defined in the same compilation unit (file) as the target region where it is used, so the compiler will create a device version of it.

When the compiler cannot see the definition, however, it will not compile the function for the device, and the linker will not be able to build the final executable.

In these cases, where functions called on the device are defined in other places in our program's collection of source files, we need to tell the compiler to create the device versions explicitly. We use the `declare target` directive, or the pair of directives `begin declare target` and `end declare target`, as shown in Table 7.3.

When one of these `declare target` directives lists a function, and the definition of that function is in the same compilation unit as where the `declare target` directive appears, a device version of that function is created.

There are three ways we can use these `declare target` directives to build device versions. As an example, when building a neural network, we often try a number of different activation functions. We decided to write this library of functions in a

---

[3]As a brief reminder, the function declaration details only the name and arguments a function takes, while the function definition additionally includes the body of the function itself.

Table 7.3: **The declare target directive in C/C++** – The declare target directive lists which functions and variables are mapped to a device.

C/C++ directive format
#pragma omp declare target(*list***)**
or
#pragma omp declare target enter(*list***)**
or
#pragma omp begin declare target *[clause[[,] clause]. . .]*
declarations-definition
#pragma omp end declare target

device_type *(any | host | nohost)*
enter *(list)*
indirect *(scalar-logical-expression)*
link *(list)*

different file in order to keep our main network code less cluttered. In order to build these functions for the device, as they are only used in a target region in a different compilation unit, we should list the functions in the `declare target` directive, as shown in Figure 7.8. Alternatively, we can list the functions in the `enter` clause on a `declare target` directive instead of listing the functions as arguments to the directive, as in Figure 7.9. In fact, the former syntax is identical to this one, with the compiler automatically listing the functions in an `enter` clause; the two spellings are the same. Finally, we can wrap our list of function definitions with a begin/end pair of `declare target` directives, as shown in Figure 7.10.

```
1   float identity(float x) { return x;}
2   float step(float x) { return (x < 0.0f) ? 0.0f : 1.0f; }
3   float hytan(float x) { return (expf(x) − expf(−x)) / (expf(x) + expf(−x)); }
4
5   #pragma omp declare target (identity, step, hytan)
```

Figure 7.8: **Building device versions of activation functions with the declare target directive** – The functions are listed in the `declare target` directive in order to create device versions of them.

```
1   float identity(float x) { return x;}
2   float step(float x) { return (x < 0.0f) ? 0.0f : 1.0f; }
3   float hytan(float x) { return (expf(x) − expf(−x)) / (expf(x) + expf(−x)); }
4
5   #pragma omp declare target enter(identity, step, hytan)
```

Figure 7.9: **Building device versions of activation functions with the declare target directive and the enter clause** – The functions are listed in the **enter** clause of the **declare target** directive in order to create device versions of them.

```
1   #pragma omp begin declare target
2   float identity(float x) { return x;}
3   float step(float x) { return (x < 0.0f) ? 0.0f : 1.0f; }
4   float hytan(float x) { return (expf(x) − expf(−x)) / (expf(x) + expf(−x)); }
5   #pragma omp end declare target
```

Figure 7.10: **Building device versions of activation functions with a pair of begin and end declare target directives** – The functions listed in between the pair of **declare target** directives will also be built for the device.

We do not necessarily need to wrap the function definitions with the **declare target** directives. We can write the function declaration, as long as the function definition is in the same compilation unit as where the declaration is used with a **declare target** directive. In all three cases, the directives mean the same thing and allow us to use these functions in a target region in another file.

Functions are not the only thing we can put in the **declare target** directives. We can provide a list of variables as well. Variables that appear in the **declare target** directive will be allocated space in the device data environment on all devices. For variables placed in the device data environment using the **declare target** directive, they will have a reference count of positive infinity and will never be removed from the data environment.

For example, consider the code in Figure 7.11, which allocates a large array at compile time. By the implicit mapping rules in Section 3.2, the array would normally be mapped **tofrom** at the beginning and end of the target region on lines 7–9. The **declare target** directive is used to place this array in the device data environment on all devices (on line 4). Therefore, when the target region on line 7 executes, there will be *no* mapping of the array, as it already exists on the device.

```
1    #define N 10000
2    int A[N];
3
4    #pragma omp declare target (A)
5
6    int main(void) {
7      #pragma omp target
8      for (int i = 0; i < N; ++i)
9        A[i] = i;
10
11     // etc
12   }
```

Figure 7.11: **The declare target directive can also be used on variables** – The `declare target` directive is used to place variables directly in the device data environment of all devices.

Note that just like functions referenced in target regions in the same compilation unit, any static variables declared in a target region will implicitly be created in the device data environment automatically as if a `declare target` directive was used.

We can turn off this implicit mapping of static variables with the `link` clause. When static variables appear in a `link` clause of a `declare target` directive, those variables are *not* mapped to the device data environment. This gives us back the control to map them on demand using the `map` clauses. For example, Figure 7.12 uses the `link` clause to prevent the `A` array from being put in the device data environment. Instead, a `map` clause is used to copy only part of the array to the device. Without using `link`, the entire array would be placed on the device. Note, the `link` clause is only valid on `declare target` and not for `begin declare target`.

The `declare target` directives also have a `device_type` clause to control the devices that functions are built for and which static variables are mapped. When the `device_type(host)` clause is used, those variables and functions will only be available to the host device and not any non-host devices. When the `device_type(nohost)` clause is used, those variables and functions will be available to all non-host devices (i.e., all devices in the system excluding the host itself). Without using this clause, the variables and functions are available to all devices, including the host device; we can equivalently write `device_type(any)` to express this default behavior.

So far we have only considered how to call functions directly inside a target region. If those functions are called and the compiler can see them, then a device version

```
1    #define N 10000000
2    int A[N];
3
4    #pragma omp declare target link(A)
5
6    int main(void) {
7
8      #pragma omp target map(tofrom:A[0:N/2])
9      for (int i = 0; i < N/2; ++i)
10       A[i] = i;
11
12     // etc.
13   }
```

Figure 7.12: **Preventing implicit creation of static variables in the device data environment with the link clause** – Variables that appear in the link clause will not be placed in the device data environment and, if required in a target region, must be mapped explicitly.

will implicitly be built; if not, we need to put the function in a `declare target` directive. We say that we call a function indirectly when we do so through a function pointer. If our program is calling functions on the device via function pointers, we need to tell the compiler about it.

The code in Figure 7.13 has a target region that calls one of our earlier activation functions (from Figures 7.8–7.10) via a function pointer `activate`. The function pointer can be set to any of the functions, and the `activate()` function can later be called instead, thereby providing a more generic interface. If we want to use the function many times in a region, function pointers give us a way to swap in and out different functions without having to edit the source in many places. The `indirect(1)` clause is added to the `declare target` directive to allow the functions to be called indirectly. That is, the functions may be called via a function pointer and not just directly by their original name.

When the `indirect` clause is used, we cannot use the `device_type(host)` or `device_type(nohost)` clauses; we must omit the `device_type` clause or use only `device_type(any)`. The `indirect` clause takes a Boolean expression, and when set to true, the functions can be called indirectly; the default (or specifying false in the clause) behavior is that calling functions indirectly is not allowed.

```
1  float identity(float x) { return x;}
2  float step(float x) { return (x < 0.0f) ? 0.0f : 1.0f; }
3  float hytan(float x) { return (expf(x) − expf(−x)) / (expf(x) + expf(−x)); }
4
5  #pragma omp declare target enter(identity, step, hytan) indirect(1)
6
7  // Choose an activation function (activate is a function pointer)
8  float (*activate)(float) = hytan;
9
10 int N = 100000;
11 float *input, *output;
12 alloc_init(&input, &output, N);
13
14 // Use the activation function indirectly in a target region
15 #pragma omp target map(to: input[:N]) map(from: output[:N])
16 for (int i = 0; i < N; ++i) {
17   output[i] = activate(input[i]);
18 }
```

Figure 7.13: **Calling device functions indirectly via a function pointer** – The **indirect** clause is used with an argument that evaluates to the value *true* (i.e., 1) to allow functions to be callable on the device indirectly using a function pointer. Without this clause, functions need to be called directly by name.

7.3 User-Defined Mappers

Sometimes we need to create complex data types to represent our data. In C, we might create a **struct** with many fields, creating what is in essence a variable as an aggregate of many other variables. OpenMP can often map our structures to and from the device automatically using the implicit rules (recall Section 3.2.3). A **struct** along with all its members will be mapped **tofrom**. When the compiler has enough knowledge of the contents of the **struct**, this might be enough. But there are many other data structures where this is not the case, such as structures containing pointers.

For example, consider a wrapper around an array that contains the pointer to the data along with the number of double-precision elements of the allocation:

```
struct span {
  int N;
  double *ptr;
};
```

While OpenMP will implicitly map any variables to the device as if we used `map(tofrom)`, the target of the pointer will not be available on the device.

For most of the data-sharing clauses (e.g., `private`, `firstprivate`, etc.), OpenMP forbids using a variable that is inside another variable, which is exactly the case for a `struct`; it is illegal to write `firstprivate(s.ptr)`, for example. This restriction is removed for the `map` clause. Therefore we can explicitly map aggregate variables and their constituents using `map` clauses.

Consider the vector addition code in Figure 7.14 that uses the `span` structure defined above rather than the regular pointers we used in earlier versions of this program. To make the data available inside the target region on the device, we rely on the implicit mapping rules to map the structures themselves (the A, B, and C structures, which contain the integer and pointer fields) and add `map` clauses to map the data reached via the pointers: for example, `map(A.ptr[:A.N])`.

For such a simple structure, explicitly mapping all components of the structure is not too arduous. For complex structures with multiple member variables, some of which may be structures themselves, using `map` clauses to map each member variable quickly becomes cumbersome. In particular, we must remember to map all the member variables every time we need to transfer the data between the host and device.

We can set up OpenMP to map our user-defined structures with the `declare mapper` directive as shown in Table 7.4. With this directive, we can define how `struct` and `union` types are to be mapped between the host and device data environment.

Table 7.4: **The declare mapper directive in C/C++ and Fortran** – The declare mapper directive describes how variables are mapped to the device.

C/C++ directive format
#pragma omp declare mapper ([mapper-identifier :] type var) *[clause[[,] clause]...]*
Fortran directive format
!$omp declare mapper ([mapper-identifier :] type :: var) *[clause[[,] clause]...]*

map *([[map-type-modifier[,]] map-type:] list)*

The code in Figure 7.15 shows the directive used to describe how our `span` structure is to be mapped. When the structure is mapped, we also need to map the data available via the pointer member variable. Instead of mapping it for each

```
1   struct span {
2     int N;
3     double *ptr;
4   };
5
6   struct span A, B, C;
7   int N = 10000;
8   A.N = N;
9   B.N = N;
10  C.N = N;
11  A.ptr = malloc(sizeof(double) * A.N);
12  B.ptr = malloc(sizeof(double) * B.N);
13  C.ptr = malloc(sizeof(double) * C.N);
14
15  for (int i = 0; i < N; ++i) {
16    A.ptr[i] = 1.0;
17    B.ptr[i] = 2.0;
18    C.ptr[i] = 0.0;
19  }
20
21  #pragma omp target map(A.ptr[:A.N], B.ptr[:B.N], C.ptr[:C.N])
22  #pragma omp loop
23  for (int i = 0; i < N; ++i) {
24    C.ptr[i] = A.ptr[i] + B.ptr[i];
25  }
```

Figure 7.14: **Manually mapping a deep copy of a structure** – By default, OpenMP can't map allocations inside structures, but we can map the structure elements in **map** clauses.

instantiation of the structure (each of the variables), we instead use the **declare mapper** directive so OpenMP knows how to map the structure in general. This mapper is then used when mapping variables of that type. Once known to the OpenMP runtime system, the default mapper thus defined by the **declare mapper** directive will be used each time variables of that type are mapped to the device by future **target** directives.

The **declare mapper** directive shows how a variable of a named type is mapped. The mapper takes an argument that looks like a declaration of a variable: we specify the type and create a variable name to use within the clauses of the construct. Following the directive, a number of **map** clauses are used to define the mapping behavior of the component variables. These map clauses use the variable name defined in the **declare mapper** argument to refer to the members of the structure.

```
1   struct span {
2     int N;
3     double *ptr;
4   };
5
6   struct span A, B, C;
7   int N = 10000;
8   A.N = N;
9   B.N = N;
10  C.N = N;
11  A.ptr = malloc(sizeof(double) * A.N);
12  B.ptr = malloc(sizeof(double) * B.N);
13  C.ptr = malloc(sizeof(double) * C.N);
14
15  for (int i = 0; i < N; ++i) {
16    A.ptr[i] = 1.0;
17    B.ptr[i] = 2.0;
18    C.ptr[i] = 0.0;
19  }
20
21  #pragma omp declare mapper (struct span s) map(tofrom: s, s.ptr[0:s.N])
22
23  #pragma omp target
24  #pragma omp loop
25  for (int i = 0; i < N; ++i) {
26    C.ptr[i] = A.ptr[i] + B.ptr[i];
27  }
```

Figure 7.15: **Mapping a deep copy of a structure with a user-defined mapper** – By default, OpenMP can't map allocations inside structures, but by defining a mapper, OpenMP can map these complex data structures.

By default, the construct describes how variables of the specific type will be mapped by default (i.e., how they are to be mapped along with mapping defined by other implicit rules). In Figure 7.15, the structure is no longer mapped tofrom by default; this is because we defined a new default mapper. We must remember to include all the member variables in a map clause on the declare mapper directive; if not, those missing variables *will not* be mapped. This extends to the variable itself. In the example, we can simply map the variable, which will include a copy of all the member variables.

We can optionally name our mapper by specifying the mapper-identifier tag in the declare mapper directive. For example, we could define multiple mappers for the span structure giving them unique names, as shown in Figure 7.16. Three mappers are defined: the default mapper maps entire `span` structure `tofrom`; the `left` mapper maps the first half of the array `tofrom`; and the `right` mapper maps the second half of the array `tofrom`.

Defining multiple mappers and giving them names gives us extra control of how we map structures. To invoke a named mapper for a `struct span` variable S, we would use the mapper identifier. For example, the `map(mapper(left):  S)` clause would use our `left` mapper. If we do not use a named mapper, such as `map(S)`, the default mapper would be invoked.

This can be useful when we want special behavior for the data to be mapped that depends on the direction of the data transfer (i.e., copying to the device, copying back from the device, allocating on the device). For example, the directives in Figure 7.16 define mappers that copy only part of the array held within the structure.

```
1   struct span {
2      int N;
3      double *ptr;
4   };
5
6   #pragma omp declare mapper (struct span s) \
7                          map(tofrom: s, s.ptr[0:s.N])
8
9   #pragma omp declare mapper (left: struct span s) \
10                         map(tofrom: s.N, s.ptr[0:s.N/2])
11
12  #pragma omp declare mapper (right: struct span s) \
13                         map(tofrom: s.N, s.ptr[s.N/2:s.N/2])
```

Figure 7.16: **Naming a mapper to give control of structure mapping** – Named mappers are created to map the different halves of the array to the device data environment.

When using named mappers, we must also specify the map type in the `map` clause (i.e., `tofrom`). This leads to the question of how the map type in the `map` clause on the `target` directive interacts with the map types in the `map` clause defined in the `declare mapper` directive. The grid shown in Table 7.5 shows the resulting map type given the combination.

Declaring mappers gives us a convenient way to express how complex data structures need to be transferred to and from the device. By defining a mapper, we

Table 7.5: **Resulting map-type when map-types are used in map clauses on both the target and mapper directives** – For the map-type in parenthesis, when the `target exit data` construct specifies a map-type of from and the mapper declares `alloc` or `to`, the resulting map-type is `release`.

		target construct map					
		alloc	to	from	tofrom	release	delete
mapper construct map	alloc	alloc	alloc	alloc (release)	alloc	release	delete
	to	alloc	to	alloc (release)	to	release	delete
	from	alloc	alloc	from	from	release	delete
	tofrom	alloc	to	from	tofrom	release	delete

do not need to remember to explicitly transfer all components of the structure on each target region, simplifying the code we have to write. They can also describe more complex behaviors by defining multiple named mappers to copy only parts of the data structures. We can also use the structure member variables directly in `map` clauses.

7.4   Team-Only Memory

Back in Section 1.1.3, we introduced GPUs at an architectural level, built of Compute Units (multithreaded SIMD processors) and Processing Elements and organized around a memory hierarchy. So far we've only shown how OpenMP manages the device memory: the memory available to all Processing Elements on the GPU. Processing Elements on each Compute Unit, however, have a region of memory that they share. This memory can be explicitly managed, and depending on how much reuse it has across the Processing Elements in a Compute Unit, it can provide substantial performance benefits.

It is unusual for a CPU to give direct control of where memory allocations exist in the memory hierarchy. On a modern GPU, however, this is common. This means we can write programs that allocate memory directly into the memory shared between Processing Elements. In essence, we treat this memory as it if is a scratchpad. Due to its proximity to the Processing Elements, this scratchpad memory is much faster to access than the main device memory. It is also small compared to main memory and only accessible by the threads scheduled to run within a single Compute Unit. Just as those threads within a single team make forward progress together and therefore can participate in synchronization events, the threads (or work-items) running as a team on a GPU can as well. This means they can work with that shared memory scratchpad together. It is important to appreciate, however, that due to the execution model of a GPU, threads in one team cannot directly synchronize with threads from another team.

When OpenMP maps variables into the device data environment, they are mapped into the main device memory and available to all threads, or else, for scalar variables they are mapped as `firstprivate` variables so each thread has its own copy. We use the `map` clause to control how variables are mapped into the device data environment.

In order to place data into local memory, we need to change how OpenMP allocates memory. In OpenMP, we can change where a variable is allocated by using an *allocator*. The memory allocator will change where a variable will be stored in the memory hierarchy. The OpenMP API defines a number of allocators to allocate memory in a specific memory space.

The OpenMP standard must work with any GPU hardware. It does not stipulate exactly what the underlying hardware should look like. Hence, the different memory spaces in OpenMP are described in terms of the properties of the memory, including its visibility to the threads running on the GPU. All good implementations of OpenMP for GPUs today make the local memory available to each team. Memory allocators are included in the OpenMP API to expose local memory spaces on a GPU.

There are two memory spaces that are useful for allocating variables in local memory on the GPU: `omp_pteam_mem_alloc` and `omp_cgroup_mem_alloc`. In both cases, one thread requests memory to be allocated.

- `omp_pteam_mem_alloc`: This allocator makes the memory available to the thread that called the allocator and all the threads in the team it belongs to. This means that the allocated data is available to all the threads in a team running within a single parallel region.

- `omp_cgroup_mem_alloc`: This allocator makes the memory available to the thread that calls the allocator, the other threads in its team, and all descendant threads spawned by any threads in the team (this is called a *contention group*).

On current GPUs, the two allocators behave the same way since GPUs do not support nested parallel regions. Hence, we will only work with `omp_pteam_mem_alloc`. We only mention `omp_cgroup_mem_alloc`, however, since it is possible a future GPU might support nested parallelism, and `omp_pteam_mem_alloc` would not grant descendant threads access to local memory.

When optimizing the matrix multiplication loops, in order to increase reuse of data loaded from main memory, it is very common to transform loops so they work over blocks. This is called blocking the loops (though it is also called tiling or strip mining). Rather than running a simple triple-nested loop as shown in Figure 7.17, each of the loops are broken into two: loops over a block and loops within a block. We show the result of this transformation in Figure 7.18. It is worth taking some time to derive the blocked version yourself if you've not applied this sort of loop transformation before.

```
1  for (int i = 0; i < Ndim; i++) {
2    for (int j = 0; j < Mdim; j++) {
3      for(int k = 0; k < Pdim; k++) {
4        C[i*Mdim+j] += A[i*Pdim+k] * B[k*Mdim+j];
5      }
6    }
7  }
```

Figure 7.17: **Matrix multiplication routine** – The dense matrix multiplication kernel uses three tightly nested loops to compute the matrix-matrix product.

We can build on Figure 7.18 by storing tiles of A and B in local memory on the GPU. Our parallel scheme is then as follows: launch one team per block of matrix C. Each team contains one thread per element in the square block ($32 \times 32 = 1024$ threads). The threads in each team will loop over tiles of the A and B matrices, copy them into local memory, and then, using these local copies, compute the matrix multiplication within each block. By using the local memory as a scratchpad, we ensure that the tiles of A and B are highly reused.

The blocked routine is shown in Figure 7.19. It uses the hierarchical parallelism constructs from Chapter 6. We first use a **target data** region to make sure the data exists in the device data environment and is available to all threads running on the device. We use clauses to specify the number of teams in the league (**num_teams**) to be one per tile of matrix C and also limit the number of threads available to each team to the tile size with the **thread_limit** clause; this step ensures that when we create the same number of threads in the parallel region, we will get the number of threads we expect. On the parallel region, we use the **num_threads** clause to launch one thread per tile.

```
1   #define BSIZE 32
2
3   // Number of block in each dimension
4   int Nblk = Ndim / Bsize;
5   int Mblk = Mdim / Bsize;
6   int Pblk = Pdim / Bsize;
7
8   // Loop over blocks of matrix C
9   for (int ib = 0; ib < Nblk; ib++) {
10    for (int jb = 0; jb < Mblk; jb++) {
11
12      // Loop over blocks of rows of A
13      for (int kb = 0; kb < Pblk; kb++) {
14
15        // Matrix multiplication within a block
16        for (int i = ib * Bsize; i < ((ib+1)*Bsize); i++) {
17          for (int j = jb * Bsize; j < ((jb+1)*Bsize); j++) {
18            for(int k = kb * Bsize; k < ((kb+1)*Bsize); k++) {
19              C[i*Mdim+j] += A[i*Pdim + k] * B[k*Mdim+j];
20            }
21          }
22        }
23      }
24    }
25  }
```

Figure 7.18: **Blocked matrix multiplication routine** – Each of the three loops in the matrix multiplication kernel is split into two loops: looping over blocks and looping within the block. This optimizes data reuse within each block. Note that we assume each matrix dimension is evenly divided by our blocksize (Bsize).

We create variables to store the tiles of the A and B matrix, Awrk and Bwrk. Notice that these variables are just small arrays in host memory. If we did nothing, these would be mapped into the device data environment as tofrom by the implicit data movement rules. We need these to be allocated instead in local memory on the target device. For that, we use the allocate clause.

The allocate clause can be placed on the same constructs that take the usual data-sharing clauses (private, firstprivate, etc.). The data-sharing constructs define how variables are made available in the region. The private clause (taken as an example since we'll use it shortly for blocked matrix multiplication) when used on a parallel construct, will create a new copy of the variable for each of the threads in the team. Similarly, when used on a teams construct, the private clause will cause a new copy of the variable for the initial thread in each team in the league.

The `allocate` clause sets the allocator used to create the copies of those variables. The clause takes as an argument a list of variables along with the memory allocator to use for those variables. So, when the variables are privatized, they will be allocated in the memory space chosen by the `allocate` clause.

For matrix multiplication, therefore, we use two clauses: `private(Awrk, Bwrk)` to make a copy of these arrays that is private for each team (so each team has their own copy to use as scratchpad arrays) and the `allocate(omp_pteam_mem_alloc: Awrk, Bwrk)` clause to allocate those per-team private copies in GPU local memory. Recall the `omp_pteam_mem_alloc` memory allocator makes those allocations available to all threads in the parallel region, so when the parallel region starts to process each block, all threads will be able to access these team-local allocations.

Finally, we must tell the `target` construct that a memory allocator will be used inside the target region using the `uses_allocators` clause. This takes the name of the allocator. For the blocked matrix multiplication example, we use the clause `uses_allocators(omp_pteam_mem_alloc)`.

With the `Awrk` and `Bwrk` arrays now allocated in team-local memory, the blocked matrix multiplication proceeds through the now-familiar algorithm. The threads in the team copy tiles of the A and B matrices into the team-local memory, synchronizing at the implicit barrier at the end of the second `for` worksharing construct. This ensures that when threads compute the matrix multiplication, the arrays contain all the data needed. Again, the implicit barrier at the end of the `for` worksharing construct ensures all threads have finished processing the current tile before starting working on the next tile, which overwrites the team-local memory.

The variables declared before the target region can be made team-only as follows:

1. Add the `uses_allocators(omp_pteam_mem_alloc)` clause on the `target` construct.

2. Add the variables to a `private(var)` clause on the `teams` construct.

3. Add the `allocate(omp_pteam_mem_alloc:  var)` clause on the `teams` construct to ensure the private copies are allocated in memory available to all threads in the team.

Our earlier attempts at running matrix multiplication on a GPU used a triple-nested loop (recall Figure 3.9). With matrix order of 11,200 on an NVIDIA®

```
1  #define Bsize 32
2  int Nblk = Ndim / Bsize;
3  int Mblk = Mdim / Bsize;
4  int Pblk = Pdim / Bsize;
5
6  double Ablk[Bsize*Bsize]; // Team—local copies of tiles
7  double Bblk[Bsize*Bsize];
8
9  #pragma omp target data map(tofrom:C[0:Ndim*Mdim]) \
10                       map(to:B[0:Pdim*Mdim], A[0:Ndim*Pdim])
11 {
12   #pragma omp target uses_allocators(omp_pteam_mem_alloc)
13   #pragma omp teams distribute collapse(2) num_teams(Nblk*Mblk) \
14                     thread_limit(Bsize*Bsize) \
15                     allocate(omp_pteam_mem_alloc: Awrk, Bwrk) \
16                     private(Awrk, Bwrk)
17   for (int ib = 0; ib < Nblk; ib++) {   // Loop over blocks of C
18     for (int jb = 0; jb < Mblk; jb++) {
19       for (int kb = 0; kb < Pblk; kb++) {   // Loop over blocks
20
21         #pragma omp parallel num_threads(Bsize*Bsize)
22         {
23           // Copy block of A into pteam memory
24           #pragma omp for collapse(2) nowait
25           for (int i = ib*Bsize; i < ((ib+1)*Bsize); i++) {
26             for (int k = kb*Bsize; k < ((kb+1)*Bsize); k++) {
27               Awrk[(i%Bsize)*Bsize + (k%Bsize)] = A[i*Pdim+k];
28           }}
29
30           // Copy block of B into pteam memory
31           #pragma omp for collapse(2)
32           for (int j = jb*Bsize; j < ((jb+1)*Bsize); j++) {
33             for (int k = kb*Bsize; k < ((kb+1)*Bsize); k++) {
34               Bwrk[(k%Bsize)*Bsize + (j%Bsize)] = B[k*Mdim+j];
35           }}
36
37           // matrix multiply block
38           #pragma omp for collapse(2)
39           for (int i = ib*Bsize; i < ((ib+1)*Bsize); i++) {
40             for (int j = jb*Bsize; j < ((jb+1)*Bsize); j++) {
41               for (int k = kb*Bsize; k < ((kb+1)*Bsize); k++) {
42                 C[i*Mdim+j] += Awrk[(i%Bsize)*Bsize + (k%Bsize)] *
                                  Bwrk[(k%Bsize)*Bsize + (j%Bsize)];
43           }}}
44         }
45   }}}
46 }
```

Figure 7.19: **Blocked matrix multiplication on the GPU** – The blocked matrix multiplication is mapped to the GPU hierarchy, with one team per tile. Each team launches 1,024 threads, which copy tiles of the A and B matrices into local memory.

A100-40GB GPU with the open-source LLVM 16 compiler, the triple-loop nest scheme attains 41 GFLOPS. The blocked version shown in Figure 7.19 attained 991 GFLOPS! Using the cuBLAS implementation of the DGEMM kernel, we can attain 6,762 GFLOPS, close to the peak of 9.7 TFLOPS. The blocked version is a significant performance boost over the original version, showing the power of minimizing data movement. It is also important to note that we are not using optimized matrix multiply kernels for the innermost DGEMM operations as the cuBLAS version is. It is likely that if we did, we'd come very close to the performance of cuBLAS.

7.5   Becoming a Cartographer: Mapping Device Memory by Hand

The `map` clause makes moving data between the host and device straightforward. We refer to the data by the same variable name whether we process it on the host or the device. Whether it is in the host or device data environment, as an original variable or a corresponding variable, it keeps its name. This shackles together a memory allocation on the device with one on the host. The variables operate in pairs, which means that when the mapped variables do not share storage, we have twice the memory footprint. The host and device have their own distinct but coupled copies. This is great for productivity, but sometimes we need to chart our own view of the device data environment without replicating it on the host.

The general pattern of all our OpenMP target programs has been to allocate data on the host, map it to the device, and compute on it there, using the large amount of parallelism available on the GPU. Let's consider a different pattern, where we program the host and device data environments separately. Each variable will have a single location either on the host or the device but not both. To do this, we need to walk away from the `map` clause and use the memory management functions available in the OpenMP API.

To allocate memory in the host data environment, we use the mechanisms from the host programming language's standard libraries. In C, this is typically done through a call to `malloc()`. To allocate memory on the device data environment, we use a function from OpenMP's API, `omp_target_alloc()`, shown in Table 7.6. As with `malloc()`, `omp_target_alloc()` allocates a particular number of bytes. The device number argument is used to identify on which device the memory is allocated. We'll learn more about this in Chapter 8, but for now, all we need to know is the devices in the system are given an integer index: the first device, assuming there is a non-host device, is numbered zero.

Table 7.6: **OpenMP C/C++ library function for allocating and freeing memory in the device data environment** – These OpenMP API routines allocate and free memory on a particular device.

void* omp_target_alloc(size_t *size*, **int** *device_num***)**
void omp_target_free(void *device_ptr, **int** *device_num***)**

Once we have allocated memory and finished using it, we need to deallocate it. For the allocator on the host, `malloc()`, we have the deallocator `free()`. For OpenMP using the device allocator `omp_target_alloc()`, we have `omp_target_free()` (shown in Table 7.6).

The code in Figure 7.20 shows the device memory allocation functions in use. The three pointers, `A`, `B`, and `C`, now point to data in *device* memory. As these are device pointers, the host must not attempt to access the data by dereferencing the pointers. The device, on the other hand, can access the pointers during the execution of a target region.

It is important to remember to use the `is_device_ptr` clause on the `target` regions. This clause tells the OpenMP runtime that the pointers are device pointers already and hence do not need to be mapped to the device. If we omit this clause, then the runtime instead will assume the pointers are host pointers and attempt to map them into the device address space. The `is_device_ptr` clause prevents this from happening, ensuring that the runtime will pass the pointer through directly, as the programmer is promising that the pointer is safe to use on the device.

The example in Figure 7.20 shows how to allocate memory on the device and pass the pointers through to the target region safely. The data only exists on the device; there is no host copy. However, if we leave the data only on the device, inaccessible from the host, how can we get our answers back for post-processing? The OpenMP API provides a number of routines to copy data between devices. These are shown in Table 7.7.

These memory copy functions will copy data from one data environment to another. They can be used to copy data from the host to a device, from a device to the host, or from one device to another. To bring the result of the vector addition where the arrays were only allocated on the device, the `omp_target_memcpy` routine is used to bring the results back to the host at the end of the program, as shown in

```
1   int N = 100000;
2   int dev = 0;
3
4   // Allocate
5   double *A = omp_target_alloc(sizeof(double)*N, dev);
6   double *B = omp_target_alloc(sizeof(double)*N, dev);
7   double *C = omp_target_alloc(sizeof(double)*N, dev);
8
9   // Initialize
10  #pragma omp target is_device_ptr(A, B, C)
11  #pragma omp loop
12  for (int i = 0; i < N; ++i) {
13    A[i] = 1.0; B[i] = 2.0; C[i] = 0.0;
14  }
15
16  // Use A, B, and C on the device
17
18  // Free
19  omp_target_free(A, dev);
20  omp_target_free(B, dev);
21  omp_target_free(C, dev);
```

Figure 7.20: **Using the target allocators and is_device_ptr** – The OpenMP target memory allocator API is used to directly allocate data on the device without an original host variable copy. The **is_device_ptr** is used to tell OpenMP that the pointer is safe to use directly, without any interference.

Figure 7.21. Until we cover device numbering in Chapter 8, the host and device IDs are stored in the `host_id` and `dev_id` variables. The data is copied from the source, with an offset of zero (i.e., the beginning of the array), to the destination, again with an offset of zero. The amount of data copies is specified in bytes.

In addition to setting offsets into the source and destination memories, there are routines in the OpenMP API for rectangular copies. In these cases, the allocated memory is imagined as multidimensional arrays. A rectangular copy allows strides as well as offsets to be specified, resulting in a portion (subvolume) of the array to be transferred. The ordering of the data is assumed to be C-style row-major. This means that the right-most index in multidimensional arrays is the fastest-moving iterator for the array laid out contiguously in memory. All OpenMP implementations must support at least three-dimensional rectangular copies.

Figure 7.22 shows a two-dimensional 8-by-5 grid, allocated as a single memory allocation of 40 elements. The cells are numbered to show the layout in memory,

Table 7.7: **OpenMP C/C++ functions for copying data between devices.**

int omp_target_memcpy(void **dst*, **const void** **src*, **size_t** *length*, **size_t** *dst_offset*, **size_t** *src_offset*, **int** *dst_device_num*, **int** *src_device_num***)**
int omp_target_memcpy_async(void **dst*, **const void** **src*, **size_t** *length*, **size_t** *dst_offset*, **size_t** *src_offset*, **int** *dst_device_num*, **int** *src_device_num*, **int** *depobj_count*, **omp_depend_t** **depobj_list***)**
int omp_target_memcpy_rect(void **dst*, **const void** **src*, **size_t** *element_size*, **int** *num_dims*, **const size_t** **volume*, **const size_t** **dst_offsets*, **const size_t** **src_offsets*, **const size_t** **dst_dimensions*, **const size_t** **src_dimensions*, **int** *dst_device_num*, **int** *src_device_num***)**
int omp_target_memcpy_rect_async(void **dst*, **const void** **src*, **size_t** *element_size*, **int** *num_dims*, **const size_t** **volume*, **const size_t** **dst_offsets*, **const size_t** **src_offsets*, **const size_t** **dst_dimensions*, **const size_t** **src_dimensions*, **int** *dst_device_num*, **int** *src_device_num*, **int** *depobj_count*, **omp_depend_t** **depobj_list***)**

where the elements are next to the numerical neighbors. The border (halo) cells are colored gray and the central grid of 6-by-3 is colored white. We can use the rectangular copy routine from the OpenMP API to extract the white section, as shown in the example in Figure 7.23.

There are many parameters to define in the `omp_target_memcpy_rect()` function:

- The destination and source of the data are listed first.

- The size of each element is stated, with the other arguments to the routine defined in terms of a number of elements of the given size, rather than in bytes.

- The array is two-dimensional, so a number of small two-dimensional arrays are defined to express the amount of data to copy (the `volume` array) along with offsets from the origin of the arrays (`dst_offsets` and `src_offsets`) and the extents of the allocations as a two-dimensional array (`dst_dimensions` and `src_dimensions`).

```
1
2   extern int host_id;
3   extern int dev_id;
4
5   int N = 1000000;
6   double *A = omp_target_alloc(sizeof(double)*N, dev_id);
7   double *B = omp_target_alloc(sizeof(double)*N, dev_id);
8   double *C = omp_target_alloc(sizeof(double)*N, dev_id);
9
10  init(A,B,C,N);
11
12  #pragma omp target is_device_ptr(A,B,C)
13  #pragma omp loop
14  for (int i = 0; i < N; ++i)
15    C[i] = A[i] + B[i];
16
17  double *result = malloc(sizeof(double)*N);
18
19  omp_target_memcpy(result, C, sizeof(double)*N, 0, 0, host_id, dev_id);
20
21  check_solution(result, N);
```

Figure 7.21: **Explicitly copying a device allocation back to the host** – The
OpenMP memcpy function is used to bring data from a device back to the host.

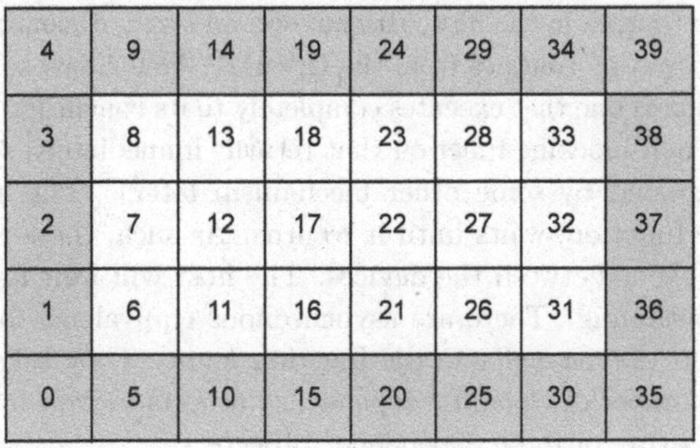

Figure 7.22: **Picture of a 2D grid** – The gray "halo" cells border the white inner
rectangle of 6-by-3 elements.

```
1   double *arr = omp_target_alloc(sizeof(double)*8*5, dev_id);
2   double *center = malloc(sizeof(double)*6*3);
3
4   init(arr);
5
6   // Amount of data to copy
7   size_t volume[2] = {6, 3};
8
9   // Offset from corner of array
10  size_t dst_offsets[2] = {0, 0};
11  size_t src_offsets[2] = {1, 1};
12
13  // Dimensions of the allocations
14  size_t dst_dimensions[2] = {6, 3};
15  size_t src_dimensions[2] = {8, 5};
16
17  omp_target_memcpy_rect(center, arr, sizeof(double), 2, volume,
        dst_offsets, src_offsets, dst_dimensions, src_dimensions, host_id,
        dev_id);
```

Figure 7.23: **Copy a central rectangle from a device allocation to the host**
– The rectangular copy function is used to copy the white cells of the allocation (see
Figure 7.22) from the device to the host.

This routine will then copy the white-colored cells from the device allocation **arr**
into the **center** array on the host. Notice how these arrays are different sizes, which
are passed to the routine in the **dst_dimensions** and **src_dimensions** parameters.

The two memory copy routines from the OpenMP API shown so far are blocking.
A blocking function is one that executes completely to its conclusion before returning
(in contrast to a non-blocking function that returns immediately, so we must check
that it has completed by some other mechanism later). This means the host,
when calling the function, waits until it returns. As such, these routines define a
synchronization event between the devices. The host will wait for the data to be
copied before continuing. There are asynchronous equivalents for both routines,
which append the **_async** suffix to the function name. They take two additional
arguments: the number of OpenMP dependency objects to wait for before starting
the copy, and an array of those dependency objects.

The dependency objects are, in C, of type **omp_depend_t**. They are created with
the **depobj** construct, which can depend on other OpenMP tasks. Section 8.5 is all
about asynchronously offloading target regions to the device. With the information

from that section (which we will discuss later), complex task graphs can be set up to asynchronously offload computation and memory transfers with OpenMP devices.

The memory routines in the OpenMP API give us the control we need to manage the location of data on the host and all the devices in the system explicitly. It breaks the coupling between mapped variables, and variables can exist in only one data environment rather than on both the host and device data environments. The memory copy routines give us a way to copy data between devices, including the host. We'll revisit some of this explicit management of device data when we discuss how to interoperate with external libraries in Chapter 9.

7.6   Unified Shared Memory for Productivity

Efficient control of data transfer between the host and device is crucial for good performance on GPUs. Keeping the data resident for as long as possible close to where it is being processed is key. The mechanisms in OpenMP for transferring data between host memory and device memory gives us the control we need to move data only when needed.

Some systems do not require data to be mapped between memory spaces at all; the hardware provides a Unified Shared Memory (USM). With suitable hardware support, the GPU is able to just read and write data that was allocated on the CPU, and the host is able to read and write data allocated on the GPU. There is no magic here, however. The CPU and the GPU, in all likelihood, still have physically separate memory spaces. The system migrates data, usually one page at a time, between the memory spaces. Typically, it is more efficient for the GPU to access its own memory than to access the CPU memory.

With USM, however, we can simply write programs without `target data` regions, without the `target enter data` and `target exit data` constructs, without `target update`, and without `map` clauses. We are able to write programs for these systems that only consider offloading *execution* with the `target` directive and rely on USM for data management. Parallel programming is hard, so thinking just about the parallelism is attractive.

This can be a boon for productivity, as explicitly writing constructs and routines into our programs to move data around can be time-consuming. Data movement, however, is time-consuming, too. We can rely on USM to move our data, but if we don't take into account where the data should be moving, we can end up with programs that do not perform well. So while USM is helpful for programmers, it is still crucial to think about data movement and write our programs in a manner that minimizes it, however that movement is notated.

We can write an OpenMP target program and omit all the memory movement clauses and directives. If we wrote it for a system that does support USM and only run it there, then we will be fine. In the future, however, we might want to run on a system that does not support USM. We need to make it clear in our program that we wrote it with the *assumption* that USM was available. OpenMP gives us the `requires` directive to make it clear to the programmer, the compiler, and the runtime that our program is written in a way that needs a particular feature to be supported. This construct will ensure that the program will compile for the system only where support is available.

The `requires` construct needs to be used before any target constructs. In addition, if we split our program across multiple files (compilation units), all must use the directive.

The first step in enabling USM is for the system to provide a single address space across the host and device. This means a pointer to an address in memory points to only that one location in memory and that memory address is consistent across all the devices and the host. From the perspective of any device in the system, that pointer is to one location in memory that makes sense for all devices. Any device can perform the pointer arithmetic, and the result points to the new, single location in memory.

Even without automatic migration of data between memory spaces, ensuring unified addressing can be important for building complex data structures on one device and accessing them on a different device. For example, a CPU could build a complex data structure out of device pointers, and that data structure is then later accessed on the GPU. Unified addressing ensures that all the pointers in that data structure are correct.

Note that unified addressing does not alone provide the ability to access the data anywhere, just that the pointers and their representations are consistent across the devices.

If our program assumes a unified address space, we should state that requirement. In OpenMP, we use the following directive:

```
#pragma omp requires unified_address
```

This means we can safely write our program assuming this property and safely pass pointers around, including using host pointers and device pointers interchangeably in the device memory routines from Section 7.5. Unlike general device pointers allocated using the OpenMP memory allocation routines from Section 7.5, we do not need to use the `is_device_ptr` clause to pass these pointers into target regions when using a unified address space.

Building on unified addressing is unified shared memory. This adds the ability to dereference those unified addresses on any device. On a system that supports it, we can dereference a pointer to anywhere from anything, assuming that the pointer is valid, of course (i.e., not `NULL`), and within the bounds of an allocation.

When writing programs that assume USM, we should add the following directive:

```
#pragma omp requires unified_shared_memory
```

The requirement `unified_shared_memory` also implies the `unified_address` requirement, so we do not also need to include that.

With the requirement of USM in place with the `requires` directive, we can omit all `map` clauses on our `target` constructs. Any data accessed within the target region will be made available by system. Our familiar vector addition program is shown in Figure 7.24, but this time using USM. Notice how the memory is allocated on the host using a standard `malloc()` system call. Rather than copying the data in this allocation to the device explicitly using a `map()` clause, we instead use USM. The need for USM is stated using the `requires` directive before any target regions. The target region then uses pointers directly, with no explicit mapping between the host and the device. The system ensures that the data is available on the device when it is used inside the target region.

We can also check that the data is accessible on the device. The OpenMP API routine `omp_target_is_accessible`, shown in Table 7.8, can be run on the host to check if a host allocation of `size` bytes is accessible on a particular device. The function returns a true (1) value if the allocation is indeed accessible directly from the device.

There are some restrictions to be aware of. The `target` construct will still implicitly map scalar values as `firstprivate` variables (recall Section 3.2.1).

Table 7.8: **OpenMP C/C++ API for querying if a host allocation is accessible from the device** – This routine checks that a pointer to data allocated on the host can be accessed on a device.

```
int omp_target_is_accessible(const void *ptr, size_t size, int device_num)
```

```
1   int N = 1000000;
2   double *A, *B, *C;
3   // Notice *host* allocation
4   A = malloc(N*sizeof(double));
5   B = malloc(N*sizeof(double));
6   C = malloc(N*sizeof(double));
7   init(A, B, C, N);
8
9   #pragma omp requires unified_shared_memory
10
11  #pragma omp target
12  #pragma omp loop
13  for (int i = 0; i < N; ++i)
14    C[i] = A[i] + B[i];
15
16  check_solution(C, N);
```

Figure 7.24: **Vector addition on a device with Unified Shared Memory** – This vector addition program omits the mapping of heap allocated data, relying on Unified Shared Memory.

In addition, although the data is available to be accessed on any device in the system, we must be careful about when it is *safe* to access that data. We must still synchronize the devices to ensure that changes to data made by one device will become visible to the other. The devices can synchronize with each other, or they can both synchronize with the host. After this synchronization, the second device can see the changes.

For our example in Figure 7.24, the host checks the solution in the check_solution function. We must ensure that the host and device synchronize between the end of the execution of the target region on the device and that the host uses the updated data. The target region as shown in this example executes synchronously, with the host waiting for the target region to finish before it continues executing. This defines a synchronization event between the host and device. When we look at asynchronous execution in Chapter 8, it will remain the programmer's responsibility to ensure that synchronizations events are placed in the right locations in the code.

For USM in OpenMP 5.2, there is limited opportunity to tune the data movement for performance. The program is at the whim of the system's support of USM for exactly when data is migrated between the discrete memory spaces, including whether it is cached to take advantage of temporal locality of repeated access by one device. Given the current and near-future trends in hardware designs, the data should migrate between the memory spaces and remain there until it is required elsewhere, therefore behaving much like caches in a NUMA system. In this sense, the explicit mapping of data between the data environments gives us the control we need to minimize data movement. USM is certainly great for productive programming, particularly when evolving existing and very large code-bases to heterogeneous platforms. It remains important, however, that we still make the effort to design our codes to carefully consider the movement of data to ensure good performance.

7.7   Summary

Managing the transfer of data between the host and device is a large but important topic when learning to program with any heterogeneous parallel programming model. OpenMP is no exception.

The `map` clause is straightforward to use, as we can refer to variables in the host and device data environments with the same name. The variables are reference counted, which lets the runtime system safely decide when data transfers between the host and device can be skipped for certain cases. We can be more explicit with our `map` clauses by using modifiers and prevent copying of uninitialized data with additional map types. Defining mappers allows us to map complex data structures, too.

The memory routines in the OpenMP API allow us to take explicit control of the device data environment. Built-in memory allocators give us greater control of where in the device data might be stored, allowing programs to use higher-performance local memory in order to code for high data reuse.

USM provides an alternative view of the memory spaces in a system. All memory is available to all devices, so mapping is not required. This can be useful for productivity, especially when working with only a small portion of a large, complex data structure. The majority of this chapter, however, has not been about USM. It has instead emphasized how to take control of the memory spaces. Programming heterogeneous systems requires thinking about the movement of data between physically distinct memory spaces. As hardware improves support for USM, increasing numbers of applications may find it provides both the performance and productivity needed. For most current systems, however, the detailed control provided by the mechanisms outlined in this chapter will be key for keeping the memory footprint and memory traffic low.

8 Asynchronous Offload to Multiple GPUs

The era of heterogeneous computing has arrived! Modern computer systems are typically composed of CPUs, GPUs, and other diverse processors. So far, we have only discussed programming a single target device. In this chapter, we consider programming multiple GPUs. We will also discuss how to get even more performance from a system by programming these devices so they execute asynchronously.

Before we discuss OpenMP programs that execute over multiple GPUs, let's consider the overall system design of a modern supercomputer. The fastest super-computers in the world[1] are designed around GPU-accelerated nodes connected through a high-speed interconnect. Each node contains multiple high-performance GPUs; four or six GPUs per node is not unusual.

Memory is distributed about the nodes of the system. In other words, each node has its own memory; there is no shared address space across the full system. Data is shared between nodes by passing messages using a standard message-passing API, most commonly, the Message Passing Interface (MPI).

How, then, might we map our application onto such a system? To make our discussion more concrete, let's consider a specific class of applications. Many problems (such as structural engineering applications and fluid dynamics) model a physical system over a spatial domain. A mesh is superimposed over the spatial domain to convert a continuous problem (e.g., over differential operators) into a discrete problem (over algebraic operators). To a so-called *mesh code* in parallel, we would first perform a domain decomposition to partition the mesh, mapping each partition to a different node in our supercomputer. Each node contains one or more multi core CPUs that share an address space. The partition assigned to a particular node is further decomposed onto a mixture of processes (that interact through MPI) and threads which, of course, are managed through OpenMP (as discussed in Chapter 2). The worksharing constructs in OpenMP make this step simple using the `parallel for` combined construct. Finding the right mix between threads and processes, however, is not simple. Programmers can run one process per core and dispense with threads altogether. This wastes memory, however, so depending on the details of a problem and how it interacts with memory, a programmer may want to have fewer processes (maybe one per memory controller) then add threads to keep cores fully occupied. In practice, programmers write hybrid MPI-OpenMP

---

[1]As ranked by the TOP500 list at www.top500.org.

programs and then experiment to find the best mix of processes and threads for their specific problem.

To distribute a problem across a system with multiple GPUs per node, we face a similar choice to that between processes and threads. The most common approach is to assign one process for each GPU. In a node with four GPUs, we would run four MPI processes per node. The application therefore would use OpenMP to target a single GPU, and communication between processes (and GPUs) would occur via the host (for CPU/GPU interactions) through a message passing interface (between different host devices). This is simple, as we only need perform the decomposition of concurrent work once (for the distributed memory). Each process also needs only be aware of a single target device. Environment variables and the system queue are used to ensure processes are distributed across the machine, and each process has exclusive access to a single GPU.

OpenMP offers us an alternative strategy. OpenMP lets us target multiple accelerators within a single OpenMP program. This functionality is enabled by the `device` clause, which can be used with nearly all of the `target` directives. As these directives can be made asynchronous via the tasking model in OpenMP with the `nowait` clause, the program is able to run different target tasks in parallel across multiple target devices. We'll cover these clauses and other related aspects of OpenMP in this chapter.

When dealing with multiple GPUs, however, the distribution of work is left up to the programmer. There are no worksharing constructs to generate target tasks automatically to keep each device fully occupied. Therefore, the programmer must implement another level of decomposition to further decompose the mesh-partition across the local system. This extra level of decomposition is complicated and usually results in programs using just one device per MPI process, using a single level decomposition.

In other domains, where distribution of the problem across nodes that do not share memory is less common, the ability to target multiple devices within the same program is valuable. This chapter will look at how to write OpenMP programs that can run on multiple target devices in parallel. We will first remind ourselves how the OpenMP task model interacts with offloading work to a GPU so target regions can run asynchronously with the host (and each other) and how to define the dependencies between them. We will then show how this can be combined with the `device` clause so that different tasks can be run on different devices in parallel.

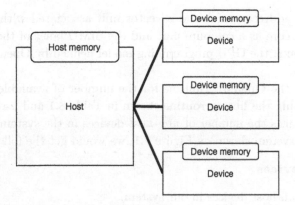

Figure 8.1: **The OpenMP host/device model** – The platform model consists of a host device (the CPU) where execution begins and zero or more attached devices. The memory spaces of each device are distinct.

8.1   Device Discovery

From Part II, we've seen how to offload regions of code and copy data to and from a device, all centered around the `target` construct. But we've left out a detail of how OpenMP manages the platform, how it differentiates between the host and the device, and how to deal with multiple devices.

Heterogeneous programming models by necessity define a high-level abstraction of the platform: to hide hardware details and support portability across systems. Until now, we've seen this platform as a host CPU plus a device such as a GPU. OpenMP naturally extends this model to include all devices in the system, including the host CPU itself.

Figure 8.1 shows a host with three connected target devices. This model, a host with attached devices, is the common way to think of computing in heterogeneous programming models. This is how the platform is seen in OpenMP as well. Each device has a dedicated, discrete memory space called the *device data environment*. We've seen how the `map()` clause is used to copy data between the host data environment and the device data environment.

OpenMP also enables the host as a device. This means it is possible to use the constructs and runtime library routines for a GPU to write OpenMP programs that run on the CPU [16]. A modern CPU has multiple cores (multithreaded execution

within a shared address space) and a vector unit associated with each core. By
thinking of each core as a compute unit and the SIMD lanes of the vector unit as
processing elements, the GPU programming model defined by OpenMP maps quite
well onto a CPU.

We can query the OpenMP runtime for the number of available target devices
in the system using the library routine shown in Table 8.1 and used in Figure 8.2.
This routine returns the number of *non-host* devices in the system. If we ran this
program on the system shown on Figure 8.1, we would get the following output:

There are 3 devices

We have three non-host devices in our system.

Each device in the system is assigned a number to identify it to the OpenMP
runtime. Devices have IDs that range from zero to the total number of non-host
devices (i.e., the number returned by **omp_get_num_devices()**) minus 1, inclusive.

Table 8.1: **OpenMP C/C++ API routine querying the number of devices.**

int omp_get_num_devices(void)

```
1   #include <stdio.h>
2   #include <omp.h>
3
4   int main() {
5     printf("There are %d devices\n", omp_get_num_devices());
6   }
```

Figure 8.2: **Program to query the number of OpenMP devices** – The
omp_get_num_devices() function is used to query the OpenMP runtime for the number of
OpenMP devices (*not* including the host device) available in the system.

8.2   Selecting a Default Device

When a program begins its execution, one of the devices in the system is designated
as the *default device*. This device is the one that will be used unless another is
explicitly selected using clauses to OpenMP directives or by resetting the default

device through a call to the appropriate function from the OpenMP runtime library. Prior to this chapter in the book, we have been using the default device.

For a program written to use the default device, we can manage execution across multiple devices by changing the default device. We do this with the pair of OpenMP API functions shown in Table 8.2 to query which device is the default device and to change the default device when we want to use a different device.

Table 8.2: **OpenMP C/C++ API routines for getting and setting the default device.**

int omp_get_default_device(void)
void omp_set_default_device(int *dev***)**

For example, if the OpenMP runtime labeled the devices in our system in Figure 8.1 as 0–2 from top to bottom, `omp_get_default_device()` might return 0, indicating the top-most GPU in the figure. If instead we wanted to use the middle device, we could set the default device by calling `omp_set_default_device(1)`. Future calls to `omp_get_default_device()` would now return 1.

The host CPU is also treated as a device in OpenMP; it is called the *host device*. This host device is given a device ID equal to the value returned by `omp_get_num_devices()`. Notice that this ID will always be equal the number of *non-host* devices in the system. For our system in Figure 8.1, the host would have ID 3, and the three attached devices would be given IDs 0, 1, and 2. We can also use the function from the OpenMP runtime library shown in the first line of Table 8.3 to find out the ID of the initial device. This numbering scheme will let us program all devices, including the host device, using the same constructs in OpenMP.

Table 8.3: **OpenMP C/C++ API routines for querying the initial device.**

int omp_get_initial_device(void)
int omp_is_initial_device(void)

The host device is also the *initial device*: the device the OpenMP program starts running on. As we saw in Section 2.4, everything in OpenMP is explained in terms of tasks. When our program runs, it's running a task. We can query which device that task is running on with the runtime library function shown in Table 8.4.

Table 8.4: **OpenMP C/C++ API routine for querying the ID of the device currently executing a target task.**

> int omp_get_device_num(void)

Just as we can find out which device a task is currently executing on, we can query if the task is running on the host using the routine on the final line of Table 8.3. If we're currently running on the host, this will return a value of *true* (which for C is equal to 1).

Usually the devices are all contained within a single system, but the OpenMP platform model is flexible enough to express other topologies. For example, some have even used this model to offload OpenMP target tasks to all the GPUs in a distributed system [17]. In other words, the GPUs targeted by OpenMP are hosted by distinct nodes across a distributed memory supercomputer.

Summarizing this section, the OpenMP platform model is relatively simple. It consists of the host CPU (the initial device) with zero or more other devices. The devices are enumerated and given an integer ID. OpenMP gives us a small number of functions from its API for querying ID numbers for the devices in the system and to support introspection, so tasks can determine which devices they are executing upon.

8.3   Offload to Multiple Devices

Our programs so far have used a single target device. Platforms, however, often contain multiple devices. Hence, we may wish to write OpenMP programs that offload to more than just one device.

For controlling device selection in a fine-grained manner, OpenMP provides the `device()` clause. This clause can be used on all varieties of `target` constructs that cause execution or data to transfer (i.e., `target`, `target data`, `target enter data`, `target exit data` and `target update`). This gives us the control we need to direct the execution and copy data to different devices.

The `device()` clause takes a single integer argument. This is the ID of the device for which the target construct should be applied. The code in Figure 8.3 runs the target region on the last non-host device in the system and assumes one is available.

The syntax of the device clause is shown in Table 8.5. To offload to a device with ID=i, use `device(i)` or equivalently with a modifier: `device(device_num:i)`.

```
1   int num_dev = omp_get_num_devices();
2   assert(num_dev > 0);
3
4   int last_dev = num_dev - 1;
5
6   #pragma omp target device(last_dev)
7   {
8       // Target region
9   }
```

Figure 8.3: **Using the device clause to run on the last non-host device** –
This program assumes that at least one non-host device exists.

Table 8.5: **OpenMP device clause.** The *device-modifier*, ancestor, can only be
used on the target construct.

device([*device-modifier:*] *integer-expression***)**

device-modifier
device_num
ancestor

OpenMP does not give us a way to automatically distribute work between multiple
devices, but we can share work manually using the SPMD pattern. We show this
for our vector addition program in Figure 8.4. We divide the total work between
all devices in the system. The number of devices in the system is queried using
the `omp_get_num_devices()` function, and the one-million element array is shared
equally between those devices. An assert statement on line 6 verifies that the number
of devices evenly divides the problem size.

Each target region is synchronous with the host; that is, the thread on the host
that encounters the target construct on lines 18–19 blocks until the target task
completes. To run on multiple GPUs at the same time, we launch multiple host
threads, one for each target device. These threads launch a target task on each
device. Later, in Section 8.5, we will see how we can create asynchronous target
tasks without the need for additional host threads.

We have explicitly requested a number of threads equal to the number of devices
by using the `num_threads()` clause on the parallel region on line 9. On lines 11

and 12, we verify that we got that number of threads and exit the program if we did not. Since the devices and the threads are numbered with IDs that range from zero, we can assign thread zero to device zero, thread one to device one, and so on. On lines 18 and 19, we use the host thread ID to associate each target region with the corresponding device by passing the ID to the `device` clause.

The SPMD pattern is used to divide the work between devices. On lines 15 and 16, the thread ID and length of each array section (`len`) are used to set `start` and `end`, which define the segment of the arrays that will be mapped to each device. This means that we copy different parts of the arrays to the different devices using the map clauses on lines 18 and 19. No device receives the entire array. We then carry out the vector add for each segment of the arrays on the GPU with the loop on lines 22–24.

Each host thread blocks for each target region, and they will all synchronize at the implied barrier at the end of the parallel region. This ensures that the work on each device has finished.

8.3.1   Reverse Offload

We use the term *offload* to refer to the host (generally a CPU) sending work to execute on a target device (typically a GPU). OpenMP also supports the opposite: work can be sent from a device to a host device. This is defined for the general case where there may be a chain of devices in the offload-chain: a device offloads to another, which offloads to another, and so on, forming a chain. Hence, the way to reference this host device is with the modifier to the `device` clause of `ancestor`, as shown in Table 8.5.

In this case, we are *reverse offloading* from the device executing the target region to the ith level up. When $i = 1$, we offload to the parent of the device executing the current target region. The thread that schedules the reverse offload task will wait for that task to finish before continuing.

This can be useful when we want to cause the device to schedule work on the parent. Consider the example in Figure 8.5 (adapted from Kwack [18]), which uses this clause to print a message on the host after the work in each iteration is complete.

We can extend this to perform far more complicated operations. For example, if a device targeted by a reverse offloaded task is running on the host, it could initiate an MPI communication event with another node or cause some I/O to occur. The

```
1   int N = 1000000;
2   double *A, *B, *C;
3   // Allocate and initialize A, B, and C (code not shown)
4
5   int num_devices = omp_get_num_devices();
6   assert (N % num_devices == 0);
7   int len = N / num_devices;
8
9   #pragma omp parallel num_threads(num_devices)
10  {
11    #pragma omp single
12        if (num_devices != omp_get_num_threads()) exit(EXIT_FAILURE);
13
14    int tid = omp_get_thread_num();
15    int start = tid * len;
16    int end = start + len;
17
18    #pragma omp target map(to: A[start:len], B[start:len]) \
19                       map(from: C[start:len]) device(tid)
20    {
21      #pragma omp loop
22      for (int i = start; i < end; ++i) {
23              C[i] = A[i] + B[i];
24      }
25    }
26  }
```

Figure 8.4: **Distributing a vector add between multiple devices** – The vector addition is distributed in a SPMD-style across multiple devices. One OpenMP thread on the host CPU is used to launch each device asynchronously.

```
1   #pragma omp requires reverse_offload
2
3   #pragma omp target
4   #pragma omp teams distribute
5   for (int i = 0; i < N; ++i) {
6     compute(i);
7
8     #pragma omp target device(ancestor: 1)
9     printf("Completed iteration %d\n", i);
10  }
```

Figure 8.5: **Reverse offloading to the parent** – The ancestor modifier to the device clause is used to reverse offload back to the host.

`map` clause can be used to send data back to the parent with the usual directional values, meaning we can communicate data between the host and the target region that initiates the reverse offload.

At the time we are writing this chapter, not all implementations of OpenMP support the reverse offload functionality. If a program uses reverse offload, the code should tell the runtime system that this is required. You can do this with the `requires` directive from Table 8.6. If an implementation of OpenMP doesn't support reverse offload and this `requires` pragma is present, the compiler will report an error and gracefully exit.

Table 8.6: **OpenMP C/C++ directive for requiring reverse offload.**

C/C++ directive format
#pragma omp requires reverse_offload

8.4   Conditional Offload

Each of the target constructs (`target`, `target data`, `target enter data`, `target exit data`, and `target update`) uses the default device and its data environment when transferring data and control of execution. When running on a GPU, it's important to create enough concurrent work to keep the device busy (recall Section 5.2.4). However, sometimes we need to write programs that work for both large and small problems.

The `if` clause can be applied to these directives to conditionally offload to the device, based on a logical expression. The expression is evaluated at runtime when the construct is encountered.

The vector addition in Figure 8.6 is very similar to the examples from Part II. An `if` clause has been added, but otherwise it should be familiar. The conditional in the clause will be checked to see if the size of arrays, N, is at least as large as a `threshold` value, set to 10 million in this case. For large values of N, the code executes on the default device, but when N is smaller, the expression in the `if` clause evaluates to false, and the code does not execute on the default device. Instead, the code is executed by the initial device (the host) and runs with data in the host data environment.

Note that when the `if` clause expression evaluates to false, any `device()` clauses are also ignored. The target region will always be executed by the host (initial device).

```
1   // A, B, C are initialized arrays of length N
2   void vecadd(double *A, double *B, double *C, int N) {
3     int threshold = 10000000;
4
5     #pragma omp target map(to: A[:N], B[:N]) map(from: C[:N]) if(N >=
          threshold)
6     {
7       #pragma omp loop
8       for (int i = 0; i < N; ++i) {
9             C[i] = A[i] + B[i];
10      }
11    }
12  }
```

Figure 8.6: **Conditionally offloading only large vector additions to the device using the if clause** – The vector addition kernel is only run on a GPU when the problem size is "large." For small cases, it is run on the host device in the host data environment.

8.5   Asynchronous Offload

As we have seen, the `target` construct synchronously offloads execution of the target region to the device (i.e., the host waits for the execution on the device to complete before proceeding). As we saw in Figure 8.4, we used multiple host threads so the host could use all GPUs at the same time. Without using multiple threads, the transfer of execution to and from each device would be serialized, with each target region executed in turn. As with all OpenMP constructs, the execution model for `target` constructs is based on tasks. For a review of tasking in OpenMP, see the summary in Section 2.4.

The `target` construct generates a task called the *target task*. Unlike explicit tasks (recall Section 2.3.3.1) with deferred execution, the target task is an *included task*. This causes the (host) thread that created the task to execute it immediately. This means that the host thread that created the target task will wait until that target task has finished execution on a device before continuing with the statements following the target region. This defines a synchronous (blocking) offload to the GPU.

We are already familiar with the `nowait` clause. It can be added to any worksharing construct (such as the `for` construct) to remove the implicit barrier at the end of the construct. It allows the threads to continue executing the parallel region once they finish the worksharing construct without waiting for all the threads in the team to finish.

The `nowait` clause can also be used to turn the target task from an included task to a deferred task. This means that the task (the target region) can be deferred, allowing the thread that generated the task to continue execution beyond the target region without waiting for it to start or complete. This lets us use the `nowait` clause to execute an *asynchronous* (non-blocking) offload to the target device.

The asynchronous target tasks are otherwise just regular OpenMP tasks and so, just as in our divide-and-conquer π program in Figure 2.13, we can use the `taskwait` construct to wait for all tasks generated by the encountering thread to finish.

Let's revisit our previous example in Figure 8.4 for vector addition over all devices in the system. Using the `nowait` clause and `taskwait` construct, we no longer need to launch one thread per device to synchronously offload. We can instead *asynchronously* offload to all devices with just a single host thread. Our vector addition example is updated for asynchronous offload in Figure 8.7.

8.5.1 Task Dependencies

We now know how to defer target tasks to support asynchronous execution between a target device and the host. Asynchronous execution, however, means that the various tasks run concurrently with each other. Depending on the algorithm, we may need to add order constraints for execution across devices (i.e., we may need to synchronize the tasks and ensure some execute after others). In our previous example in Figure 8.7, all the tasks are active and execute in any order (i.e., concurrently), which lets us utilize all the devices in the system at the same time. The `taskwait` construct was used to wait for all tasks to complete.

We can support more fine-grained synchronization by defining explicit dependencies between the tasks. We do this with the `depend()` clause. The `depend` clause on a `target` directive works exactly the same as it does with explicit OpenMP tasks. The syntax of the `depend()` clause is shown in Table 8.7.

```
1    int N = 1000000;
2    double *A, *B, *C;
3    // Allocate and initialize A, B, and C (code not shown)
4
5    int num_devices = omp_get_num_devices();
6    assert (N % num_devices == 0);
7    int len = N / num_devices;
8
9    for (int dev = 0; dev < num_devices; ++dev) {
10
11     int start = dev * len;
12     int end = start + len;
13
14     #pragma omp target map(to: A[start:len], B[start:len]) \
15                     map(from: C[start:len]) device(dev) nowait
16     {
17       #pragma omp loop
18       for (int i = start; i < end; ++i) {
19             C[i] = A[i] + B[i];
20       }
21     }
22   }
23   #pragma omp taskwait
```

Figure 8.7: **Distributing a vector add between multiple devices asynchronously** – The vector addition is distributed in a SPMD-style across multiple devices. One OpenMP thread creates a deferred target task for each device, so all devices can run together.

Table 8.7: **OpenMP depend clause for task dependencies.**

depend([*depend-modifier,*] dependence-type : *list***)**

dependence-type
in
out
inout
mutexinoutset
inoutset
depobj

The `depend` clause has a list of variables on which a dependence is applied to the task, along with a dependence modifier that states the direction of that dependence. The `list` is formatted as with the data-sharing clauses (recall Section 2.3.2). The `dependence` modifier can be one of the following:

- `in`: the task will use the data as input and depend on previously generated sibling tasks that have the data as an output (`out`, `inout`, `mutexinoutset`, or `inoutset`).

- `out` and `inout`: the task will use the data as output and depend on previously generated sibling tasks that have the data as an input or an output (`in`, `out`, `inout`, `mutexinoutset`, or `inoutset`). Note that `out` and `inout` are equivalent.

- `mutexinoutset`: two tasks that have this dependency on the same data can be run in either order but never at the same time; in addition, the task will depend on previously generated sibling tasks that have the data as an input or output (`in`, `out`, `inout`, or `inoutset`).

- `inoutset`: the task will have a dependency on sibling tasks that use the data but not with the `inoutset` clause (a dependence happens only for `in`, `out`, `inout`, or `mutexinoutset`).

- `depobj`: the task depends on a previously constructed dependency object, which can be useful for creating a specific non-data object using the `depobj` construct on which other dependencies can be set.

In all cases, the dependency is defined with regard to sibling tasks. These are tasks that were created by the same thread.

We can explore how these tasks might be used in practice by building a vector addition code that initializes the data on the device before computing the vector addition. We want to do this asynchronously, though, so the host thread that creates all the target tasks can proceed to other work while waiting for the tasks to finish. We show the code in Figure 8.8, along with a sketch of a task graph in Figure 8.9, which shows the dependencies between the target tasks. A target task is created to initialize each array. These initialization operations may execute concurrently. When the size of each kernel is small, some GPUs are able to schedule multiple kernels simultaneously. For this example, the three initializations can be scheduled concurrently. The vector addition loop must wait for all the tasks initializing the data before starting.

```
1   #pragma omp target enter data map(alloc: A[:N], B[:N], C[:N])
2
3   // Task: init A
4   #pragma omp target nowait depend(out:A[:N])
5   #pragma omp loop
6   for (int i = 0; i < N; ++i)  A[i] = 1.0;
7
8   // Task: init B
9   #pragma omp target nowait depend(out:B[:N])
10  #pragma omp loop
11  for (int i = 0; i < N; ++i)  B[i] = 2.0;
12
13  // Task: init C
14  #pragma omp target nowait depend(out:C[:N])
15  #pragma omp loop
16  for (int i = 0; i < N; ++i)  C[i] = 0.0;
17
18  // Task: vector add
19  #pragma omp target nowait depend(in: A[:N], B[:N]) depend(inout: C[:N])
20  #pragma omp loop
21  for (int i = 0; i < N; ++i)  C[i] = A[i] + B[i];
22
23  // Host can wait for it all to finish
24  #pragma omp taskwait
```

Figure 8.8: **Asynchronous array initialization and vector addition** – Asynchronous target tasks are created with the **nowait** clause, with the runtime dependence between the tasks set with the **depend** clause.

We can also use asynchronous tasks to share work between different devices with the **device** clause. The OpenMP tasks are all siblings, so they can synchronize with each other. Using dependencies and the **taskwait** construct, we can create tasks that run on different target devices, and ensure they run in the correct order. The code in Figure 8.10 shows how expressive these clauses can be. It is important to state this is not necessarily a sensible program, as it copies the array to the device at the start of each task, and copies the data back at the end of each task; there are many host-to-device copies in this program. The program runs the initialization of the three arrays on the first three devices in the system, all asynchronously. A good runtime will be able to schedule the data transfers and target executions to each

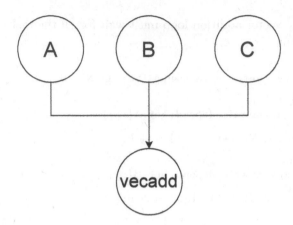

Figure 8.9: **A graph of the tasks and their dependencies** – This graph is based on the code in Figure 8.8.

device so they happen in parallel. The final vector addition task is enqueued to the final device but will not start until the three initialization tasks finish.

This program also highlights *when* the memory transfers occur. The transfers happen when the target tasks starts executing. This means that the addition task will copy the data from the host to the device *after* the three initialization tasks have completed copying the updated data to the host. This of course means the correct values are copied to the fourth device for that final task to use.

We'll use these asynchronous tasks along with the `depend` clause when combining OpenMP programs with external libraries in Chapter 9.

8.5.2   Asynchronous Data Transfers

In the previous examples, we've shown how the transfer of execution to the device can be made asynchronous using the `nowait` clause, and we set up dependencies between those tasks with the `depend` clause to make sure they run in the correct order. The very same mechanisms are also available for the data copying constructs: `target update`, `target enter data`, and `target exit data`.

Each of these constructs move data on demand by copying data between the host and device data environments. For `target update`, that data already exists in the data environment, having been mapped previously by a `target enter data` or a `target data` region.

```
1    #pragma omp target nowait depend(out:A) map(tofrom:A[:N]) device(0)
2    #pragma omp loop
3    for (int i = 0; i < N; ++i)  A[i] = 1.0;
4
5    #pragma omp target nowait depend(out:B) map(tofrom:B[:N]) device(1)
6    #pragma omp loop
7    for (int i = 0; i < N; ++i)  B[i] = 2.0;
8
9    #pragma omp target nowait depend(out:C) map(tofrom:C[:N]) device(2)
10   #pragma omp loop
11   for (int i = 0; i < N; ++i)  C[i] = 90.0;
12
13
14   #pragma omp target nowait depend(in:A,B) depend(inout:C) map(to:A[:N],
            B[:N]) map(tofrom: C[:N]) device(3)
15   #pragma omp loop
16   for (int i = 0; i < N; ++i)  C[i] = A[i] + B[i];
17
18   #pragma omp taskwait
```

Figure 8.10: **Splitting the asynchronous vector addition task graph across four devices** – This program runs each task of vector addition on a different device, assuming there are four devices in the system. Memory is mapped to and from each device via the host, so this program is clearly not optimal but does show the flexibility that the **nowait**, **depend**, and **device** clauses can provide.

The three constructs listed above all generate a target task in the same way as the **target** construct generates a target task. The task they generate does not have a target region to execute on the device, but otherwise behave the same. This means the same clauses used to support asynchronous execution for the target tasks can be used.

As with the code in Figure 8.10, the data transfer occurs when the target task is *executed* or scheduled by the OpenMP runtime. The transfer itself does not happen when the construct is encountered, although as we saw with the pointer swapping in Section 4.4.4, the location of the copies is determined at this point.

These data movement constructs work with the OpenMP tasking model in the same way as constructs for execution. This means we can use the synchronous constructs (omitting the **nowait** clause) that depend on prior asynchronous tasks as an alternative way to wait for all the tasks to finish. This means the host thread can wait and use these as a blocking synchronization point instead of **taskwait**.

The example in Figure 8.8 uses `taskwait`, but we can use a synchronous `target update` instead, as shown in Figure 8.11.

The `target data` construct does not operate asynchronously. This means that the data transfers occur when the construct is encountered and at the end of the region, and the construct does not synchronize with any tasks created within the data region. In this instance, do not forget to wait for the tasks with the `taskwait` construct!

```
1   #pragma omp target enter data map(alloc: A[:N], B[:N], C[:N])
2
3   // Task: init A
4   #pragma omp target nowait depend(out:A[:N])
5   #pragma omp loop
6   for (int i = 0; i < N; ++i)  A[i] = 1.0;
7
8   // Task: init B
9   #pragma omp target nowait depend(out:B[:N])
10  #pragma omp loop
11  for (int i = 0; i < N; ++i)  B[i] = 2.0;
12
13  // Task: init C
14  #pragma omp target nowait depend(out:C[:N])
15  #pragma omp loop
16  for (int i = 0; i < N; ++i)  C[i] = 0.0;
17
18  // Task: vector add
19  #pragma omp target nowait depend(in: A[:N], B[:N]) depend(inout: C[:N])
20  #pragma omp loop
21  for (int i = 0; i < N; ++i)  C[i] = A[i] + B[i];
22
23  #pragma omp target update from(C[:N]) depend(in: C[:N])
```

Figure 8.11: **Asynchronous vector addition synchronizing on data transfer** – Asynchronous target tasks are created with the **nowait** clause, with the runtime dependence between the tasks set with the **depend** clause. The host waits in the **target update** construct until the C array is copied back to the host.

8.5.3   Task Reductions

We can use reductions with target tasks so they cooperate on updates to a reduction variable even when they are running asynchronously. By cooperating, the tasks apply the reduction semantics to the shared reduction variable and together update it safely to produce the final value. When we use a worksharing construct (e.g., `parallel for`) for a loop with a reduction variable, we use the `reduction` clause, but we need to consider what happens when we want to carry out a reduction between independent tasks.

The code in Figure 8.12 is similar to our previous vector addition example, but this time it computes a dot product across multiple GPUs using the SPMD pattern. The division of work remains the same as with our earlier vector addition examples, with each device in the system taking a portion of the work. Two changes to our constructs are present: the addition of a `reduction` clause with a `task` modifier to the parallel region and the inclusion of the `in_reduction` clause on the target task. These clauses are in addition to the usual `reduction` clause we used on the `loop` or other parallel constructs such as `teams`, `parallel`, and so on. We must use these together to ensure the reduction is correct.

First, we must ensure that the host threads work together to reduce the `sum` variable by adding the `reduction` clause to the parallel region. The reduction is a summation, so we use the `reduction(+:  sum)` clause. We must also include a reduction modifier to state that any tasks that will be generated will participate in the reduction. This means that when tasks are generated, they can join the reduction. For any implicit tasks, the reduction modifier is sufficient, but our target tasks are explicit, and so we need the task modifier. The clause would therefore read `reduction(task, +:sum)`.

Second, once our top-level reduction is aware that tasks need to participate in the reduction, any explicit tasks we create, including target tasks created with the `target` construct, need to use the `in_reduction` clause. This takes a matching operator and variable just as the `reduction()` clause does. The `in_reduction()` clause should match the outer `reduction()` clause, excluding the task modifier.

When the `in_reduction` clause is used on a `target` construct, the reduction variable will be implicitly mapped `tofrom`. We do not need to add our own `map` clause, as the default behavior is to map reduction variable to and from the device data environment automatically.

A `taskgroup` construct can be used to group explicit tasks generated within its scope. When the scope of the construct ends, there is an implicit synchronization, of sibling tasks *and* their descendants. The `taskgroup` construct is a more extensive synchronization point than a `taskwait`, which only waits on sibling tasks.

When reductions are used with a `taskgroup`, we need two clauses. On the `taskgroup` construct, we need to set up the reduction and tell the system that

```
1   int N = 1000000;
2   double *A, *B;
3   // Allocate and initialize (not shown)
4   double sum = 0.0;
5
6   int num_devices = omp_get_num_devices();
7   assert (N % num_devices == 0);
8   int len = N / num_devices;
9
10  #pragma omp parallel num_threads(num_devices) reduction(task, +:sum)
11  {
12      int tid = omp_get_thread_num();
13      int start = tid * len;
14      int end = start + len;
15
16      #pragma omp target map(to: A[start:len], B[start:len]) device(tid)
                in_reduction(+:sum)
17      {
18          #pragma omp loop reduction(+:sum)
19          for (int i = start; i < end; ++i) {
20              sum += A[i] * B[i];
21          }
22      }
23  }
```

Figure 8.12: **Distributing a dot product between multiple devices** – The dot product is distributed using the SPMD pattern across multiple devices. One OpenMP thread on the host CPU is used to launch each device asynchronously.

tasks in the taskgroup may participate in a reduction. We do this with the `task_reduction(op:list)` clause. Then, for any task in the group (which includes `target` constructs), we need to specify the `in_reduction(op:list)` clause.

Figure 8.13 shows a dot product using the `taskgroup` construct. Asynchronous target tasks are launched within the region and contribute to the reduction due to the `in_reduction()` clause.

8.6   Summary

Chapter 5 spoke of the importance of asynchronous execution when running on GPUs. The host queues up a large amount of asynchronous work for the GPU, hiding any latency in offloading work or moving data. Up until now, all the target regions have been executed synchronously with the host; that is, the CPU waits for

```
1   int N = 1000000;
2   double *A, *B;
3   // Allocate and initialize
4   double sum = 0.0;
5
6   int num_devices = omp_get_num_devices();
7   assert (N % num_devices == 0);
8   int len = N / num_devices;
9
10  #pragma omp taskgroup task_reduction(+:sum)
11  {
12    for (int dev = 0; dev < num_devices; ++dev) {
13      int start = dev * len;
14      int end = start + len;
15
16      #pragma omp target map(to: A[start:len], B[start:len]) device(dev)
                in_reduction(+:sum) nowait
17      {
18        #pragma omp loop reduction(+: sum)
19        for (int i = start; i < end; ++i) {
20          sum += A[i] * B[i];
21        }
22      }
23    }
24  }
```

Figure 8.13: **Distributing a dot product between multiple devices asynchronously in a taskgroup** – The dot product is distributed using the SPMD pattern across multiple devices. One OpenMP thread creates a deferred target task for each device so all devices can run together and synchronize at the end of the **taskgroup** region.

each and every target region to execute before offloading the next one. This chapter provided mechanisms in OpenMP for asynchronous offload.

OpenMP is defined in terms of tasks. The various **target** constructs are no exception. These target tasks can run asynchronously with the **nowait** clause, with data dependencies between them specified with the **depend** clause. With the host free to enqueue the offload tasks, we can use several GPUs simultaneously by directing the tasks to different devices with the **device** clause. And because it's all OpenMP tasks, we can synchronize between them and orchestrate reductions using familiar task-oriented approaches.

9 Working with External Runtime Environments

It is rare that we are given the opportunity to write an application anew in High Performance Computing. Large applications in particular aren't rewritten as new technologies emerge. Instead, they evolve and adapt, switching to new parallel programming models as a wholesale transformation is extremely expensive and rarely occurs. A common adaptation strategy is to build a program around reusable software components from external libraries to provide functionality tuned to the specific features of new platforms. A common example is the linear algebra routines found in the Basic Linear Algebra Subprograms (BLAS) to perform operations with vectors and matrices.

External libraries are a crucial part of the application ecosystem. Vendors are able to supply high-quality and high-performance implementations of common routines. This improves programmer productivity as they do not need to optimize these routines themselves but still benefit from fast implementations.

OpenMP programs, therefore, must interoperate with external libraries, sharing data, synchronizing execution, and sharing compute resources. Data movement is costly, so we must ensure that data stays resident on the device for use inside a library or, for data allocated by a library, to be available for our OpenMP programs. For the best performance, we may write asynchronous applications that call both OpenMP target tasks and external library target tasks. Our program must interact with the tasks enqueued by these libraries to ensure all the tasks execute in the correct order.

Using and interacting with external libraries is part of many large applications, so in this chapter, we show how to interact with external libraries in our OpenMP programs. We work through both use cases: sharing our OpenMP data with an external library and using data allocated by an external library on the device within our OpenMP program. We also show how tasks synchronize with those running in a library so they can execute asynchronously.

9.1 Calling External Library Routines from OpenMP

An OpenMP program relies on the OpenMP runtime system to look after the devices in a system, fork and join threads on the host, offload target regions, manage dependencies between tasks, and more. The runtime system is an integral part of an OpenMP application. The libraries and software modules that enable the runtime system are combined with user-written code by the linker as the application's executable is created. A full application generally interacts with a range of libraries, which are linked into the executable as it is created.

Just as OpenMP is tightly coupled with its runtime system, so too are the low-level programming systems that vendors provide with their devices. These programming systems are important to programs that need to exploit a large fraction of the peak performance of a system. These vendor-specific programming models are often used to implement highly optimized versions of common routines provided as a library. As OpenMP programmers, we're much better off, in terms of performance, if we use those vendor-optimized libraries than writing and maintaining our own implementation of key routines. That means our OpenMP applications will often need to interoperate with libraries that are not based on OpenMP.

The OpenMP runtime system is implemented on top of the low-level features specific to a particular device [19]. Generally, this requires the implementer of OpenMP to use vendor-specific runtimes inside OpenMP. For example, if we wish to run our OpenMP program on NVIDIA® GPUs, the OpenMP runtime would most likely be written (in part) with CUDA™.

The result is mostly transparent to the OpenMP programmer, but it does give us the opportunity to interact with the rest of the vendor's ecosystem. However, the OpenMP programmer will need the interoperability functionality in OpenMP to gain access to objects provided by a vendor-specific runtime. For example, we might wish to access data already stored on the device and pass it directly to CUDA, or pass data allocated by CUDA directly into our OpenMP target regions without moving the data through the host. We may need access to CUDA objects such as streams so we can enqueue external tasks to the CUDA stream and ensure that CUDA's kernels run in the correct order with respect to tasks from our OpenMP program.

OpenMP calls these other runtimes a *foreign runtime*. In general, the foreign runtime could be any runtime that OpenMP can interoperate with, sharing the devices in the system, sharing data between them, and ensuring any execution happens in the correct order.

These foreign runtimes follow a similar model of execution to OpenMP. They provide an API with functions that a host calls to enqueue execution on the device. They come with their own names, semantics, syntax, and mechanisms for interoperability. Generalizing to *any* foreign runtime is not particularly useful, so in this discussion we will focus on a couple of concrete foreign runtimes. We will start with CUDA.

CUDA™ is an API for programming NVIDIA® GPUs. We introduced much of the language used to describe how work is run on a GPU device back in Chapter 1 in Table 1.1. A kernel is a function that executes on a GPU. The kernel is submitted to a queue for execution. This queue is called a *stream*. When it runs, an instance of the kernel executes at each point in an abstract index space. For CUDA, this index space is called a *grid*. The instance of a kernel at each point in the index space is called a *thread*. When we need to disambiguate the threads in CUDA from threads in OpenMP, we use the term *CUDA-threads*. The CUDA-threads are organized into *thread-blocks* that execute together on the GPU. We can see this execution model in Figure 3.7 if we equate *work-items* to CUDA-threads and *work-groups* to thread-blocks.

The grid is defined when a CUDA kernel is enqueued. This is done with a "chevron" notation, as shown in lines 23–25 in Figure 9.1. This example creates a CUDA stream and enqueues three kernels on it. The CUDA kernel submission is non-blocking, and the host will enqueue all three to the queue in turn. The stream will process the kernels in the queue in the order they were submitted. As the kernel enqueue operations are non-blocking, the host must wait for them all to finish by calling `cudaStreamSynchronize()`.

A foreign runtime might also abstract some of these details away and provide a library of common functions. For example, the cuBLAS library is an implementation of linear algebra routines (vector and matrix operations) optimized for NVIDIA GPUs. The library defines a host API for enqueuing functions on the GPU. Instead of calling a CUDA kernel directly (with the "chevrons"), the programmer calls a library routine that itself will enqueue the right combination of complex kernels. cuBLAS, as its name might suggest, is built on top of CUDA and borrows the ideas of a CUDA stream. It will use the default CUDA stream, but a specific stream can also be set.

In either case, the host will call a *foreign function*. These are kernels, functions, routines and library calls in the foreign runtime. They are initiated by the host and are usually non-blocking, so the host uses some mechanism to order the execution of the foreign functions (a CUDA stream or an OpenCL queue), depending on the details of the foreign runtime. OpenMP calls this object the *foreign synchronization object*. The name is perhaps rather vague, and it is intuitively best understood as a queue of work (foreign functions) executed in the foreign runtime.

Many of the examples in this chapter will show how OpenMP kernels interoperate with the CUDA and cuBLAS foreign runtimes. Although they are specific to CUDA, the concepts are transferable to other the foreign runtimes supported by OpenMP, which currently includes HIP, OpenCL, SYCL, and others.

```
1   // A CUDA kernel
2   __global__ void init(double *A, int N, double val) {
3     const int i = blockDim.x * blockIdx.x + threadIdx.x;
4     if (i < N)
5       A[i] = val;
6   }
7
8   int main(void) {
9     int N = 1024 * 1024;
10    double *A, *B, *C;
11
12    cudaMalloc(&A, sizeof(double)*N);
13    cudaMalloc(&B, sizeof(double)*N);
14    cudaMalloc(&C, sizeof(double)*N);
15
16    // Create a CUDA stream
17    cudaStream_t s;
18    cudaStreamCreate(&s);
19
20    // Launch three CUDA kernels in the stream
21    int blocks = N / 64;
22    int threads = 64;
23    init<<<blocks, threads, 0, s>>>(A, N, 1.0);
24    init<<<blocks, threads, 0, s>>>(B, N, 2.0);
25    init<<<blocks, threads, 0, s>>>(C, N, 0.0);
26
27    // Wait for work in stream to finish
28    cudaStreamSynchronize(s);
29
30    use(A,B,C,N); // Use on the host
31
32    // Destroy stream
33    cudaStreamDestroy(s);
34    cudaFree(A);
35    cudaFree(B);
36    cudaFree(C);
37
38    return 0;
39  }
```

Figure 9.1: **Enqueuing a CUDA kernel on a stream** – A CUDA stream is created and a CUDA kernel enqueued on it. Note that kernel enqueue is a non-blocking operation, and the host will not wait for it to complete before progressing.

With the general concepts of foreign runtimes defined, we can now show how these foreign functions can be called in our OpenMP programs and, more importantly, how data can be shared between OpenMP and a foreign runtime. Later, in Section 9.4, we will show how to order our non-blocking OpenMP tasks with the non-blocking foreign runtime tasks by interoperating with the foreign synchronization object. However, we'll build up to this slowly. In the next two sections, we will focus on sharing data allocated in an OpenMP program with a foreign runtime and sharing data allocated in the foreign runtime with OpenMP programs.

9.2   Sharing OpenMP Data with Foreign Functions

In earlier chapters, we used matrix multiplication as a running example to show how to run on a device using OpenMP. Optimizing matrix multiplication is a specialist profession, and we can take advantage of all that effort by using an optimized library implementation when possible. In a large, scientific application, matrix multiplication is only part of the entire computational workload, and so we need to be able to mix our own code with code that calls functions from a library.

The key to calling foreign functions in a performant way is to leave the data resident on the device. Just as we keep the data on the device between consecutive target tasks, we need to use that same approach and keep the data on the device for use by the library. Without interoperability between OpenMP and the foreign runtime, we would need to bring all the required data back to the host so the host could launch the foreign function using the native vendor-specific runtime. This means it would pass data from the host to the device using the approach specific to the library. Then, when the library routine completes, it would pass the data back to the host. The host would then move data back to the device to be used by the OpenMP program. In other words, without interoperability, data would move back and forth between the host and the device with every call to an external library function. As is hopefully clear, this is enormously wasteful. We should keep the data stationary and simply grant the library access to it.

We turn back to the `target data` construct we introduced in Chapter 4. We used this construct to map data onto the device data environment for the duration of the structured block associated with the `target data` construct. This means any target tasks would not need to remap data as it was already present in the device data environment.

The **target data** construct can also be used to pass device data into supported foreign runtimes. To do this, we use the **use_device_addr** clause, shown in Table 9.1. This clause lists any variables mapped to the device that we wish to convert to their device addresses for the duration of the target data region. This mapping between host addresses and device addresses for each variable usually occurs when a target task starts. The variables inside the target region use the device addresses, and OpenMP translates them for us. We can allow that translation to happen on demand by using the **use_device_addr** clause to the **target data** construct. All use of the variables listed in the clause are replaced by their device equivalents for the duration of the target data region. This means we can gain access to the native address of the data and can pass it to a foreign runtime.

Table 9.1: **The use_device_addr clause in C/C++ and Fortran** – The variables listed in the clause will be converted to their device addressed for the duration of the structured block.

C/C++ directive format
#pragma omp target data use_device_addr *(list)*
structured_block
Fortran directive format
!$omp target data use_device_addr *(list)*
structured_block
!$omp end target data

A straightforward way to see this in action is by printing out the addresses of variables. Look at the code Figure 9.2, which allocates a variable on the host called **var**. The variable is mapped to the device, and we print out its address (the location of the variable in memory) from inside and outside target data regions.

Compiling the code in Figure 9.2 with the NVIDIA HPC SDK compiler 22.1 and running it on a Linux machine hosting an NVIDIA® GeForce® RTX 2080 Ti GPU, the following output was produced:

```
Host address of var is 0x7ffdf5323e5c
Address of var in target data region is 0x7ffdf5323e5c
Device address of var is 0x7fafb4cfa000
```

The first line of output corresponds to the print of the address of **var**. This prints out where the variable is stored in host memory. We then map the variable to the

```
1    int var = 42;
2
3    printf("Host address of var is %p\n", &var);
4
5    // Map var to the device
6    #pragma omp target data map(var)
7    {
8
9      // Update var on the device
10     #pragma omp target
11     var = var + 1;
12
13     printf("Address of var in target data region is %p\n", &var);
14
15     // Use device address of var
16     #pragma omp target data use_device_addr(var)
17     {
18       printf("Device address of var is %p\n", &var);
19     }
20
21   }
```

Figure 9.2: **Printing pointers in target data regions** – This program uses the use_device_addr() clause to translate host pointers to device pointers in host code.

device using a **target data** region and update it on the device inside a target region by incrementing it by one. The address of the variable is again printed out, and this will once again produce the address where the variable is stored on the *host* since it is the host that is calling the **printf()** routine. Only inside the target regions (*not* the target data regions) do the variables take on their device equivalents.

To do the translation in other places, a second target data region is created, nested inside the first target data region. Here we use the **use_device_addr** clause to replace the address of the variable. This means we reference the device copy of the variable, the copy that was mapped by the outer **target data** construct. The final message printed by the host now shows the *device* address. Notice how we are executing on the host but obtaining the address of the variable that exists on the device (the corresponding variable). This means we can recover the location of mapped variables for use in foreign runtimes that operate using the addresses of variables already present in device memory.

For pointer data types, we use the **use_device_ptr** clause instead of the previous clause, **use_device_addr**, shown in Table 9.2. The clause is used on the **target**

data directive in the same way as **use_device_addr**. It is restricted to pointer types, whereas **use_device_addr** works for all mapped variables. When we use **use_device_addr** on a pointer mapped array, OpenMP creates a new variable of the same name locally inside our target data region containing the translated base pointer. This means the pointer variable inside the target data region is available on the host and contains the address of where the array exists on the device.

Table 9.2: **The use_device_ptr clause in C/C++ and Fortran** – The pointer variables listed in the clause will be translated to their corresponding device pointers for the duration of the structured block.

C/C++ directive format
#pragma omp target data use_device_ptr *(list)*
structured_block
Fortran directive format
!$omp target data use_device_ptr *(list)*
structured_block
!$omp end target data

Once a variable has been transformed by the **use_device_addr** clause on the **target data** construct, any references to it will use the device address. This will also be the case for any target regions inside the target data structured block. As the variables will now be taking the device address already, thanks to the transformation by the **use_device_addr** clause, we need to also list them in a **has_device_addr** clause on the **target** construct, as shown in Figure 9.3 and listed in Table 9.3.

Table 9.3: **The has_device_addr clause in C/C++ and Fortran** – The has_device_addr clause on the **target** construct is used to stop additional translation of variables with device addresses converted previously, using a **use_device_addr** clause on a **target data** construct.

C/C++ directive format
#pragma omp target has_device_addr *(list)*
structured_block
Fortran directive format
!$omp target has_device_addr *(list)*
structured_block
!$omp end target

```
1   int var = 42;
2   #pragma omp target enter data map(to: var)
3
4   #pragma omp target data use_device_addr(var)
5   {
6     #pragma omp target has_device_addr(var)
7     {
8       // use var ...
9     }
10  }
```

Figure 9.3: **Example of using the has_device_addr clause** – The `has_device_addr` clause is used on target regions where that variable has already appeared in an earlier `use_device_addr` clause on a `target data` construct.

9.2.1   The Need for Synchronization

The preceding example shows how we can use the device addresses of mapped variables. We can use them in calls to external libraries and foreign runtimes. But before we do, we must consider synchronization between an OpenMP program and the external library.

The `target data` construct is not a blocking operation and does not define a synchronization event between the host and the device. This means that when the host encounters the inner `target data` construct with the `use_device_addr` clause, there is again no synchronization. Programmers must ensure that any outstanding asynchronous target tasks (any target regions that started with the `nowait` clause) are finished before allowing a foreign runtime (external library) to generate tasks that use the same data. We showed how to synchronize with the `taskwait` directive in Chapter 8. Alternatively, we can use blocking target tasks by omitting the `nowait` clause. We will also need to make sure that the foreign runtime has completely finished executing before allowing future OpenMP tasks that may use that data to begin. We must synchronize twice: once before leaving OpenMP and handing control over to the foreign runtime and again before returning control back to OpenMP. For now, we will use these blocking target regions. However synchronization occurs, we must ensure that all our OpenMP target tasks finish before calling a foreign function in an external library. In Section 9.4 we will show how these synchronization events can be made non-blocking on the host.

9.2.2   Example: Sharing OpenMP Data with cuBLAS

In this section we show how to share data allocated on the device using OpenMP with the external library cuBLAS. We must ensure that our OpenMP implementation supports NVIDIA GPUs, and that our program is offloading our data and execution to it. We will assume that we are using the default device, and cuBLAS will likewise use the same device. Note we also synchronize before calling cuBLAS, and synchronize again before continuing with our OpenMP program.

As a brief aside before we begin, the command line arguments shown in Figure 9.4 are passed to the NVIDIA HPC SDK compiler 22.5 to build the example program in Figure 9.5 that uses OpenMP and the cuBLAS library together. The example is otherwise complete, including the cuBLAS headers, with the exception of the `check_solution()` routine to confirm the answers are correct (which we have omitted so the example fits on a single page).

```
nvc −O3 −mp=gpu −gpu=cc75 −lm −lcudart −lcublas −L/path/to/hpc_sdk
    /22.5/Linux_x86_64/22.5/cuda/lib64/
```

Figure 9.4: **Invoking the NVIDIA HPC SDK compiler to build a program using OpenMP and cuBLAS.**

The program computes the multiplication of two matrices, A and B, and stores the result in matrix C. We use OpenMP to allocate the data and initialize the arrays on the device. However, we know we will run this code on an NVIDIA GPU, so instead of implementing matrix multiplication ourselves, we can use the highly optimized implementation `cublasDgemm()` available in the cuBLAS library. The program in Figure 9.5 shows how we can acquire the device addresses (pointers) of the data mapped to the device by OpenMP and pass them to the cuBLAS library for direct use without any additional memory transfers.

The size of the matrix is saved to the variable N. The cuBLAS library is then initialized. We won't explain how cuBLAS works. Our focus will be on the flow of the application itself.

The host allocates data for the matrices. They are mapped to the device using the `target enter data` construct. As the data is uninitialized on the host, we map using `alloc` to simply reserve space on the device without copying data from the host to the device. The matrices are then initialized on the device in a straightforward target region using the `target teams loop` directive.

Crucially, this target task will block until it is completed. We need to make sure that the matrices are initialized before we compute the matrix product. This means we must wait for the target region to complete before we call out to our external library, cuBLAS. We ensure this synchronization by waiting on the host for the target task to finish before continuing with a call to our external library.

We now use the `target data` construct with the `use_device_addr` clause to use the device addresses for the matrix variables. We need these to pass to the cuBLAS library call `cublasDgemm`. The data is expected to be on the device, so we must convert the host addresses for variables into the device addresses. For the duration of this `target data` region (lines 29–35), all uses of the pointer variables A, B, and C are replaced with the corresponding device pointer instead.

Notice in Figure 9.5 that we must once again synchronize after our external library call and before returning to our OpenMP program. In this program, we do this using the `cudaDeviceSynchronize()` function from the CUDA API.

Our data is copied back to the host and deallocated on the device using the `target exit data` directive. Notice that the C matrix holds the result of the matrix product computed by our external library. The program finishes by checking that the matrices were multiplied correctly.

In summary, to pass data mapped to the device by OpenMP to an external library, we must first synchronize to ensure all target tasks finish execution. Then, we use a `target data` region with the `use_device_addr` clause to translate use of those variables inside that region from the host addresses to the device addresses. The variables can then be used by an external library. Finally, we must ensure the library has finished with our data before returning to OpenMP, requiring some form of synchronization.

9.3   Using Data from a Foreign Runtime with OpenMP

In the previous section, we discussed how to share data mapped to the device by OpenMP with a foreign runtime. In this section we look at the reverse: how to make use of data allocated by a foreign runtime inside an OpenMP target region. The motivation is similar to what we explained before. We do not want to redundantly move data back and forth between the device and host. We just need to leave the

```
1   #include <cuda_runtime.h>
2   #include "cublas_v2.h"
3
4   int main(void) {
5     int N = 10000;
6
7     // Initalize cuBLAS Library
8     cublasHandle_t handle;
9     cublasCreate(&handle);
10
11    double *A = malloc(sizeof(double)*N*N);
12    double *B = malloc(sizeof(double)*N*N);
13    double *C = malloc(sizeof(double)*N*N);
14
15    #pragma omp target enter data \
16                map(alloc: A[0:N*N], B[0:N*N], C[0:N*N])
17
18    #pragma omp target teams loop collapse(2)
19    for (int i = 0; i < N; ++i) {
20      for (int j = 0; j < N; ++j) {
21        A[i*N+j] = 1.0;
22        B[i*N+j] = 2.0;
23        C[i*N+j] = 0.0;
24      }
25    }
26    // Note: Blocking target call to synchronize OpenMP
27
28    #pragma omp target data use_device_addr(A, B, C)
29    {
30      double alpha = 1.0;   double beta = 0.0;
31      cublasDgemm(handle, CUBLAS_OP_N, CUBLAS_OP_N, N, N, N, &alpha, A,
32          N, B, N, &beta, C, N);
33      // Synchronize with CUDA device before returning (ensure all work
34          finished)
34      cudaDeviceSynchronize();
35    }
36
37    #pragma omp target exit data map(from: C[0:N*N]) \
38            map(delete: A[0:N*N], B[0:N*N])
39
40    // Check solution
41    check_solution(C, N);
42
43    cublasDestroy(handle);
44  }
```

Figure 9.5: **Passing OpenMP data to cuBLAS** – This program uses the target data construct with the **use_device_addr** clause to share data with cuBLAS.

data resident on the device and ensure OpenMP maps the addresses inside the target region.

The requirements for synchronization that we discussed in Section 9.2.1 still apply. Unless we use the constructs discussed later in Section 9.4, we must ensure the foreign functions have finished with the data before OpenMP acts on it, and vice versa. The methods of synchronization are the same as in our earlier discussion, so we won't repeat them here, but don't forget to synchronize!

When a foreign runtime allocates data on a device, it creates a pointer to that data in the address space of the device memory. That pointer can be used by code running on the device. In a heterogeneous application, programmers usually need variables on the host and the device that mirror each other for access to device data from the host or host data from the device. A common convention for such mirrored variable names in heterogeneous applications is the prefix h_ for the host data and d_ for the device data.

OpenMP makes the programmers life much simpler by handling these mirror copies for us as *mapped variables*. We create our variables on the host, and they are mapped to and from the device. The device copy uses the name from the host in the scope of the target region running on the device. The implicit data transfers and explicit mapping controls ensure that the correct version of that variable is used depending on the scope. Inside a target region, we use the device address while on the host we use the host equivalent.

Table 9.4: **The omp_target_associate_ptr function in C/C++.**

C/C++ library routine
int omp_target_associate_ptr(const void *host_ptr, const void *device_ptr, size_t size, size_t device_offset, int device_num)

However, if we wish to use externally allocated data inside OpenMP, we must perform these steps ourselves. We do this with the function from the OpenMP API shown in Table 9.4. This function sets up the correspondence between the host pointer (host_ptr) and the device pointer (device_ptr) so that when the host pointer is mapped to the target data environment on entry to a target region, the device will use the data stored at the device pointer.

The size and device_offset parameters are expressed in bytes. They describe the extent of the association and any offset from the beginning of the device allocation for where the association begins. In most common situations, the size parameter will be the size of the allocation and the offset will be zero, indicating the start of the array.

Notice that we must supply the device number. This should match the device we use for our later target constructs. If we do not use the `device` clause, then those target tasks will use the default device. We can discover the number of that device with the `omp_get_default_device()` function.

The function returns a non zero value in the case of an error. The host pointer should point to allocated memory (i.e., the host pointer should not be `NULL`). This is so that when the OpenMP runtime maps the host pointer, it is translating a non-NULL address.

The code in Figure 9.6 shows how the host and device pointers are associated. On line 4, the host memory for the array A is allocated. Recall that the host pointer must be a valid pointer, so we must allocate some memory on the host. The device memory is allocated by a CUDA API routine on line 9. Notice we are using the convention of `h_A` to represent the host variable and `d_A` for the device variable. We now have two separate memory allocations: one on the host and one on the device.

On line 11, we collect the default device. We will need this in the next step when we associate the pointers. On line 13, the host and device allocations are associated with each other. This means that when we use the `h_A` variable inside target regions, OpenMP will translate it to the device variable `d_A`. This will happen for our target region on lines 15–19. The association of the pointers is removed on line 21, as the application winds down.

We have seen how to associate host and device pointers manually and how this enables OpenMP to learn about device allocations made outside the OpenMP environment. This lets us pass external data into OpenMP. We can remove this association with the routine shown in Table 9.5. The contents of the device allocation becomes invalid, however, so we must not use that allocation externally once OpenMP has released it.

In summary, we can access device data that has been allocated by an external library inside OpenMP by associating that data with a host allocation. For this, we use the `omp_target_associate_ptr()` function, which sets up the connection between the two. The host variable is then used in our code, and when mapped to the device on reaching a target construct, the device allocation will be used.

```
1   const int N = 1000;
2
3   // Allocate array on the host
4   double * h_A = malloc(sizeof(double) * N);
5
6   double * d_A = NULL;
7
8   // Allocate on device using external library
9   cudaMalloc((void **)&d_A, sizeof(double)*N);
10
11  int dev = omp_get_default_device();
12
13  omp_target_associate_ptr(h_A, d_A, sizeof(double)*N, 0, dev);
14
15  #pragma omp target device(dev)
16  #pragma omp teams loop
17  for (int i = 0; i < N; ++i) {
18    h_A[i] = (double) i;
19  }
20
21  omp_target_disassociate_ptr(h_A, dev);
22  cudaFree(d_A);
23  free(h_A);
```

Figure 9.6: **Associating existing device pointers with host allocations** – This program joins host and device allocations by association so that the OpenMP runtime will map the host pointer to the associated device pointer in target regions.

Table 9.5: **The omp_target_disassociate_ptr function in C/C++.**

C/C++ library routine
int omp_target_disassociate_ptr(const void *_ptr_, int _device_num_)

9.3.1   Example: Sharing cuBLAS Data with OpenMP

The example in Figure 9.7 shows how we might access data allocated on the device by the CUDA library inside OpenMP. The code is similar to our previous example in Figure 9.5 in that we use the cuBLAS library to calculate the matrix product. Again, the data in initialized by OpenMP, but here in Figure 9.7, the data is no longer allocated by OpenMP; the data is allocated by the CUDA function **cudaMalloc** (on lines 6–8).

```
1    int N = 10000;
2    cublasHandle_t handle; cublasCreate(&handle);
3
4    // Device pointers, allocated by CUDA
5    double *d_A, *d_B, *d_C;
6    cudaMalloc((void**)&d_A, sizeof(double)*N*N);
7    cudaMalloc((void**)&d_B, sizeof(double)*N*N);
8    cudaMalloc((void**)&d_C, sizeof(double)*N*N);
9
10   // Host pointers — must allocate space for all variables
11   double *A = malloc(sizeof(double)*N*N);
12   double *B = malloc(sizeof(double)*N*N);
13   double *C = malloc(sizeof(double)*N*N);
14
15   // Get the default OpenMP target device
16   int dev = omp_get_default_device();
17
18   // Associate external device pointers
19   omp_target_associate_ptr(A, d_A, sizeof(double)*N*N, 0, dev);
20   omp_target_associate_ptr(B, d_B, sizeof(double)*N*N, 0, dev);
21   omp_target_associate_ptr(C, d_C, sizeof(double)*N*N, 0, dev);
22
23   // Use blocking OpenMP target task to initalize CUDA arrays
24   // Notice implicit mapping of host pointers to device pointers
25   #pragma omp target
26   init_arrays(A, B, C, N);
27
28   // Use cuBLAS for DGEMM, using the device pointers directly
29   double alpha = 1.0; double beta = 0.0;
30   cublasDgemm(handle, CUBLAS_OP_N, CUBLAS_OP_N, N, N, N, &alpha, d_A,
           N, d_B, N, &beta, d_C, N);
31
32   // Copy back with *blocking* operation to ensure DGEMM completes
33   cudaMemcpy(C, d_C, sizeof(double)*N*N, cudaMemcpyDeviceToHost);
34
35   // Release pointers, invalidating the device memory
36   omp_target_disassociate_ptr(A, dev);
37   omp_target_disassociate_ptr(B, dev);
38   omp_target_disassociate_ptr(C, dev);
39
40   check_solution(C, N);
41
42   cudaFree(d_A); cudaFree(d_B); cudaFree(d_C);
43   free(A); free(B); free(C);
44   cublasDestroy(handle);
```

Figure 9.7: **Using CUDA data in OpenMP** – This program uses the association functions to connect host data with device data allocated by the CUDA runtime so it can be used in OpenMP target regions.

In order to access CUDA allocations inside OpenMP, we need to allocate matching host variables and associate them with the device allocations. On lines 11–13, we allocate arrays on the host using `malloc`, resulting in host pointers to the matrices: `A`, `B`, and `C`.

We need to associate the host pointers with the device allocations: `d_A`, `d_B`, `d_C`. We collect the OpenMP default device number using the `omp_get_default_device()` function on line 16 and use this in the function to associate the host and device pointer-pairs on lines 19–21.

In our target task on lines 25–26, we use the host pointer variable names to run on the device. Thanks to our association between pointers and the implicit mapping rules of pointer variables, the CUDA allocation will be used for this target region. Note that we use a blocking target task (the `nowait` is omitted) to ensure the target region has finished initializing our arrays before we call the external library routines.

Our cuBLAS call occurs on line 30 and uses the device pointer variables directly. This API expects the arguments representing the matrices to be device pointers, and so we can just pass in the device pointers previously allocated.

Finally, we copy the data from the device to the host on line 33. For this we have used `cudaMemcpy` and the host and device pointers manually. This function will block on the host until all previous asynchronous tasks, including the `cublasDgemm` routine, have completed.

On lines 36–38 we remove the association between the host and device pointers. This invalidates the contents of the device allocations.

In summary, to pass external data to OpenMP, we allocate host and device data from the host and then associate the pointers with the `omp_target_associate_ptr` function. In future target constructs, we use the host variable name, and the implicit mapping rules translates it to the associated device pointer as required. When finished, we disassociate the pointers, at which point the contents of the device memory allocation is invalidated.

9.3.2   Avoiding Unportable Code

Our example of accessing device data allocated externally to OpenMP shows that care needs to be taken when stitching together host and device pointers. Using the `omp_target_associate_ptr()` functions ensures the program will work on all OpenMP 5.2 implementations supporting NVIDIA GPUs and CUDA.

Table 9.6: **Summary of where different *_device_* clauses are used** – The clauses in this table are all used for passing and converting host variables into device variables.

Clause	Valid constructs	Use
is_device_ptr	target	The listed pointers are device pointers and do not need to be mapped for the target region. This is useful when the variables were allocated in device memory by the `omp_target_alloc` function.
	dispatch	The listed pointers are passed to the function variant as device pointers and do not need to be mapped.
has_device_addr	target	Input one or more variables; for each, indicate to the runtime system that they are device addresses and do not need to be mapped for the target region. This is useful when the address has already been converted by the `use_device_addr` clause.
use_device_ptr	target data	Input one or more pointers; for the duration of the target data region, when the host uses the pointer variables, the pointer value is replaced by the corresponding device pointer.
use_device_addr	target data	Input one or more variables; for the duration of the target data region, when the host references the variables, they are converted to references (i.e., pointers) to the corresponding device variable.

However, there are cases where a simpler approach works that relies on the particular behavior of certain implementations. The `is_device_ptr` clause can be used on the target construct to indicate that the pointer variables listed are device addresses. OpenMP requires that the pointers in this clause must have been allocated with the `omp_target_alloc` routine from the OpenMP API. This means that OpenMP is responsible for allocating the data.

Some implementations also allow external device pointers to be passed into the target region using the `is_device_ptr` clause. While this is not forbidden by OpenMP as it allows an implementation to support this behavior, there is no guarantee that this will work in general.

You have by now seen several clauses with similar-sounding names: `is_device_ptr`, `use_device_ptr`, `has_device_addr`, and `use_device_addr`. They are all used for managing the representation of variables and pointers in a target region or a target data region. We summarize their use in Table 9.6.

9.4   Direct Control of Foreign Runtimes

In the last two sections, we discussed how to share data between OpenMP and a foreign runtime. That data might be allocated by OpenMP and used by the foreign runtime or vice versa. When running code between OpenMP and an external runtime system (such as CUDA), the programmer must ensure they do not get in each other's way. For example, it would be easy in such scenarios to create data races as an OpenMP target region might start to modify data that was still being computed by CUDA. We dealt with these synchronization problems by using the blocking features of tasks in OpenMP. If you do not use the `nowait` clause, the various `target` constructs will cause the host to wait until the target region has completed before proceeding to subsequent instructions. This means the host has to wait for OpenMP target regions to finish before transferring control to the external library, and wait once again for the library to finish. These blocking synchronization events can add considerable overhead.

OpenMP gives us more fine-grained control of interactions with a foreign runtime using the `interop` construct, shown in Table 9.7. This construct principally provides two functions: querying properties of the foreign runtime and device and establishing synchronization between OpenMP and the foreign runtime.

Alongside the `interop` construct, OpenMP uses an *interop handle* to provide a bridge into the foreign runtime. This handle is used to access implementation-specific objects we might need for managing interoperability with the foreign runtime. The interop handle is an opaque type `omp_interop_t`, and no matter how we use the `interop` construct (for querying or synchronization), we must first create it.

To create the interoperability object, we use the `init` clause on the `interop` construct. The clause takes as an argument the interop object and the type of interoperability required. At least one of the two interop-type modifers must be provided:

- `target`: provides access to the foreign runtimes resources associated with the device, platform and context.

- `targetsync`: provides access to the synchronization object used to establish happens-before relations between OpenMP and the foreign runtime.

No matter which interop-type is used, the interop object can additionally be queried for foreign runtime properties.

To create the interop handle, we include the pattern shown in Figure 9.8 in our program. The interop handle `iobj` is first set to `omp_interop_none` (which is equal to the integer zero). This means that the handle is not initialized and is not connected to the foreign runtime. The `interop init()` construct connects OpenMP to the available foreign runtime and creates the handle in the variable we pass to the clause. We must use at least one modifier (`target` and/or `targetsync`) in the `init` clause. Once we have finished using it, the handle can be destroyed, which also sets the handle to `omp_interop_none` by calling the `interop destroy()` construct.

Establishing the rules and regulations of how OpenMP and the foreign runtime interact to enable asynchronous heterogeneous programming is an involved topic that we will discuss in depth in Section 9.4.2. Therefore, we will begin exploring the `interop` construct by first seeing how it can provide introspection of the foreign runtime.

```
 1   // Declare the interop object
 2   omp_interop_t iobj = omp_interop_none;
 3
 4   // Initialize the interop object
 5   #pragma omp interop init(target: iobj)
 6
 7
 8   // later...
 9
10   // Destroy the interop object
11   #pragma omp interop destroy(iobj)
```

Figure 9.8: **Creating and destroying an interop handle** – The `interop` construct is used with the `init` clause to create an interop handle for a foreign runtime. It is destroyed with the `destroy` clause.

Table 9.7: **The interop construct in C/C++ and Fortran** – The `interop` construct supports interoperability between OpenMP and external runtimes. The functionality differs depending on how the *interop-var* is initialized. If initialized with the *interop-type* `target`, the interop-var can be used to query properties of the foreign runtime. If initialized with the interop-type `targetsync`, the interop-var is used to access the queue (or stream) used to submit kernels to a GPU. It also establishes synchronization behaviors between the OpenMP and foreign runtimes.

C/C++ directive format
#pragma omp interop *[clause[[,] clause]...]*
Fortran directive format
!$omp interop *[clause[[,] clause]...]*

depend *(dependence-type: list)*
destroy *(destroy-var)*
device *([device-modifier:] integer-expression)*
init *([interop-modifier,] interop-type: interop-var)*
nowait
use *(interop-var)*

9.4.1   Query Properties of the Foreign Runtime

The opaque interop handle gives us a view into the foreign runtime. It can be queried to learn more about the foreign runtime. We can also gain access to the fundamental objects inside the foreign runtime such as handles to devices, queues, and other objects.

The first question that naturally arises when the interop handle is constructed is what the foreign runtime actually is. Depending on which foreign runtime is available at runtime, we might need to call a different code path.

The interop handle can be queried with one of the library routines shown in Table 9.8. The correct one to use will depend on the type of the property in question; for instance, if the property is an integer, the `omp_get_interop_int` routine should be used, and for properties that are pointers, the `omp_get_interop_ptr` routine should be used.

Table 9.8: **OpenMP API functions for querying properties of a foreign runtime.**

Function	Description
omp_intptr_t omp_get_interop_int(**const omp_interop_t** *interop*, **omp_interop_property_t** *property_id*, **int ****ret_code***)**	Get the integer property specified by the property ID
void *omp_get_interop_ptr(**const omp_interop_t** *interop*, **omp_interop_property_t** *property_id*, **int ****ret_code***)**	Get the pointer property specified by the property ID
char *omp_get_interop_str(**const omp_interop_t** *interop*, **omp_interop_property_t** *property_id*, **int ****ret_code***)**	Get the string property specified by the property ID

The example in Figure 9.9 shows how we might choose a different execution path based on the particular runtime available (where the various options are defined in the OpenMP 5.2 specification).

The currently supported foreign runtimes are listed in the example with their IDs defined in a common form as `omp_ifr_*`. It is important to check that the external runtime is the one expected. This is especially important when we request resource handles to the native object in the foreign runtime (e.g., queues, devices) as they must be cast to the correct type depending on the specific foreign runtime.

```
1   omp_interop_t iobj = omp_interop_none;
2   #pragma omp interop init(target: iobj)
3   int err;
4
5   omp_intptr_t id = omp_get_interop_int(iobj, omp_ipr_fr_id, &err);
6   assert(err < 0);
7
8   switch (id) {
9     case omp_ifr_cuda:
10      call_cuda_code(iobj);
11      break;
12    case omp_ifr_cuda_driver:
13      call_cuda_driver_code(iobj);
14      break;
15    case omp_ifr_opencl:
16      call_opencl_code(iobj);
17      break;
18    case omp_ifr_sycl:
19      call_sycl_code(iobj);
20      break;
21    case omp_ifr_hip:
22      call_hip_code(iobj);
23      break;
24    case omp_ifr_level_zero:
25      call_level_zero_code(iobj);
26      break;
27    default:
28      // No interop object available
29      ;
30  }
```

Figure 9.9: **Querying the interop handle** – The interop handle is queried to identify the underlying runtime in order to call the appropriate function.

In addition to the ID of the foreign runtime, a number of other properties are available. The mandatory ones that will be available for all supported foreign runtimes are listed in Table 9.9, but additional ones may be made available for the specific foreign runtime. The number of properties available to query is discovered by calling the OpenMP library routine in Table 9.10 and subtracting the special value omp_ipr_first. More details about the properties can be programmatically obtained using the routines in Table 9.11, which produce human-readable descriptions of the properties and the return types available in the foreign runtime.

Table 9.9: **Mandatory foreign runtime properties available to query** – For
some properties to be available, a particular `interop-type` must be used when creating
the interop handle with the `init()` clause. The return type of the properties are also given.
Where the return type is a pointer, the OpenMP library routine returns a `void *`, which
should be cast to the correct type depending on the foreign runtime.

Property	Interop type	Return type	Description
omp_ipr_fr_id	All	intptr_t	Foreign runtime ID
omp_ipr_fr_name	All	char *	Name of foreign runtime
omp_ipr_vendor	All	intptr_t	Foreign runtime vendor ID
omp_ipr_vendor_name	All	char *	Name of foreign runtime vendor
omp_ipr_device_num	All	int	OpenMP device ID of the device used by the foreign runtime
omp_ipr_platform	target	Pointer	Handle to foreign runtime platform
omp_ipr_device	target	Pointer	Handle to foreign runtime device
omp_ipr_device_context	target	Pointer	Handle to foreign runtime device context
omp_ipr_targetsync	targetsync	Pointer	Handle to foreign runtime synchronization object (e.g., CUDA stream)

Table 9.10: **OpenMP API function for querying the number properties of
a foreign runtime.**

Function	Description
int omp_get_num_interop_properties(const omp_interop_t *interop***)**	Get number of properties available to the interop handle

Once we have a handle to the runtime, we can pull other objects from it aside
from its ID. The objects available depend on the type of interoperability. With
`targetsync`, we can get a synchronization object, which for the runtimes supported
by OpenMP is a native runtime task queue.

Table 9.11: **OpenMP API functions for querying properties of a foreign runtime.**

Function	Description
const char * omp_get_interop_name(const omp_interop_t *interop*, omp_interop_property_t *property_id*)	Get the name of a property
const char * omp_get_interop_type_desc(const omp_interop_t *interop*, omp_interop_property_t *property_id*)	Get description of the type of a property
const char * omp_get_interop_rc_desc(const omp_interop_t *interop*, omp_interop_rc_t *ret_code*)	Get description of the return code of a previous property query

```
1  omp_interop_t iobj = omp_interop_none;
2  #pragma omp interop init(targetsync: iobj)
3
4  // Check we have a CUDA runtime
5  int err;
6  assert(omp_get_interop_int(iobj, omp_ipr_fr_id, &err)==omp_ifr_cuda);
7
8  // Get CUDA stream
9  cudaStream_t s = (cudaStream_t) omp_get_interop_ptr(iobj,
       omp_ipr_targetsync, NULL);
10
11 // Use the stream...
12
13 #pragma omp interop destroy(iobj)
```

Figure 9.10: **Obtain a CUDA stream from an OpenMP interop handle** – The interop handle is used to get a synchronization object from the OpenMP runtime. In the case of a CUDA runtime, this is a CUDA stream.

The code in Figure 9.10 pulls a CUDA stream from the OpenMP runtime interoperating with CUDA. The `omp_get_interop_ptr` function returns the synchronization object appropriate for the runtime. The function returns a `void *` pointer that we must typecast to the particular object type for that backend. For CUDA, this is a stream; for OpenCL, it will be a queue. We are able to use this in our external library to enqueue additional native kernels. Finally, we close the interoperability session by using the `destroy` clause on the `interop` construct. This will release any objects pulled from the backend (such as the queue) and set the handler back to `omp_interop_none`, where it can no longer be used.

9.4.2   Using the Interop Construct to Correctly Synchronize with Foreign Functions

We've seen how OpenMP can interact with a foreign runtime in order to share data (in both directions) using the `target data` directive, appropriate clauses, and API routines. We've also seen how the `interop` construct lets us gain more information about the foreign runtime. We have not yet, however, discussed the synchronization semantics associated with `interop` to give us a way to ensure an ordering of OpenMP target tasks and foreign functions running on the same device. This is what we need to address now, so we can enable truly asynchronous programming.

In the examples so far (particularly Figure 9.5 and Figure 9.7), synchronization between OpenMP target tasks and foreign runtime tasks was orchestrated by ensuring all OpenMP tasks where finished before calling a foreign function and then ensuring those finished before creating more OpenMP tasks. The host program was responsible for ensuring this heavy-handed regime for synchronization.

We can reduce our synchronization overhead when using the `interop` construct. This construct includes a way to integrate OpenMP tasks with foreign functions asynchronously. This means we are able to enqueue OpenMP tasks, switch over to an external library routine, and return to enqueuing OpenMP tasks—all without blocking on the host.

Let's take a moment to discuss relationships and ordering of operations. The finer details of happens-before relationships sit in the realm of programming language semantics, which we'll avoid in this book. But we'll start with a simple example. The example in Figure 9.11 modifies and prints out the value of its argument. We expect this code to output N = 42. That is, the variable is set to the value 42 before the value of that variable is printed to the screen. This is an example of a *happens-before* relation. Technically, the first statement is *sequenced-before* the second.

Now imagine that we put the assignment and printing of N in separate threads. The threads are concurrent (i.e., unordered), and we no longer have a happens-before relation between when the variable is set and when it is output. There would be no reason to expect the program to output N = 42.

```
1  void update(int *N) {
2    *N = 42;
3    printf("N = %d\n", *N);
4  }
```

Figure 9.11: **A function to demonstrate program order** – The value of N is updated, with the new value realized in subsequent statements.

Synchronization is a complex topic. It is surprisingly easy to get the sequences of happens-before relations in a program wrong. Fortunately, the OpenMP tasking model gives us a synchronization mechanism that is straightforward and covers many of the patterns of synchronization we are likely to need. In OpenMP, we can set up task dependencies with the **depend()** clause (see Chapter 8). This means we ensure that one task won't begin until the task it depends on has finished. These dependencies establish happens-before relations between tasks, where precursor tasks happen before those enqueued later that depend on them.

The happens-before relationship is important to understanding the **interop** construct. When we switch from OpenMP to our foreign runtime, we want all our OpenMP tasks to happen before those foreign functions that the foreign runtime might then enqueue. Likewise, when we return to OpenMP, we want all those foreign functions to happen before any future OpenMP tasks we might create. The challenge is to accomplish these order constraints without stopping work anymore than the actual dependencies require and in particular to avoid blocking on the host.

We can use the **interop** construct to ensure an ordering between OpenMP tasks and foreign functions that are enqueued on the foreign synchronization object. The basic pattern in shown in Figure 9.12. We create the interop handle with the **targetsync** interop-type and extract the foreign synchronization object. Foreign functions are then enqueued on that foreign synchronization object (the CUDA stream in our example). OpenMP tasks prior to the **interop init()** construct will happen before the foreign functions that are enqueued on the foreign synchronization object. When the interop handle is destroyed, those enqueued foreign functions will happen before further OpenMP tasks. Note that all uses of the **interop** construct are blocking, but the enqueue of the foreign functions are not. We will address the non-blocking behavior in a moment.

```
1   omp_interop_t iobj = omp_interop_none;
2   #pragma omp interop init(targetsync: iobj)
3
4   // Check we have a CUDA runtime
5   int err;
6   assert(omp_get_interop_int(iobj, omp_ipr_fr_id, &err)==omp_ifr_cuda);
7
8   // Get CUDA stream
9   cudaStream_t s = (cudaStream_t) omp_get_interop_ptr(iobj,
        omp_ipr_targetsync, NULL);
10
11  // Enqueue a CUDA kernel, a non-blocking operation
12  kernel<<<blocks, threads, 0, s>>>(/* args */);
13
14  #pragma omp interop destroy(iobj)
15  // kernel will be finished here
```

Figure 9.12: **Enqueuing foreign functions** – The `interop` construct is used to extract a foreign synchronization object that can be used to enqueue foreign functions. Note that in practice, the compiler may require the CUDA kernel invocation to be wrapped inside a function in a different file, which is compiled as a CUDA code, and linked to the OpenMP program.

Using this pair of constructs, the interop handle is created and destroyed. This means the foreign synchronization object is likely destroyed, but this is inefficient: we want to set up the interoperability once, extract the foreign synchronization object, and use it multiple times in our program. We also need to ensure the happens-before relations happen at the correct times so we can switch back and forth between OpenMP tasks and foreign functions. For this, we need the `interop use()` construct; the syntax is shown in Table 9.7.

The happens-before behavior of the `interop` construct occurs whenever the interop handle was (previously) created with a `targetsync` interop type. Whenever we wish to switch between enqueuing OpenMP tasks and foreign functions, or vice versa, we insert an `interop use` construct. For example, the program in Figure 9.13 creates a foreign synchronization object (a CUDA stream), and between enqueuing CUDA kernels and launching OpenMP target tasks, the `interop use` construct appears to ensure these happen in the correct order.

This basic pattern can be used to support the asynchronous behavior we want. We use a pair of `interop` constructs to manage the creation of an interop handle: the first creates the handler; the second destroys it. We then use the handler to

```
1   omp_interop_t iobj = omp_interop_none;
2   #pragma omp interop init(targetsync: iobj)
3
4   // Check we have a CUDA runtime
5   int err;
6   assert(omp_get_interop_int(iobj, omp_ipr_fr_id, &err)==omp_ifr_cuda);
7
8   // Get CUDA stream
9   cudaStream_t s = (cudaStream_t) omp_get_interop_ptr(iobj,
        omp_ipr_targetsync, NULL);
10
11  for (int t = 0; t < 1000; ++t) {
12    #pragma omp interop use(iobj)
13    // Previous OpenMP target tasks
14
15    // Enqueue a CUDA kernel, a non-blocking operation
16    kernel<<<blocks, threads, 0, s>>>(/* args */);
17
18    #pragma omp interop use(iobj)
19    // kernel will be finished here
20
21    #pragma omp target
22    {
23      // Some target task
24    }
25  }
26
27  #pragma omp interop destroy(iobj)
```

Figure 9.13: **Enqueuing multiple foreign functions and OpenMP tasks** –
The **interop** construct is used to extract a foreign synchronization object that can be used
to enqueue foreign functions. The **use** clause on the **interop** construct ensures the correct
ordering.

gain access to a queue (foreign synchronization object) from the backend runtime
and enqueue foreign functions *using that queue* for execution in between the pair of
interop constructs. When we wish to switch from generating OpenMP tasks and
enqueuing foreign functions, we use the **interop use** construct, and when we wish
to switch back from enqueuing foreign functions to generating OpenMP tasks, we
use another **interop use** construct.

9.4.3   Non-blocking Synchronization with a Foreign Runtime

So far we have not operated in a truly asynchronous manner, as those `interop` constructs will be executed when they are encountered. To go asynchronous, we use the same approach as for asynchronous target tasks that we discussed in Chapter 8. We will use two clauses: `nowait` and `depend`. The `nowait` ensures the constructs create a task and the host continues without blocking, and the `depend` clause ensures that those tasks occur in the correct relative order.

Consider the case where we have created a number of target tasks running on the device. We have set the dependencies with the `depend` clause. We can specify that the `interop` construct also operates asynchronously, and we can specify a dependency on it, too. The construct will create the interoperability handle object when used with the `init` clause. At this point, OpenMP ensures any foreign functions enqueued on the foreign synchronization object obtainable from the interop handle have finished before the task generated by the `interop` construct completes. There are no such foreign functions because the interop handle has only just been created! We point this out because only foreign functions enqueued using the queue extracted from the interop handle provide any ordering guarantees.

Because we additionally specify an OpenMP dependency on the `interop init` construct, we know that the point at which that ordering of foreign functions occurs will also ensure than those OpenMP tasks with the same dependency history will also complete before external tasks created *after* the `interop` construct. Note that there is otherwise no specified ordering of foreign and OpenMP tasks: they can happen in any order. We make use of the happens-before relationship provided by the `interop` construct to know that foreign functions after the construct happen after all previous OpenMP tasks (because of the dependency on the `interop`) before the construct finishes. This means we know that those prior OpenMP tasks happen before any external tasks occurring after the construct. Again, if we mix OpenMP and external tasks after the construct, there is no way to guarantee an ordering, and we must use an `interop use` construct to switch between OpenMP tasks and foreign functions.

Let's walk through an example with the snippet in Figure 9.14 from a program that wants to interoperate between OpenMP and CUDA.

We create a non-blocking (deferred) target task on line 5 with a dependency on the `A` array. We populate our interop handle object on line 10 and ensure the backend is of the correct type (CUDA) on line 14. This means we also get a valid CUDA

```
1   int N = 100000;
2   int *A = (int *)malloc(sizeof(int) * N);
3   #pragma omp target enter data map(alloc: A[:N])
4
5   #pragma omp target teams loop nowait depend(out: A)
6   for (int i = 0; i < N; ++i)
7     A[i] = i;
8
9   omp_interop_t iobj = omp_interop_none;
10  #pragma omp interop init(targetsync: iobj) nowait depend(inout: A)
11
12  // Check we have a CUDA runtime
13  int err;
14  assert(omp_get_interop_int(iobj, omp_ipr_fr_id, &err)==omp_ifr_cuda);
15
16  // Get CUDA stream
17  cudaStream_t s = (cudaStream_t) omp_get_interop_ptr(iobj,
        omp_ipr_targetsync, NULL);
18
19  // Asynchronously enqueue CUDA kernel on the stream
20  #pragma omp target data use_device_ptr(A)
21  cuda_kernel<<<N, 16, 0, s>>>(A);
22
23  #pragma omp interop use(iobj) nowait depend(inout: A)
24
25  #pragma omp target teams loop nowait depend(inout: A)
26  for (int i = 0; i < N; ++i)
27    A[i] += 1;
28
29  #pragma omp interop use(iobj) nowait depend(inout: A)
30
31  #pragma omp target data use_device_ptr(A)
32  cuda_kernel<<<N, 16, 0, s>>>(A);
33
34  #pragma omp interop destroy(iobj) nowait depend(inout: A)
35
36  #pragma omp taskwait
```

Figure 9.14: Non-blocking synchronization with an asynchronous CUDA kernel – This program enqueues a CUDA kernel on the CUDA stream obtained by an interop handle. The **nowait** clause is used, so all tasks are deferred (non-blocking). The **interop** construct ensures the target tasks and CUDA kernels execute in the correct order.

stream on line 17, which we will use to enqueue CUDA kernels. We enqueue the first CUDA kernel to this stream on line 21. Don't forget that CUDA kernels execute in a non-blocking manner with respect to the host. The **target data** construct is used to translate the array A into its corresponding variable for use directly in the CUDA kernel.

In order to ensure that CUDA kernel completes before any further OpenMP tasks, we use the `interop` construct with the `use` clause on line 23. This again is a deferred task with a dependency on A, ensuring it happens after the previous OpenMP tasks with a relevant dependency: the task on line 10. The happens-before semantics of the `interop` construct ensure that the CUDA kernel on line 21 happens before the deferred task generated as part of the `interop` construct on line 23, which itself happens before any future OpenMP tasks such as that on line 25. The pattern repeats in much the same way before we destroy the interop handler after this on line 34. Notice how we do not synchronize the device after the CUDA kernel enqueues. Throughout this entire code snippet, the host does not block: it will proceed without stopping until it reaches the `taskwait` at the end of this example.

The ordering guarantees provided by the `interop` construct ensure that the following occurs in this order:

1. The target task on line 5 executes.

2. The `interop` construct causes a non-blocking synchronization to occur on line 10 as a result of the `depend` and `nowait` clause and the semantics of the `interop` construct. Note that there can be no prior foreign functions at this point.

3. The CUDA kernel enqueued on line 21 executes.

4. The `interop` construct synchronization occurs on line 23, ensuring foreign functions previously enqueued on the foreign synchronization object (the CUDA stream) will complete before the deferred task here completes.

5. The target task on line 25 executes after the deferred task on line 23.

6. The interop task likewise completes after the target task on line 25, due to the dependencies.

7. Again, the CUDA kernel on line 32 executes.

8. Again, the interop task on line 34 completes after the CUDA kernel has finished.

This means we know that the CUDA kernel will run *after* our target task and will finish before any further OpenMP tasks that depend on array A. But note that the host has not been blocked from making progress due to the asynchronous nature of these constructs.

In our example, the array A is used in CUDA kernels and OpenMP target tasks, but this is immaterial to the dependency tracking. It is important to also notice that the ordering is determined by the interaction of the OpenMP task dependencies (the **depend** clause) and the **interop** construct synchronizations on the foreign synchronization object. Do not forget that the foreign functions need to be enqueued on the foreign synchronization object. There are otherwise no guarantees about the ordering of foreign functions and OpenMP tasks; the **interop use** construct should be used to create the synchronization points when switching between creating OpenMP (target) tasks and enqueuing foreign functions.

There is a lot to take in here, so we will walk through a specific example in the next section.

9.4.4   Example: Calling CUDA Kernels without Blocking

We can improve on our earlier example from Section 9.2.2 where we shared data allocated on the device using OpenMP **map()** clauses with the cuBLAS library. To translate the host pointers into device pointers ready for use with the cuBLAS functions, we used **target data** regions with the **use_device_addr** clause. But we needed to synchronize with OpenMP before the call to cuBLAS and synchronize again with cuBLAS before returning to OpenMP. We will now use the **interop** construct to remove this host synchronization in order to make the program operate asynchronously.

Our program in Figure 9.15 follows the same general outline as our previous example in Figure 9.5. The matrix size is set on line 1, and three matrices are allocated on the host. We map these to the device using the **target enter data** construct. However, the program differs here in that this mapping happens asynchronously because we have now included the **nowait** clause. This will cause the construct to return immediately, and the allocation of data on the device will occur in the background. In addition, because the construct is running in the background, we have set up a dependency with the **depend** clause. This lets us ensure that future asynchronous tasks can operate in order after the data allocation has finished.

```
1    int N = 10000;
2    cublasHandle_t handle; cublasCreate(&handle);
3
4    double *A = malloc(sizeof(double)*N*N);
5    double *B = malloc(sizeof(double)*N*N);
6    double *C = malloc(sizeof(double)*N*N);
7
8    #pragma omp target enter data \
9            map(alloc: A[0:N*N], B[0:N*N], C[0:N*N]) \
10           nowait depend(out: C[0:N*N])
11
12   #pragma omp target nowait depend(inout: C[0:N*N])
13   init_arrays(A, B, C, N);
14
15   omp_interop_t o = omp_interop_none; // interop object
16
17   #pragma omp interop init(targetsync: o) nowait \
18         depend(inout: C[0:N*N])
19
20   // Get and set CUDA stream (assuming it's a CUDA backend)
21   cudaStream_t s = omp_get_interop_ptr(o, omp_ipr_targetsync, NULL);
22   cublasSetStream(handle, s);
23
24   // Replace pointers with device pointers
25   #pragma omp target data use_device_ptr(A, B, C)
26   {
27     // Call DGEMM
28     double alpha = 1.0; double beta = 0.0;
29     cublasDgemm(handle, CUBLAS_OP_N, CUBLAS_OP_N, N, N, N,
30                    &alpha, A, N, B, N, &beta, C, N);
31   }
32
33   #pragma omp interop destroy(o) nowait depend(out: C[0:N*N])
34   // NB: If I wanted to reuse the stream, I would instead have
35   // #pragma omp interop use(o) nowait depend(out: C[0:N*N])
36
37   // Copy C back to the host, blocking to ensure host
38   // waits for previous tasks
39   #pragma omp target update from(C[0:N*N]) depend(in: C[0:N*N])
40
41   check_solution(C, N);
42
43   #pragma omp target exit data \
44           map(delete: A[0:N*N], B[0:N*N], C[0:N*N])
45
46   cublasDestroy(handle);
```

Figure 9.15: **Non-blocking calls to cuBLAS** – This OpenMP program interoperates completely asynchronously with the cuBLAS library using the **interop** construct and non-blocking OpenMP tasks.

To that end, a target task is started to initialize the data, beginning on line 13. Again, this is asynchronous (`nowait`) and depends on the `target data` due the `depend` clause. Our target task will run once the data is allocated and initialize the matrices on the device.

We create our interoperability handler on line 15, initialize it using the `interop` construct on lines 17–18, and extract the CUDA stream on line 21. The `nowait` and `depend` clauses ensure that the host doesn't wait for the previous OpenMP tasks to finish, allowing it to continue on and enqueue a cuBLAS kernel. We will know, however, that the enqueued cuBLAS kernel will happen after any previous OpenMP tasks on which the `interop` construct has a dependency. The `depend` clause is crucial here to ensure an ordering of OpenMP tasks before the `interop` construct and those after. Note, however, that all tasks must have appropriate dependencies, as they do in our example.

The CUDA stream obtained on line 21 is used to configure the cuBLAS library on line 22 to ensure that cuBLAS kernels use this specific queue, rather than the default queue the library might otherwise use. This is important to make sure that we are able to respect the task dependencies that the interoperability features in OpenMP allow: that the foreign functions must use the foreign synchronization object.

The `target data` region on line 25 converts the A, B, and C variables from their host pointer values to the mapped device values for that target data region. This means when we call cuBLAS on line 29, the function arguments will contain pointers to device memory. This function call is asynchronous. It will happen after the initialization of the arrays by the target region on lines 12–13 because our `interop` construct on line 17 depends on that initialization target task.

Notice that instead of synchronizing the host and device as we did in our previous example in Section 9.2.2 with a call to `cudaDeviceSynchronize()`, we do not stop the host from running after the call to cuBLAS. We destroy the interoperability object on line 33. Just as with the creation of the interoperability object, this ensures that our cuBLAS kernel will execute before any OpenMP tasks that occur after, and depend on, this `interop` construct. The `depend` clause ensures that future OpenMP tasks with the same dependency will also occur after the cuBLAS kernel call.

On line 39, we finally allow the host to block on a `target update` construct to copy matrix C onto the host from the device. Note that this is blocking as there is no `nowait` clause. The `depend` clause ensures that the copy will wait until the dependency on C is resolved. By using a chain of **depend** clauses on our **target enter data**, **target** task, both **interop** constructs surrounding the cuBLAS API call, and finally the **target update**, we ensure the tasks execute in this order and that the host enqueues all this work before waiting for it to finish for the first time in the **target update**. When the host continues, we know that the result is available on the host ready for checking that the answer is correct.

This example shows the overall structure of asynchrony with interoperability in OpenMP. We use the **nowait** clause for asynchrony and the **depend** clause to ensure that those non-blocking OpenMP tasks execute in the correct order. The non-blocking use of **interop** constructs that also share the dependencies gives us the synchronization and ordering of tasks, removing the need for the host to unnecessarily synchronize with the device.

9.5   Enhanced Portability Using Variant Directives

We started this chapter by talking about application programs in high performance computing. Source code is generally *not* rewritten from scratch as new technologies emerge. Instead, programs evolve and change incrementally, so a large code-base continues to run on legacy systems as it changes in response to new (and increasingly heterogeneous) hardware. We then launched into the main body of the chapter and described how to call functions from foreign runtime libraries and the constructs in OpenMP to support interoperability with non-OpenMP runtime systems. The result was that we learned several ways to write customized code to insert into a program—which kind of misses the point of this chapter. If you don't get to rewrite your application from scratch as new systems emerge, then going through hundreds of thousands of lines of code to implement interfaces to foreign functions is not practical. We need a way to leave function interfaces inside a code-base alone and to specialize functions behind a fixed interface.

This can be done using C/C++ preprocessor macros. We show an example of function specialization using the preprocessor in Figure 9.16. A macro (**USE_AVX512**) is defined and used by the preprocessor to select an external function optimized for the indicated architecture instead of the generic code-block in the body of the function. This approach works. C programmers do this sort of thing all the time.

Using preprocessor macros, however, is error prone. Building an application that specializes code based on preprocessor macros forces the programmer to ensure that these preprocessor-defined variables are set appropriately, consistently, and do not

```
1    #define USE_AVX512
2
3    void vecadd(int N, float *A, float *B, float *C) {
4        #ifdef USE_AVX512
5            vecadd_avx512(N, A, B, C);
6        #else
7            for (int i = 0; i < N; ++i) {
8                C[i] = A[i] + B[i];
9            }
10       #endif
11   }
12
13   int main()
14   {
15       int N = 4000;
16       float A[N], B[N], C[N];   // initialization not shown
17
18       vecadd(N, A, B, C);
19
20       // Check results omitted
21   }
```

Figure 9.16: **Using preprocessor macros to specialize functions** – The macro **USE_AVX512** can be defined at compile time to replace the body of the **vecadd** function with a call to an external function optimized for the x86 architecture with AVX512 vector instructions.

conflict with similar variables set by the compiler or other parts of a program. Macros are rigid and do not permit the flexibility needed to transparently modify interfaces (i.e., modifications that happen automatically without programmer intervention) to meet the needs of different systems.

Fortunately, in OpenMP 5.0, constructs to manage and substitute function-variants were added to OpenMP. This required a new concept in OpenMP: the *context* of the system at compile time. Directives were added so variant forms for a function could be substituted for a base case function based on that context. The function interface that a programmer works with inside the main body of the code does not change. The OpenMP compiler keeps track of the context and specializes functions as directed during compilation.

The way these constructs are typically used are to place them, and any associated interoperability code, inside a header file. This simplifies the application code as the OpenMP constructs and clauses needed for interoperating with foreign runtimes are hidden behind high-level interfaces. It also lets the compiler toolchain only worry about the parts of the program it needs to work with, without having to use other mechanisms, such as the preprocessor, to protect the compiler and linker from code it doesn't understand.

In this section, we will describe the variant function capability in OpenMP. This is not a simple capability to use. To help make variant functions easier to understand, we will decompose this functionality into a progression of largely distinct components:

- Declaring function variants

- OpenMP context and the match clause

- Modifying variant function arguments

- Controlling variant substitution with the dispatch construct

We will then close this important topic with an example that ties all these elements together.

9.5.1 Declaring Function Variants

Programmers break a program into distinct units that can be independently written, debugged, and tested. These units (in C and C++) are functions. A programmer writes a function. We call this the *base function*. Later, as part of the optimization process, the programmer may replace the base function with an optimized version of that function. It is a *variant* function that (hopefully) generates the same output for a given set of input values while running much faster.

When running on systems that utilize a single processor architecture, substitution of a variant for a base function is straightforward. You just change a Makefile and link in a different function variant. For heterogeneous systems, however, substituting variant functions can be considerably more complicated. Different variants are needed inside a program, depending on which processor is being used. As we've learned in this chapter, foreign runtimes may be involved that can require use of pointers to variables in different memory spaces. This all adds up to modifications to the application's source code that must be addressed at compile time, which means you can't manage these foreign functions just by changing the object files the linker uses to build an executable.

OpenMP includes a variant function capability. The first step in understanding variant functions is to consider how they are defined and how they are connected to

Table 9.12: **The declare variant directive in C/C++ and Fortran** – The declare variant directive defines the base function and associated variant functions, the context for when substitutions might occur, and potential modifications to function arguments. We also include the values for *modifier* (used by `adjust_args`) and *append-op-list* (used by `append_args`).

C/C++ directive format
#pragma omp declare variant*(variant-func-id) [clause[[,] clause]...]*
[**#pragma omp declare variant***(variant-func-id) [clause[[,] clause]...]*]   function-definition or declaration
Fortran directive format
!$omp declare variant(*[base-proc-name:] variant-proc-name***)** *[clause[[,] clause]...]*

adjust_args *([modifier :] parameter-list)*	nothing, need_device_ptr
append_args *(append-op-list)*	interop(*interop-type[[,interop-type]...])*
match *(context-selector)*	see Section 9.5.1.1

the base function. The key directive is the `declare variant` directive defined in Table 9.12. As we often do in this book, we list all the clauses in the table defining the directive, but we don't describe them all at once. It's better to learn about these clauses as we go through the next few sections and explain them in terms of how they are used in practice.

The `declare variant` directive defines a function (the base function), one or more variant functions, a `match` clause to define the context, and other optional clauses. Based on the context, one of the variant functions may be selected and substituted for locations in the program where the base function is called. There are many details to understand, but let's start with a simple example.

In Figure 9.17 we see this directive in action. The base function is defined on lines 8–12. The `declare variant` directive is on lines 6–7, right before the definition of the base function. It specifies the name of the variant function. In this case, it is a highly optimized version of the `vecadd` function, probably implemented with the AVX-512 intrinsics (code not shown) called `vecadd_avx512`.

The declare variant directive is required to have a `match` clause to define the context. We will say much more about the `match` clause in the next section. For now, we show the most basic use of the clause. A `device` selector specifies that the context for when the variant will replace the base function is that the processor uses an Instruction Set Architecture (`isa`) equal to "core-avx512." The value of `isa` is

```
1
2    #include <omp.h>
3    // Optimized version of vecadd written in AVX-512 intrinsics
4    void vecadd_avx512(int N, float *A, float *B, float *C);
5
6    #pragma omp declare variant(vecadd_avx512) \
7       match(device={isa("core-avx512")})
8    void vecadd(int N, float *A, float *B, float *C) { // Base function
9       for (int i = 0; i < N; ++i) {
10         C[i] = A[i] + B[i];
11      }
12   }
13
14   int main()
15   {
16
17      int N = 4000;
18      float A[N], B[N], C[N];   // initialization not shown
19
20      vecadd(N, A, B, C);
21
22      // Check results omitted
23   }
```

Figure 9.17: **Declare variant** – This program adds two vectors of length N. The variant function, **vecadd_avx512()**, is an optimized version of the **vecadd** function, probably based on AVX512 vector intrinsics (we don't provide the code). The **match** clause sets the context such that a device that uses the x86 instruction set architecture (ISA) with AVX512 will use the variant function.

an implementation-defined parameter that the OpenMP compiler vendor is required to document.

The main program calls the **vecadd** function on line 20. When the executable is built for a compilation target that matches the context (x86 with AVX-512), every call to the base function in the program will be replaced with a call to the variant function. If compiled on a platform that does not match the context, the compiler will use the base function.

The **declare variant** directive is repeated for each context the programmer wishes to address. For example, variant functions for ARM, AMD, RISC-V, and other processors could be handled by consecutively stacking the relevant **declare variant** directives in the code, one per processor type.

When using `declare variant` directives, the program needs a version of each variant function. You see this on line 4, where the function prototype for the variant function is provided. The linker will expect an implementation of that function for each `function variant` used. In our experience, this is not a problem, but in case it is, in OpenMP version 5.1, pragmas were added to support context-dependent definitions of variant functions. These directives are presented in Table 9.13. In between the `begin variant` and `end variant` directives, the variant function is defined. A `match` clause on the `begin variant` directive selects the context for compiling the code. By making that `match` clause consistent with the corresponding `match` clause on the `declare variant` directive, a programmer can easily specify that when the context favors a particular variant, the compiler will compile the function supporting that variant.

There is much more to cover in order to fully understand everything the `declare variant` directive does. We will do so in the next few subsections as we cover the clauses to the directive in more detail.

Table 9.13: **The begin/end declare variant construct in C/C++** – Note, however, this construct is not available for Fortran.

C/C++ directive format
#pragma omp begin declare variant match(*context-selector*)
function-definition-sequence
#pragma omp end declare variant

9.5.1.1 OpenMP Context and the Match Clause

OpenMP directives do not exist in isolation. They are embedded in a host programming language and interact with other constructs, foreign runtimes, and execution agents (such as threads). In most OpenMP programs, the context is implied. We don't spend much time thinking about it. When working with variant functions, however, interaction with the context is explicit. If a variant function is selected based on the context present where it is called, then the program needs a way to describe required features or *traits* it needs in the context.

This is done with the `match` clause. For GPU programming in OpenMP, the `match` clause is used on following directives:

- `#pragma omp declare variant`

- `#pragma omp begin declare variant`

Table 9.14: **The match clause** – The `match` clause specifies a context-selector. This is a collection of *trait-sets* consisting of a trait-set-selector and associated traits. For GPU programming, the relevant trait-set-selectors include *device*, *target device*, and *construct*.

match(_[trait-set,] trait-set_**)**
match(device={_[trait,] trait_}**)** *device* traits are `kind()`, `isa()`, `arch()`
match(target_device={_[trait,] trait_}**)** *target_device* traits are `device_num()`, `kind()`
match(construct=list) *construct* are `dispatch`, `target` and `parallel`

The `match` clause is defined in Table 9.14. It specifies the context required by a directive in terms of a collection of one or more comma-separated *trait-sets*. A trait-set is composed of a *trait-set-selector* and one or more traits. For programming target devices, the trait-sets-selectors are:

- `device`: selects kinds of devices or, in other cases, implementation-defined designations of specific devices.

- `target_device`: selects kinds of devices or specific OpenMP device numbers.

- `construct`: selects a specific construct to interact with.

The `match` clause *context-selector-specification* is expressed as a comma-separated list of trait-sets. For each trait-set, you have the name of the trait-set-selector, an equals sign, and a set of traits between curly braces. For example, a context that includes an NVIDIA GPU and the `dispatch` construct would be specified as follows:

```
match(device={arch(nvptx)}, construct={dispatch})
```

The traits used in trait-sets include specific cases defined in the OpenMP specification and others that are implementation defined. Some common traits you are likely to encounter include the following:

- **device** trait-set-selector:

  - kind(): OpenMP standard (host, nohost, gpu, cpu, fpga).

  - isa(): implementation defined (e.g., core-avx512).

  - arch: implementation defined (e.g., XeHP, gen, nvptx).

- **target_device** trait-set-selector:

  - device_num(): the number of the device ranging from zero to number of target devices minus one.

  - kind(): same set as above under the device trait-set-selector.

- **construct** trait-set-selector:

  - any OpenMP construct. For GPU programming, this is usually the **dispatch** construct (which we introduce shortly in Section 9.5.2).

We have already seen the **match** clause in action. In Figure 9.17 on line 7, we use the **device** trait-set-selector with the **isa** trait with the value *core-avx512*. This stipulates that the variant function with the name **vecadd_avx512** should be used when the device we're building the executable for is using the **core-avx512** instruction set.

9.5.1.2 Modifying Variant Function Arguments

A sufficiently motivated programmer could cover most of the variant replacement functionality we've discussed using macros and the preprocessor. When arguments need to change as part of the variant replacement, however, approaches based on the preprocessor fall apart.

In this section, we discuss the **declare variant** directive with clauses that change the argument lists when replacing the base function at a call site. This involves two different clauses:

- **adjust_args**: change pointer arguments passed into a function to *device pointers*.

- **append_args**: add an extra argument at the end of a function to expose the interop handler.

We will cover both of these clauses in this section.

The **adjust_args** clause provides the **use_device_ptr** functionality we discussed in Section 9.2. Our **adjust_args** clause takes a modifier along with the list of pointers: the **needs_device_ptr** modifier stipulates which arguments to the function should be translated into the corresponding device pointers, or **nothing** when the translation shouldn't occur.

Let's consider the case where we are given a library routine for our **vecadd** kernel that runs on an NVIDIA GPU using the **nvptx** architecture. We can use the **match** clause to check for this architecture and the **declare variant** construct to replace our usual function call with the special one for the GPU. An example is shown in Figure 9.18.

The program maps the arrays to the target device and then runs the **vecadd_target** function. However, this will be replaced by the **vecadd_nvptx** function if the device is an NVIDIA GPU. Note that the standard **vecadd_target** function expects host pointers for the variables—the function uses the **target** directive, which will translate our pointers implicitly for the target region. However, we are using some external routine that needs device pointers for the **vecadd_nvptx** function. In order to make this translation, we use the **adjust_args** clause on the **declare variant** construct to make sure that OpenMP will do this translation for us whenever the function is replaced.

There are cases where the variant function needs to interact with a foreign runtime system. As we discussed in Section 9.4, this happens through the **interop** construct. We can augment the function replacement mechanism with OpenMP's interoperability rules by using the **append_args** clause.

Let's start with how the **append_args** clause gives us access to the interop handler. Figure 9.19 shows an updated version of Figure 9.18, which called a specialized vector addition function for a GPU. There are two changes: first, the function has an additional final argument for the interop handler; second, the **declare variant** directive now includes the **append_args(interop(targetsync))** clause.

The **append_args** clause specifies the desired interoperability object (usually **targetsync**), creates the interop handler for us before the function is called, and destroys it when the variant function returns. It uses exactly the same semantics as doing it directly with the **init** and **destroy** clauses on the **interop** construct. Hence, with this clause, we get the same behavior as we observed in our example in Figure 9.15. The interop handle that is created automatically is made available to the variant function in its final (i.e., the "appended") argument.

```
1
2    // External function requiring NVIDIA GPU device pointers
3    void vecadd_nvptx(int N, float *A, float *B, float *C);
4
5    #pragma omp declare variant(vecadd_nvptx) match(device={arch(nvptx)}) \
6                            adjust_args(need_device_ptr: A, B, C)
7    void vecadd_target(int N, float *A, float *B, float *C) { // Base function
8
9      #pragma omp target loop
10     for (int i = 0; i < N; ++i) {
11       C[i] = A[i] + B[i];
12     }
13   }
14
15   int main()
16   {
17
18     int N = 4000;
19     float A[N], B[N], C[N];   // initialization not shown
20
21     // Map to the device
22     #pragma omp target enter data map(to: A, B, C)
23
24     // Run vecadd on a device
25     vecadd_target(N, A, B, C);
26
27     // Check results omitted
28   }
```

Figure 9.18: **Declare variant with adjust_args clause** – This program adds two vectors of length N using a provided NVIDIA GPU version of the **vecadd** function on supported platforms.

9.5.2 Controlling Variant Substitution with the Dispatch Construct

The variant substitution capability we've covered so far is "all or nothing." If the constraints established by the **declare variant** directive are met, replacement occurs. There are times, however, when we need to be more selective about when replacement of the base function by a variant function occurs. For this extra control over replacement, we have the **dispatch** construct defined in Table 9.15. This control applies to anywhere inside the associated structured block where variant substitution might occur.

```
 1
 2   // External function requiring NVIDIA GPU device pointers
 3   void vecadd_nvptx(int N, float *A, float *B, float *C, omp_interop_t o);
 4
 5   #pragma omp declare variant(vecadd_nvptx) match(device={arch(nvptx)}) \
 6     adjust_args(need_device_ptr: A, B, C) append_args(interop(targetsync))
 7   void vecadd_target(int N, float *A, float *B, float *C) { // Base function
 8
 9     #pragma omp target loop
10     for (int i = 0; i < N; ++i) {
11       C[i] = A[i] + B[i];
12     }
13   }
14
15   int main()
16   {
17
18     int N = 4000;
19     float A[N], B[N], C[N];  // initialization not shown
20
21     // Map to the device
22     #pragma omp target enter data map(to: A, B, C)
23
24     // Run vecadd on a device
25     vecadd_target(N, A, B, C);
26
27     // Check results omitted
28   }
```

Figure 9.19: **Declare variant with append_args clause** – This program adds two vectors of length N using a provided NVIDIA GPU version of the **vecadd** function on supported platforms using the interop handler.

To use the **dispatch** construct, you must tell OpenMP that you plan to do so by setting the **construct** *trait-set-selector* to **dispatch** in the **match** clause of the relevant **declare variant** directive. For replacement with a variant function to occur, the constraints as defined by the relevant **declare variant** directive must hold. In addition, if the logical expression on the **novariants** clause evaluates to *true*, the variant substitution will not occur.

In addition to controlling variant substitution, the **dispatch** construct affects how the variant function executes using the familiar clauses **depend**, **device**, **is_device_ptr**, and **nowait**. If we use the **append_arg** clause in the **declare variant** directive, these all interact with the **interop** object exactly as we described

Table 9.15: **The dispatch construct in C/C++ and Fortran** – The dispatch construct requests function replacement.

C/C++ directive format
#pragma omp dispatch *[clause[[,] clause]...]*
function-dispatch-structured-block
Fortran directive format
!$omp dispatch *[clause[[,] clause]...]*
function-dispatch-structured-block
!$omp end dispatch

depend *(dependence-type: list)*
device *([device-modifier:] integer-expression)*
is_device_ptr *(list)*
nocontext *(scalar-logical-expression)*
novariants *(scalar-logical-expression)*
nowait

in Section 9.4.2.

To understand the `dispatch` construct, let's consider the final version of vector addition program in Figure 9.20. In addition to adjusting and appending arguments as we did in the previous example (Figure 9.19), for this case we add the `dispatch` construct to provide additional context for function replacement. This means we need to set `construct` to `dispatch` in the `match` clause on line 7.

Everything else works as before. The interop object is exposed to the variant function. With the `nowait` and `depend` clauses on the `dispatch` construct, we get the asynchronous execution we'd expect when working with the interop synchronization object.

9.5.3 Putting It All Together

Let's wrap up this discussion with one last, and more complex, example. We can use the `dispatch` construct with the `declare variant` construct to call foreign functions that will execute asynchronously, relying on interoperability with OpenMP through the interoperability object. The example, shown in Figure 9.21, does this for dense matrix-matrix multiplication (DGEMM). This is a variation of an example

```
1
2   // External function requiring NVIDIA GPU device pointers
3   void vecadd_nvptx(int N, float *A, float *B, float *C,
4                                   omp_interop_t o);
5
6   #pragma omp declare variant(vecadd_nvptx) \
7       match(construct={dispatch}, device={arch(nvptx)}) \
8       adjust_args(need_device_ptr: A, B, C) \
9       append_args(interop(targetsync))
10  void vecadd_target(int N, float *A, float *B, float *C) {
11
12    #pragma omp target nowait
13    #pragma omp loop
14    for (int i = 0; i < N; ++i) {
15      C[i] = A[i] + B[i];
16    }
17  }
18
19  int main()
20  {
21
22    int N = 4000;
23    float A[N], B[N], C[N];  // initialization not shown
24
25    // Map to the device
26    #pragma omp target enter data map(to: A, B, C)
27
28    // Run vecadd on a device
29    #pragma omp dispatch nowait depend(inout: C[0:N])
30    vecadd_target(N, A, B, C);
31
32    // Check results and wait for non-blocking
33    // call to vecadd_target() or variant omitted
34  }
```

Figure 9.20: **Declare variant with the dispatch construct** – This program adds
two vectors of length N using a provided NVIDIA GPU version of the vecadd function
on supported platforms using the interop handler and specialization with the dispatch
construct.

we've seen before (Figure 9.15), where we called the cuBLAS library asynchronously,
using the OpenMP interop handler to gain access to a CUDA stream.

In this case, we wish to run on a variety of GPUs from different vendors and
call their optimized DGEMM routines. To do this, we write our own small library,
which implements the interop mechanisms for each of the libraries. For instance,

we write a `dgemm_nvptx` routine that, given the `omp_interop_t` interop handler, extracts a CUDA stream and enqueues a `cublasDgemm` kernel. We would also write a `dgemm_xehp` routine that works similarly but interacts with Intel's math libraries that run on XeHP GPUs. Note that we do not need a target data region with the `use_device_ptr` clause, as we can use the `adjust_args` clause on the `declare variant` directive to state that the entire function relies on device pointer replacement. With these functions in place, we can use `declare variant` directives to describe how the generic target `dgemm` function should be replaced with a variant function. We're using many clauses. Recall how the `adjust_args` clause states that the variant function expects device pointers, and the `append_args` clause creates (and, when done, destroys) an interop handler passed as the final argument to the variant function.

Consider our main routine, which we write with asynchronous work in mind. We liberally use `nowait` and `depend` clauses to allocate device memory, initialize it with an asynchronous target task, call the DGEMM routine, and copy back the result. This final step uses blocking synchronization—that is, we use the `depend` clause but we do not include a `nowait` clause. The function call to `dgemm` occurs inside a `dispatch` construct that is used to pass the `nowait` and `depend` information to the interop handler created for the execution of this function.

The function definition and declarations of their variant functions can all be hidden inside a header file. The main routine still needs to set up the `nowait` and `depend` clauses to support asynchronous execution, but all the complexity of interoperability and variant function replacement can be hidden from the main execution flow. In other words, we can use the interoperability and variant constructs to make the use of external libraries transparent to the bulk of the code, which is exactly the problem we set out to solve in this chapter.

```
 1   void dgemm_cuda(double *A, double *B, double *C, int N, double alpha,
         double beta, omp_interop_t o);
 2   void dgemm_xehp(double *A, double *B, double *C, int N, double alpha,
         double beta, omp_interop_t o);
 3
 4   #pragma omp declare variant(dgemm_cuda) match(construct={dispatch},
         device={arch(nvptx)}) append_args(interop(targetsync)) adjust_args
         (need_device_ptr: A, B, C)
 5   #pragma omp declare variant(dgemm_xehp) match(construct={dispatch},
         device={arch(XeHP)}) append_args(interop(targetsync)) adjust_args(
         need_device_ptr: A, B, C)
 6   void dgemm(double *A, double *B, double *C, int N, double alpha,
         double beta) {
 7     #pragma omp target nowait depend(inout: C[0:N*N])
 8     #pragma omp loop collapse(2)
 9     for (int i = 0; i < N; ++i) {
10       for (int j = 0; j < N; ++j) {
11         C[i*N+j] *= beta;
12         for (int k = 0; k < N; ++k) {
13           C[i*N+j] += alpha*A[i*N+k] * B[k*N+j];
14         }}}
15   }
16
17   int main(void) {
18     int N = 10000;
19
20     double *A, *B, *C; allocate_arrays(&A, &B, &C, N);
21
22     #pragma omp target enter data map(alloc: A[0:N*N], B[0:N*N], C[0:N*N
         ]) nowait depend(out: C[0:N*N])
23
24     #pragma omp target nowait depend(inout: C[0:N*N])
25     init_arrays(A, B, C, N);
26
27     // Asynchronous call to dgemm, substituted by a matching replacement
28     #pragma omp dispatch nowait depend(inout: C[0:N*N])
29     dgemm(A, B, C, N, 1.0, 0.0);
30
31     #pragma omp target exit data map(from: C[0:N*N]) map(delete: A, B)
         depend(in: C[0:N*N])
32
33     check_solution(C, N);
34   }
```

Figure 9.21: **Using the dispatch construct to call external library wrappers**
– The **dispatch** construct combined with the **declare variant** constructs allow the main
program to use a simple interface for calling asynchronous functions specialized for different
platforms.

10 OpenMP and the Future of Heterogeneous Computing

We're finished. You now know how to program your GPU with OpenMP. You've gained the knowledge you need to move beyond threads running in a shared address space to GPUs with the staggering levels of parallelism and performance they provide.

As you move forward, however, do not lose sight of the ultimate goal: to get the most from the available hardware. The GPU is a throughput-optimized device and is great for data parallel algorithms. The CPU is a latency-optimized device and is great for workloads composed of collections of tasks, each of which must make forward progress with low latency. You need to match the components that make up a workload to the processors best suited to their needs. In other words, the goal is not to offload work to a GPU while the CPU patiently waits for it to finish. The goal is heterogeneous computing where CPUs and GPUs work together to accomplish a job. You should think about writing heterogeneous programs in a holistic way to make the most of all the hardware at your disposal, which means making heavy use of asynchronous execution.

We expect a bright future for programming models such as OpenMP. It covers both latency-optimized CPUs and throughput-optimized GPUs in one consistent programming model. As the computing industry focuses on performance per unit of energy, the need to specialize processors to the needs of workloads will increase. As systems become ever more heterogeneous, we need applications that exploit all the available concurrency across *all* devices and accelerators, and OpenMP is one of the few APIs that support programming such systems.

This book has focused on the key features of the OpenMP 5.2 specification (released in 2021) for programming GPUs. The content of this book and the routines and directives in OpenMP are applicable to all manner of generally programmable accelerators. These OpenMP features for GPU programming are already widely supported across multiple vendor-supplied and open-source compilers.

However, OpenMP doesn't stand still. Way back in 1996, when work first started on OpenMP, we knew successful standards continuously evolve to adapt to new classes of applications and new hardware. Hence, OpenMP was set up organizationally from the beginning to support its ongoing evolution. As we write this book, new OpenMP specifications are released every few years. These new versions of OpenMP will not only contain new features but add clarifications and improvements to earlier versions of the specification. As new versions of OpenMP are released, updates to compilers and OpenMP runtimes will follow.

You can follow the latest in OpenMP at the OpenMP Architecture Review Board (ARB) website, `www.openmp.org`. An OpenMP specification is written for those who implement OpenMP compilers and runtime systems. For an application programmer, it is prohibitively difficult to understand a feature in OpenMP just from reading the specification. Frankly, we had to work with the OpenMP Language Committee at several points while writing this book to make sure we were correctly interpreting the OpenMP specification.

How can an application programmer keep up with new developments in OpenMP given the implementer focus of the specifications? In each new specification, there is a list of changes from previous specifications. We recommend consulting this list so you can focus on what's new in the latest versions of OpenMP. Furthermore, the OpenMP Language Committee produces an examples document (available on the OpenMP website) for each version of OpenMP. The examples are annotated and often are a better way to learn how to use a new feature of OpenMP than reading the specification.

To really master a parallel programming model, however, you need a hands-on approach. We highly recommend that you write many programs in OpenMP targeting both CPUs and GPUs. You can use the programs in this book as a starting point (source code is available on our website, `www.ompgpu.com`). Writing, compiling, and running programs on a heterogeneous system is challenging, just as writing any parallel program is challenging. With the knowledge from the GPU Common Core in Part II, you can feel confident about how much you can achieve with just a few compiler directives. Thinking about the Eightfold Path to performance from Chapter 5 will help you write programs that perform well on GPUs. Many of our own programs use only the directives from the GPU Common Core [20] and, by following the advice in the Eightfold Path, achieve close to peak available performance on a wide range of GPUs from multiple vendors. Attaining performance portability is really possible with OpenMP today [12].

Appendix: Reference Guide

When writing code, it can be frustrating to flip through a book to find the precise syntax for a particular construct or function. Therefore, we summarize in this appendix the constructs, directives, clauses, API functions, and environment variables discussed in this book. In these summaries, we use the following conventions.

- *list*: a comma separated list of items (usually variables).

- *scalar-logical-expression*: used with "binary choice" clauses such as `if`, where 0 is false and anything else (typically 1) is true.

- *reduction-identifier*: a binary operator used for reductions in OpenMP (typically +).

- *alloc-nam*: an expression of type `omp_allocator_handle_t`. Only two values are typically used for GPU programming, **omp_pteam_mem_alloc** and **omp_cgroups_mem_alloc**, though OpenMP defines several additional memory allocators (see Section 6.2 of the OpenMP 5.2 specification).

Some constructs include the option of including the clause `order(concurrent)`. This implies that the iterations of the associated loops can execute in any order and that they do not contain any OpenMP API function calls or other OpenMP constructs. This order is implied by the `loop` construct, and hence this clause is rarely needed.

A.1   Programming a CPU with OpenMP

Table A.1: **The OpenMP Common Core (CPU)** – This table summarizes the most commonly used pragmas, runtime library routines, and clauses for multithreaded programming with OpenMP. See Chapter 2.

OpenMP pragma, function, or clause	Concepts
#pragma omp parallel	Create a parallel region.
int omp_get_num_threads()	Number of threads (N)
int omp_get_thread_num()	Thread rank (0 to N-1)
void omp_set_num_threads()	Set default number of threads
double omp_get_wtime()	Time blocks of code
export OMP_NUM_THREADS=N	Default number of threads
#pragma omp barrier	Synchronization: explicit barrier
#pragma omp critical	Synchronization: mutual exclusion
#pragma omp for	Worksharing loops
#pragma omp parallel for	Combined parallel for
collapse(M)	Combine M nested loops
reduction(op: list)	Reduction
schedule(static [, chunk])	Static loop schedule
schedule(dynamic [,chunk])	Dynamic loop schedule
private(list)	Private variables, uninitialized
firstprivate (list)	Private variables, initialized
shared(list)	Shared Variables
nowait	Disable implied barriers
#pragma omp single	Work done by a single thread
#pragma omp task	Create an explicit task
#pragma omp taskwait	Wait for sibling tasks to complete

Table A.2: **The taskgroup construct in C/C++ and Fortran** – All tasks (including descendant tasks) created in the taskgroup region will complete before the encountering task continues beyond the taskgroup construct. See Section 8.5.3.

C/C++ directive format
#pragma omp taskgroup *[clause[[,] clause]...]*
structured_block
Fortran directive format
!$omp taskgroup *[clause[[,] clause]...]*
structured_block
!$omp end taskgroup

allocate *(alloc-nam: list)*
task_reduction *(reduction-identifier:list)*

Table A.3: **The depend clause for task dependencies** – Used with **task**, **target**, **target enter data**, **target exit data**, and **interop**. See Section 8.5.1.

depend(*dependence-type* **: list)**

dependence-type
in
out
inout
mutexinoutset
inoutset
depobj

Table A.4: **The in_reduction clause for tasks participating in a reduction** – Used with **target** and **task** constructs.

in_reduction *(reduction-identifier : list)*

reduction-identifier   defines the reduction operator   Sec. 8.5.3

A.2 Directives and Constructs for the GPU

Table A.5: **The target construct in C/C++ and Fortran** – The target construct packages the code in a structured block into a kernel and offloads that kernel to a device for execution. See Section 3.1.

C/C++ directive format
#pragma omp target *[clause[[,] clause]...]*   structured_block
Fortran directive format
!$omp target *[clause[[,] clause]...]*   structured_block   **!$omp end target**

allocate *(alloc-nam: list)*
defaultmap *(implicit-behavior:variable-category)*
depend *(dependence-type: list)*
device *([device-modifier:] integer-expression)*
firstprivate *(list)*
has_device_addr *(list)*
if *(scalar-logical-expression)*
in_reduction *(reduction-identifier : list)*
is_device_ptr *(list)*
map *([[map-type-modifier[,]] map-type:] list])*
nowait
private *(list)*
thread_limit *(integer-expression)*
uses_allocators *(alloc-nam)*

alloc-nam	**omp_pteam_mem_alloc, omp_cgroups_mem_alloc**	Sec. 7.4
implicit-behavior	**alloc, default, firstprivate, from, none, present,** **to, tofrom**	Sec. 7.1.3
variable-category	**aggregate, all, pointer, scalar**	Sec. 7.1.3
dependence-type	**in, out, inout**	Sec. 4.2.1
device-modifier	**device_num, ancestor**	Sec. 8.3
map-type-modifier	**always, close, present, mapper(***mapper-id***)**	Sec. 7.1.2
map-types	**to, from, tofrom, alloc, release, delete**	Sec. 4.2

Table A.6: **The target data construct in C/C++ and Fortran** – The target data construct maps data to the device data environment for the duration of the associated structured block. See Section 4.4.1.

C/C++ directive format
#pragma omp target data *[clause[[,] clause]...]*
structured_block
Fortran directive format
!$omp target data *[clause[[,] clause]...]*
structured_block
!$omp end target data

device *([device-modifier:] integer-expression)*
if *(scalar-logical-expression)*
map *([[map-type-modifier[,]] map-type:] list])*
use_device_addr *(list)*
use_device_ptr *(list)*

device-modifier	**device_num**	Sec. 8.3
map-type-modifier	**always, close, present, mapper(***mapper-id***)**	Sec. 7.1.2
map-types	**to, from, tofrom, alloc**	Sec. 4.2

270Appendix

Table A.7: **The target enter data and target exit data constructs in C/C++ and Fortran** – The target enter data and target exit data construct maps data to the device data environment. See Section 4.4.3.

C/C++ directive format
#pragma omp target enter data *[clause[[,] clause]...]*
#pragma omp target exit data *[clause[[,] clause]...]*
Fortran directive format
!$omp target enter data *[clause[[,] clause]...]*
!$omp target exit data *[clause[[,] clause]...]*

depend *(dependence-type: list)*
device *([device-modifier:] integer-expression)*
if *(scalar-logical-expression)*
map *([[map-type-modifier[,]] map-type:] list])*
nowait

dependence-type	**in, out, inout**	Sec. 4.2.1
device-modifier	**device_num**	Sec. 8.3
map-type-modifier	**always, close, present, mapper(***mapper-id***)**	Sec. 7.1.2
map-types enter	**to, tofrom, alloc**	Sec. 4.2
map-types exit	**from, tofrom, release, delete**	Sec. 4.2

Table A.8: **The target update construct in C/C++ and Fortran** – The target update construct copies data between the host and device data environment. See Section 4.4.2.

C/C++ directive format
#pragma omp target update *[clause[[,] clause]...]*
Fortran directive format
!$omp target update *[clause[[,] clause]...]*

depend *(dependence-type: list)*
device *([device-modifier:] integer-expression)*
from *(list)*
if *(scalar-logical-expression)*
to *(list)*
nowait

dependence-type	**in, out, inout**	Sec. 4.2.1
device-modifier	**device_num**	Sec. 8.3

A.2.1   Parallelism with Loop, Teams, and Worksharing Constructs

Table A.9: **The loop construct in C/C++ and Fortran** – The loop construct indicates the for-loop iterations (do-loop iterations in Fortran) can execute concurrently. See Section 3.4.

C/C++ directive format
#pragma omp loop *[clause[[,] clause]...]* for-loop
Fortran directive format
!$omp loop *[clause[[,] clause]...]* do-loop **!$omp end loop**

bind *(binding)*
collapse *(n)*
lastprivate *(list)*
order *(concurrent)*
private *(list)*
reduction *(reduction-identifier : list)*

binding	**teams, parallel, thread**	Sec. 6.4.3
n	the number of tightly nested loops to combine	Sec. 2.3.2

Table A.10: **The teams construct in C/C++ and Fortran** – The teams construct creates a league of teams. It must be directly nested inside a target region (or program scope). See Section 6.2.

C/C++ directive format
#pragma omp teams *[clause[[,] clause]...]*
structured_block
Fortran directive format
!$omp teams *[clause[[,] clause]...]*
structured_block
!$omp end teams

allocate *(alloc-nam: list)*
default(shared | none)
firstprivate *(list)*
num_teams *(integer-expression)*
private *(list)*
reduction *(reduction-identifier : list)*
shared *(list)*
thread_limit *(integer-expression)*

alloc-nam   **omp_pteam_mem_alloc, omp_cgroups_mem_alloc**   Sec. 7.4

Table A.11: **The distribute construct in C/C++ and Fortran** – The distribute
construct workshares loop iterations between teams in a league of teams. See Section 6.2.2.

C/C++ directive format
#pragma omp distribute *[clause[[,] clause]...]*
for-loop
Fortran directive format
!$omp distribute *[clause[[,] clause]...]*
do-loop
!$omp end distribute

allocate *(alloc-nam: list)*
collapse *(n)*
dist_schedule *(kind[, chunk_size])*
firstprivate *(list)*
lastprivate *(list)*
order *(concurrent)*
private *(list)*

n	the number of tightly nested loops to combine	Sec. 2.3.2
alloc-nam	**omp_pteam_mem_alloc, omp_cgroups_mem_alloc**	Sec. 7.4
kind	loop distribution schedule, currently can only = *static*	Sec. 6.2.2

A.2.2   Constructs for Interoperability

Table A.12: **The interop construct in C/C++ and Fortran** – The interop construct supports interoperability between OpenMP and external runtimes. The functionality differs depending on how the *interop-var* is initialized. If initialized with the *interop-type* **target**, the *interop-var* can be used to query properties of the foreign runtime. If initialized with the *interop-type* **targetsync**, the *interop-var* is used to access the queue (or stream) used to submit kernels to a GPU. It also establishes synchronization behaviors between the OpenMP and foreign runtimes. See Section 9.4.

C/C++ directive format
#pragma omp interop *[clause[[,] clause]...]*
Fortran directive format
!$omp interop *[clause[[,] clause]...]*

depend *(dependence-type: list)*
destroy *(destroy-var)*
device *([device-modifier:] integer-expression)*
init *([interop-modifier,] interop-type: interop-var)*
nowait
use *(interop-var)*

dependence-type	**in, out, inout**	Sec. 4.2.1
destroy-var	An object of type **omp_interop_t**	Sec. 9.4
device-modifier	**device_num**	Sec. 8.3
interop-modifier	**prefer***(prop)* to request a matching device	Sec. 9.4
prop	an object of type **omp_ipr_fr_id**	Sec. 9.4
interop-type	**target** for properties or **targetsync** for a sync-object	Sec. 9.4
interop-var	an interop-handle object of type **omp_interop_t**	Sec. 9.4

Table A.13: **Foreign Runtime Data Types** – Details of the foreign runtimes supported by OpenMP and data types of respective properties.

Foreign runtime	targetsync	device_context
omp_ifr_cuda	cudaStream_t	-
omp_ifr_cuda_driver	CUstream	CUcontext
omp_ifr_opencl	cl_queue	cl_context
omp_ifr_sycl	cl::sycl::queue	cl::sycl::context
omp_ifr_hip	hipStream_t	hipCtx_t
omp_ifr_level_zero	ze_command_queue_handle_t	ze_context_handle_t
	device	platform
omp_ifr_cuda	int	-
omp_ifr_cuda_driver	CUdevice	-
omp_ifr_opencl	cl_device	cl_platform
omp_ifr_sycl	cl::sycl::device	cl::sycl::platform
omp_ifr_hip	hipDevice_t	-
omp_ifr_level_zero	ze_device_handle_t	ze_driver_handle_t

Table A.14: **The declare variant directive in C/C++ and Fortran** – The declare variant directive defines function replacement candidates. See Section 9.5.1.

C/C++ directive format
#pragma omp declare variant *[clause[[,] clause]...]*   function-definition
Fortran directive format
!$omp declare variant *[clause[[,] clause]...]*   function-definition **!$omp end declare variant**

adjust_args *([modifier :] parameter-list)* **append_args** *(append-op-list)* **match** *(context-selector)*

Table A.15: **The dispatch construct in C/C++ and Fortran** – The dispatch
construct requests function replacement. See Section 9.5.2.

C/C++ directive format
#pragma omp dispatch *[clause[[,] clause]...]*   function-dispatch-structured-block
Fortran directive format
!$omp dispatch *[clause[[,] clause]...]*   function-dispatch-structured-block **!$omp end dispatch**

depend *(dependence-type: list)* **device** *([device-modifier:] integer-expression)* **is_device_ptr** *(list)* **nocontext** *(scalar-logical-expression)* **novariants** *(scalar-logical-expression)* **nowait**

A.2.3 Constructs for Device Data Environment Manipulation

Table A.16: **The requires directive in C/C++ and Fortran** – The requires directive lists features that the OpenMP implementation must support for the program to be correct. See Section 7.6.

C/C++ directive format
#pragma omp requires *[clause[[,] clause]...]*
Fortran directive format
!$omp requires *[clause[[,] clause]...]*

atomic_default_mem_order *(seq_cst | acq_rel | relaxed)*
dynamic_allocators
reverse_offload
unified_address
unified_shared_memory

Table A.17: **The declare target directive in C/C++ and Fortran** – The declare target directive lists which functions and variables are mapped to a device. See Section 7.2.

C/C++ directive format
#pragma omp declare target(list)
or
#pragma omp declare target *[clause[[,] clause]...]*
or
#pragma omp begin declare target *[clause[[,] clause]...]*   declarations-definition
#pragma omp end declare target
Fortran directive format
!$omp declare target(list)
or
!$omp declare target *[clause[[,] clause]...]*

device_type *(any | host | nohost)* **enter** *(list)* **indirect** *(scalar-logical-expression)* **link** *(list)*

Table A.18: **The declare mapper directive in C/C++ and Fortran** – The declare mapper directive defines a user-defined mapper for a given type, and an optional name to be used as a mapper-identifier for use in map clauses. See Section 7.3.

C/C++ directive format
#pragma omp declare mapper ([mapper-identifier :] type var) *[clause[[,] clause]...]*
Fortran directive format
!$omp declare mapper ([mapper-identifier :] type :: var) *[clause[[,] clause]...]*

map *([[map-type-modifier[,]] map-type:] list])*

mapper-identifier	A valid identifier in the base language or **default**	Sec. 7.3
type	A valid type in scope	Sec. 7.3
map-type-modifier	**always, close, present, mapper(**map-type-modifier*mapper-id*)**	Sec. 7.1.2
map-types	**to, from, tofrom, alloc**	Sec. 4.2

Table A.19: **The allocate directive in C/C++ and Fortran** – The allocate
directive describes which allocator to use for variables. See Section 7.4.

C/C++ directive format
#pragma omp allocate (list) *[clause[[,] clause]...]*
Fortran directive format
!$omp allocate (list) *[clause[[,] clause]...]*

align *(alignment)*
allocator *(allocator-handle)*

alignment	An integer of power 2
allocator-handle	type **omp_allocator_handle_t**

A.3 Combined Constructs

Table A.20: **Combined constructs for-loops in C/C++** – These combined constructs workshare the loop iterations across various levels of the parallel hierarchy.

C/C++ directive format
#pragma omp teams distribute *[clause[[,] clause]...]*   for-loop
#pragma omp teams distribute parallel for *[clause[[,] clause]...]*   for-loop
#pragma omp teams distribute parallel for simd *[clause[[,] clause]...]*   for-loop
#pragma omp teams loop *[clause[[,] clause]...]*   for-loop
#pragma omp parallel loop *[clause[[,] clause]...]*   for-loop
#pragma omp target teams distribute *[clause[[,] clause]...]*   for-loop
#pragma omp target teams distribute parallel for *[clause[[,] clause]...]*   for-loop
#pragma omp target teams distribute parallel for simd *[clause[[,] clause]...]*   for-loop
#pragma omp target teams loop *[clause[[,] clause]...]*   for-loop
#pragma omp target parallel loop *[clause[[,] clause]...]*   for-loop
#pragma omp target parallel for *[clause[[,] clause]...]*   for-loop
#pragma omp target parallel for simd *[clause[[,] clause]...]*   for-loop

Table A.21: **Combined constructs for structured blocks in C/C++** – These combined constructs launch parallel work on the target device.

C/C++ directive format
#pragma omp target teams *[clause[[,] clause]...]* structured-block
#pragma omp target parallel *[clause[[,] clause]...]* structured-block

A.4   Internal Control Variables, Environment Variables, and OpenMP API Functions

Table A.22: OpenMP Internal Control Variables (ICVs) and Environment Variables relating to target – These environment variables control the default behavior for device-related concepts in OpenMP.

ICV	Environment variable	Value
default-device-var	OMP_DEFAULT_DEVICE	Non-negative integer
nteams-var	OMP_NUM_TEAMS	Non-negative integer
target-offload-var	OMP_TARGET_OFFLOAD	`mandatory` | `disabled` | `default`

Table A.23: OpenMP API functions for SPMD-style programming in C/C++ – These OpenMP API functions are used to query IDs and numbers of threads and teams. See Section 6.2.2.

Function	Description
int omp_get_thread_num(void)	Get ID of current thread in the team
int omp_get_num_threads(void)	Get number of threads in current team
void omp_set_num_threads(int *num_threads*)	Set the number of threads per teams for future parallel regions
int omp_get_team_num(void)	Get ID of current team in the league
int omp_get_num_teams(void)	Get number of teams in current league
void omp_set_num_teams(int *num_teams*)	Set the number of teams per league for future teams regions

Table A.24: **OpenMP API functions for target device control in C/C++**
– These OpenMP API functions are used for querying and controlling the devices in a
system. See Section 8.3.

Function	Description
int omp_get_num_devices(void)	Get number of non-host devices in the system
int omp_get_device_num(void)	Get the ID of the device executing the current target region
int omp_get_default_device(void)	Get the ID of default device
void omp_set_default_device(int *dev*)	Set the default device
int omp_get_initial_device(void)	Get the ID of the host device
int omp_is_initial_device(void)	Query if the device executing the current target region is the host device

Table A.25: **OpenMP API functions for associating device pointers** – These
OpenMP API functions are used for associating device pointers allocated externally to
OpenMP with host allocations for interoperability. See Section 9.3.

Function
int omp_target_associate_ptr(const void *_host_ptr_, const void *_device_ptr_, size_t _size_, size_t _device_offset_, int _device_num_)
int omp_target_disassociate_ptr(const void *_ptr_, int _device_num_)
void * omp_get_mapped_ptr(const void *_ptr_, int _device_num_)

Table A.26: **OpenMP API functions for device memory in C/C++** – These OpenMP API functions are used for allocating, copying, and querying memory allocations in the device data environment. See Sections 7.5 and 7.6.

Function
void* omp_target_alloc(size_t *size*, int *device_num*)
void omp_target_free(void *device_ptr*, int *device_num*)
int omp_target_memcpy(void *dst*, const void *src*, size_t *length*, size_t *dst_offset*, size_t *src_offset*, int *dst_device_num*, int *src_device_num*)
int omp_target_memcpy_async(void *dst*, const void *src*, size_t *length*, size_t *dst_offset*, size_t *src_offset*, int *dst_device_num*, int *src_device_num*, int *depobj_count*, omp_depend_t *depobj_list*)
int omp_target_memcpy_rect(void *dst*, const void *src*, size_t *element_size*, int *num_dims*, const size_t *volume*, const size_t *dst_offsets*, const size_t *src_offsets*, const size_t *dst_dimensions*, const size_t *src_dimensions*, int *dst_device_num*, int *src_device_num*)
int omp_target_memcpy_rect_async(void *dst*, const void *src*, size_t *element_size*, int *num_dims*, const size_t *volume*, const size_t *dst_offsets*, const size_t *src_offsets*, const size_t *dst_dimensions*, const size_t *src_dimensions*, int *dst_device_num*, int *src_device_num*, int *depobj_count*, omp_depend_t *depobj_list*)
int omp_target_is_present(const void *ptr*, int *device_num*)
int omp_target_is_accessible(const void *ptr*, size_t *size*, int *device_num*)

Table A.27: **OpenMP API functions for querying properties of a foreign runtime** – See Section 9.4.1.

Function	Description
omp_intptr_t omp_get_interop_int(**const omp_interop_t** *interop,* **omp_interop_property_t** *property_id,* **int ****ret_code***)**	Get the integer property specified by the property ID
void *omp_get_interop_ptr(**const omp_interop_t** *interop,* **omp_interop_property_t** *property_id,* **int ****ret_code***)**	Get the pointer property specified by the property ID
char *omp_get_interop_str(**const omp_interop_t** *interop,* **omp_interop_property_t** *property_id,* **int ****ret_code***)**	Get the string property specified by the property ID
int omp_get_num_interop_properties(**const omp_interop_t** *interop***)**	Get number of properties available to the interop handle
const char * omp_get_interop_name(**const omp_interop_t** *interop,* **omp_interop_property_t** *property_id***)**	Get the name of a property
const char * omp_get_interop_type_desc(**const omp_interop_t** *interop,* **omp_interop_property_t** *property_id***)**	Get description of the type of a property
const char * omp_get_interop_rc_desc(**const omp_interop_t** *interop,* **omp_interop_rc_t** *ret_code***)**	Get description of the return code of a previous property query

Glossary

Address space The memory in a computer system is accessed by address. A variable is a name for an address in memory. The *address space* is the set of all addresses in memory. In OpenMP, a single shared address space is available to all the threads associated with a process. Each target device has its own address space distinct from the host address space unless the system supports a Unified Shared Memory (USM). As the name implies, when a system supports USM, a single address space spans the host and the devices.

Amdahl's law This simple relation shows that the part of a program that is not parallelized (the serial fraction) limits how much faster a program might run when executed in parallel with multiple processors. If *alpha* is the serial fraction, *Amdahl's* law states that, at best, a program can run $1/alpha$ times faster.

Barrier The *barrier* is the fundamental synchronization construct in OpenMP. A barrier defines a point in the execution of a program where threads in a team wait until all the threads in the team have arrived. Once all of the threads have arrived at the barrier, variables in shared memory are flushed (i.e., their values are made consistent with memory), and then threads execute statements following the barrier.

BLAS Linear algebra is the branch of mathematics behind a large fraction of high performance computing. The linear algebra operations that application developers depend on can be built from a modest number of fundamental building blocks. A standard API for these building blocks was released in three stages from the late 1970s to the late 1980s. This API is called the Basic Linear Algebra Subprograms or the *BLAS*.

Blocking Constructs and functions when invoked imply a sequence of instructions that execute to completion. The construct terminates or the function returns when the sequence of instructions complete. If the task that encounters the construct or calls the function in question waits until the instruction sequence is complete, we say that the construct or function is *blocking*. In some cases, the construct or function does not cause the encountering task to wait for the instruction sequence to complete; in this case, the function or construct is said to be *non-blocking*. Non-blocking constructs and functions support asynchronous execution. Blocking constructs and functions imply an ordered relationship with the encountering task and therefore can be called synchronous execution.

Cache A *cache* is a memory buffer that provides low latency access to a block of memory. A cache does *not* define a distinct address space. Informally, you can think of a cache as providing a window into the RAM memory of a system. Data is moved between memory and the cache in units of a *cache line*, which corresponds to a contiguous segment of addresses in memory. A typical cache line in a modern CPU is 64 bytes; on a GPU, a cache line is usually 128 bytes. There are many ways to organize the caches in a system. Typically, there are a pair of caches close to each core. These are called L1D and L1I for the *L1 data cache* and the *L1 instruction cache*. They are small but run at or near the clock of the CPU. A larger but slower cache is the *unified L2 cache*. The term "unified" is used to signify that it holds both data and instructions. The hierarchy continues through multiple levels until we reach the last-level cache, which is a larger and slower cache shared between the cores in a multiprocessor.

Cache coherence In a shared memory system with caches for each processor, a single variable may exist in multiple locations across the memory hierarchy. Most of these systems are said to be cache coherent; that is, they guarantee that in a properly synchronized, race-free program, the system maintains a single view of the memory. This means the system must keep track of the values across a cache hierarchy and update them as needed when processors read or write to shared variables.

Cluster Shared memory, in order to be effective, requires a significant investment in hardware to support a shared address space across processors with a variation in latencies to memory that is suitable for the parallel algorithms programmers write. At some point, as we scale the size of a parallel computer, the cost of maintaining shared memory becomes too high and unwieldy to implement. The solution is to transition to a distributed memory system where each computer in the system has its own distinct memory. Interaction between computers then happens as the exchange of discrete messages rather than through loads and stores into a shared address space. A cluster is the dominant way to build distributed memory systems. A cluster uses "Commercial Off-The-Shelf" (COTS) computers (nodes) with a COTS network to build large-scale distributed memory computers. Software systems organize the nodes in the cluster so they appear as a single integrated system. The most important software in a cluster is the message passing software, typically based on the MPI standard. When a cluster is particularly large, we sometimes also call it a *supercomputer*.

Concurrency A condition of a system in which two or more execution entities are active but unordered. By "active" we mean the execution entities are logically executing a sequence of operations (i.e., available to an OS to be scheduled for execution). By "unordered" we mean that we do not have global time stamps that allow us to say when operations from different execution entities are executed with respect to each other. When such ordering constraints are needed, we use *synchronization* operations.

Construct An OpenMP *executable directive* and the associated loop or *structured block*. It does not include code inside any routines called from within the structured block. The most commonly used constructs are `parallel`, `task`, `single`, `target`, and the worksharing-loop. OpenMP defines combined constructs, which are made by merging two constructs together. The semantics of a combined construct is the same as if the two separate constructs are called successively. OpenMP also defines *composite* constructs, which are constructed by merging constructs, but the resulting semantics might differ from what would follow from successive application of the individual constructs.

Core To improve aggregate performance, a processor is usually composed of multiple smaller processors. When these processors appear at an abstract level as distinct processing elements, each with their own sequence of instructions, they are called a core. The CPUs in most high performance computing systems generally have multiple cores. A core often includes hardware elements to store the execution context of multiple threads. These are called *hardware threads*. This is called Simultaneous Multi-Threading (SMT) or *hyperthreading*. Each hardware thread appears to the operating system as a *virtual core*. For example, a high-end CPU for a server may have 24 physical cores, but SMT technology might support two hardware threads per core, in which case the operating system would report 48 virtual cores. A similar model applies to GPUs, which are made up of multiple cores (e.g., Streaming Multiprocessors or Compute Units), each made up of processing elements that operate with a SIMT (Single Instruction Multiple Threads) execution model.

Corresponding variable A variable in the data environment of the host device may be mapped onto a variable in the data environment of a device. These variables use the same name. The variable in the host environment is the *original variable*, while the related (mapped) variable in the device data environment is called the *corresponding variable*. Note that the original and corresponding variables may share storage.

CPU A Central Processing Unit is a general-purpose processor optimized for low latencies and interactive use cases. By "general purpose" we mean that a CPU is expected to run any well-formed program. To support interactive use cases, a CPU typically has a cache hierarchy to hopefully keep frequently updated variables in memory buffers that run fast relative to the speed of the processing elements within the CPU. As a class of devices, CPUs are extremely common, appearing in everything from high-end servers inside data centers to tiny chips running in a cell phone. In high performance computing systems, we informally think of a CPU as the device that occupies a *socket* in a server.

Critical The critical directive plus its associated structured block defines a synchronization construct that provides mutual exclusion in OpenMP. The code in the structured block can only be executed by one thread at a time. If a thread encounters the critical construct and another thread is already executing code in the construct, it will wait until that thread has completed the work defined by the construct, made any updates to memory visible to other threads, and exited the construct. In the computer science literature, this functionality is often referred to as a *critical section*.

CUDA The low-level programming language used to program NVIDIA® GPUs is called CUDA™. It is based on the *SIMT* execution model. A CUDA program follows a host-device model where the code that runs on the GPU is called a *kernel*. An instance of the kernel (called a CUDA-thread) runs at each point in an index space (a grid). NVIDIA GPUs are designed to work closely with CUDA to optimize the throughput of the full set of CUDA-threads for each kernel. While the first release of CUDA was restricted to the SIMT model, later releases of CUDA include additional functionality that goes well beyond the original SIMT model.

Data environment The set of variables visible inside a region. This means that each construct (i.e., a directive plus its associated structured block) has its own data environment. OpenMP provides a set of clauses that define how variables move between data environments. The most common examples of these clauses are `shared`, `private`, and `firstprivate`. When working with target devices, each device has its own data environment called the *device data environment*.

Data race A data race occurs when: (1) two or more threads in a shared memory system issue loads and stores to overlapping address ranges, and (2) those loads and stores are not constrained to follow a particular order. The term "race" is used since the threads running on the different processors are "racing" to see which store lands in the shared variable. Most modern languages (including OpenMP) stipulate that a program with a data race is invalid; a compiler is not required to produce well-defined results in such cases.

DDR A clock signal drives the execution of components inside a computer. If data is transferred on the rising and falling edges of the clock signal, the data transfer is occurring at Double Data Rate (DDR). This approach is commonly used with CPUs to achieve higher bandwidths to memory. There are multiple generations of DDR memory technologies that pack increasing data transfer blocks into each clock cycle. In CPU block diagrams, the memory controllers that manage data movement to Random Access Memory (RAM) are often labeled as *DDR* regardless of the DDR generation used by the CPU.

Device A device is a logical execution engine. The details of how the logical concept of a device maps onto actual hardware is implementation defined. The device where an OpenMP program begins execution is called a *host device*. The device referenced by a directive involved with offloading execution or memory operations from one device to another is called the *target device*.

DGEMM Matrix multiplication is one of the most heavily used routines from the Basic Linear Algebra Subprograms (BLAS). Over time, the BLAS naming conventions for matrix multiplication have become standard jargon in applied linear algebra. Therefore, it is useful to understand them. If the matrices do not have specialized structure that can be exploited, they are called *general matrices*. The BLAS focus on floating point arithmetic, which traditionally means *single* precision and *double* precision. Using the rules defined by the BLAS for naming subprograms, the BLAS routine for matrix multiplication (MM) of a pair of double precision (D) general matrices (GE) is DGEMM. It is common to see the terms SGEMM for the single precision case or even GEMM when the data type of the matrix elements is not specified.

Directive A directive is a command issued to the compiler and expressed within the source code of a program. In OpenMP, a directive is introduced with the sentinels `#pragma omp` in C/C++ and a comment statement such as `!$OMP` in Fortran. OpenMP is an explicit API, so the directives tell the compiler to carry out a specific transformation to the code during compilation. OpenMP defines several types of directives. A *declarative directive* occurs among the declaration statements in a program and influences how variables are declared. An example is the `threadprivate` directive. An *executable* directive appears among the executable statements of a program and typically tells the program how to transform code during compilation to support threads. The `parallel` directive is a good example of an executable directive. A *stand-alone* directive is not associated with any declarations or blocks of code. It defines a direct action for the compiler to insert into the stream of instructions the compiler generates. The `barrier` directive is a stand-alone directive.

DRAM The memory in a typical computer system is exposed as Random Access Memory (RAM), which is usually supported by hardware modules implemented with Dynamic Random Access Memory (DRAM) chips. The term DRAM is used in this book when we want to specify a hardware element that supports the memory system.

Environment variable An environment variable is a mechanism to modify the environment within which a process executes. The details of how these variables are set and managed are not defined in OpenMP as they often vary from one operating system to another. Typically, each internal control variable (ICV) in OpenMP has an associated environment variable. This is used to set the default value of the ICV for an OpenMP execution. The most commonly used OpenMP environment variable is `OMP_NUM_THREADS`.

Flush The *flush* operation makes a thread's set of shared variables consistent with their values in memory. The original flush in OpenMP did not define a *synchronized-with* relation between threads; therefore, it was not a synchronization operation. Flush is essential, however, in controlling data consistency when combined with a synchronization operation. The flush operation forces variables in registers or buffers to be written to memory, and it marks cache lines as "dirty" so they will be refreshed from memory on the next load. In OpenMP 5.0, memory ordering clauses were added to the flush construct to support acquire/release synchronization.

Foreign runtime A runtime system is associated with a programming environment and supports the execution of a program. From the perspective of OpenMP executing on the host (i.e., multithreaded execution on a CPU), the runtime system supporting a device such as a GPU is a foreign runtime system. For example, if an OpenMP program uses `target` constructs to offload execution onto an NVIDIA GPU, the foreign runtime could be the CUDA runtime system. A function from a library whose routines execute on a target device is called a *foreign function*.

GPU Graphic Processing Units were initially designed for processing graphics data. These are throughput-optimized devices. For example, if you are rendering an image, the time to compute any particular pixel is not important. The concern is the throughput; that is, the number of images per second that can be streamed through the GPU. Over time, as more sophisticated rendering algorithms were developed, GPU processing pipelines became programmable. This led to GPGPU programming or General-Purpose GPU Programming. The execution model of GPGPU is called SIMT (Single Instruction Multiple Threads). In OpenMP, the `target` and associated device directives are used to program a GPU.

Happens-before Concurrent execution stipulates that executing threads are unordered. A synchronization event defines an ordering constraint between concurrent threads. We reason about the details of a synchronization event in terms of *happens-before* relations between two or more threads. Within a thread, instructions follow the sequenced-before relations defined by the host programming language. A synchronized-with event establishes a point between two threads where an ordering constraint is imposed between the threads. Sequenced-before relations prior to the synchronized-with event on one thread happen before operations sequenced after the synchronized-with relation on a second thread. This reasoning is the essence of how memory consistency models are defined.

Heap A contiguous block of memory reserved for a process that is shared by threads associated with that process. This memory is dynamic and managed by the programmer (using memory allocators such as malloc()).

Internal Control Variable An opaque object internal to an OpenMP implementation that manages default values, execution modes, or other behaviors for the execution of an OpenMP program. In most cases, an internal control variable (ICV) has an associated environment variable and runtime library routines to set the variable and to get the value of the variable.

Kernel A *kernel* is a function that executes on the GPU. In the GPU execution model, an index space (an *NDRange* or, for CUDA, a *grid*) is defined, typically with one, two, or three dimensions. An instance of the kernel executes at each point in the index space. Using terminology from *OpenCL*, this kernel instance is called a *work-item*. The collection of work-items are organized into groups that execute together on the compute units of a GPU; this collection is called a *work-group*. The work-groups are submitted to a queue on the device when a kernel is enqueued onto the GPU for execution. The work-groups are active and available to be scheduled for execution (they are *concurrent*, but they are not fairly scheduled).

Load balancing A team of threads working together to execute code in parallel completes their work when the last thread in the team has finished. Variation in when threads complete results in a subset of the threads waiting for other threads to finish, thereby incurring parallel overhead. *Load balancing* refers to techniques that adjust the work done by each thread so the team of threads finishes at about the same time. For OpenMP programmers, this often comes down to adjusting the parameters of the schedule clause on a worksharing-loop construct.

Map Variables may have a mapping relationship between data environments on the host and on the devices. A mapping operation (e.g., through a `map` clause) connects an original variable in the host data environment to a corresponding variable in a device data environment. Such variables are *mapped variables*.

Memory A subsystem in a computer that holds the values of variables. The memory is accessed through addresses, hence we can describe the memory as the subsystem in a computer that supports the address space for the system. Memory is organized into a hierarchy with faster/smaller memory units (cache) near the processors and slower/larger memory devices (usually as DRAM modules) further away from the processors.

Memory model The full name is "memory consistency model," though we typically call it a "memory model" for short. The memory model is the set of rules that define the value returned by a read (or *load*) operation on a variable when that variable is shared between two or more threads. The model is used when reasoning about multiple threads that issue loads and stores to overlapping address ranges to ensure that a program is free of any *data races*.

MPI The Message Passing Interface (MPI) is the dominant standard API for programming distributed memory computers. As the name implies, it defines semantics for how processes in a distributed memory system exchange messages. MPI is much more than a system for passing messages. It is a full-fledged system for coordinating the execution of processes and includes collective communication, one-sided communication, shared memory regions, and the basic constructs needed to build runtime systems for partitioned global address spaces. MPI and OpenMP have grown side by side over the years, and the two have become the dominant models of high performance computing, with MPI between nodes and OpenMP on a node. This is often called the MPI+OpenMP hybrid model.

Multicore A CPU with multiple cores is a *multicore* CPU. While technically multicore is an adjective, it is often used as a noun. In some cases, we distinguish between multicore CPUs, which connect cores through the memory hierarchy (cache coherent), as opposed to a many-core CPUs, which connects the cores through a scalable on-die network.

Multiprocessor A class of computer systems where multiple processors share a single address space supported by a physical shared memory system.

Multithreading An execution model in which a number of light-weight execution entities (threads) execute within a shared address space.

Node Large-scale parallel computers are built by connecting multiple independent computers together over a network of some variety. We call each computer in this system a *node*. Another way to think about the term is the computer network defines a graph. The nodes in the graph are the computers in the network, while the edges of the graph represent point-to-point links in the network.

NUMA A Non-Uniform Memory Architecture system is a shared memory computer for which the cost to different locations in memory varies between the processors in the system. Because of the presence of caches, most computer systems available today are NUMA systems.

OpenCL Shortly after the release of CUDA, a team was formed to define an open standard for GPU programming. That standard is called OpenCL™. It is based on the SIMT model pioneered by *CUDA*. Unlike CUDA, however, OpenCL is a portable standard and works for GPUs, CPUs, and FPGAs (Field Programmable Gate Arrays) from most vendors.

Original variable Variables appear inside the code associated with an OpenMP construct. Many of these variables are declared prior to the construct and pass into the scope of the construct by default or through one of the clauses on the construct. For such variables, there is a variable of the same name that exists immediately prior to the construct. This is called the *original variable*.

Parallelism Multiple processors running at the same time to solve a problem are running *in parallel*. Multithreading is a specific type of parallelism where a collection of concurrent threads run on multiple processors to execute in parallel.

Process Operating systems organize the execution of programs in terms of a *process*. A process includes one or more threads and handles resources to support the threads. It includes a region of memory that is shared between the threads.

Processor A generic term to refer to any hardware element on which threads can run. This includes CPUs, GPUs, Digital Signal Processors (DSPs), cores, and any other variety of processing element.

RAM When we consider memory in a computer system, we typically are referring to Random Access Memory (RAM). This is byte-addressable memory that supports arbitrary streams of memory references (i.e., random access).

Region All code encountered during a specific instance of the execution of a given *construct* or of an OpenMP library routine. The region includes code from the structured block (i.e., the lexical scope of the directive) plus any code inside functions called as the threads execute the code within the construct.

Runtime library OpenMP provides a set of library routines callable at runtime to manage features of the implementation that cannot be addressed at compile time. Examples include the `omp_thread_num()` function, which returns the ID of an individual member of a team of threads, or the `omp_num_threads()` function, which returns the number of threads in a team.

SIMD Single Instruction Multiple Data (SIMD) is an execution model in which a collection of tightly coupled processing elements (SIMD Lanes) execute a single stream of instructions in "lock-step." The execution is parallel but not concurrent since it is strictly ordered. The classic example of architectures designed around the SIMD execution model are the vector units found inside most CPUs.

SIMT Single Instruction Multiple Thread (SIMT) is an execution model for programs running on Graphics Processing Units (GPUs). A space of indices is defined (in OpenMP, by a set of nested loops), and at each point in this index space, an instance of a function called a *kernel* executes. Data is organized around this index space, which helps programmers reason about memory locality. The kernel instances are grouped into blocks. These blocks are enqueued for execution and execute as their data is available. The goal of SIMT execution is to optimize the throughput of the system; that is, any individual kernel instance may take a long time to compute, but the aggregate collection of kernel instances complete at high bandwidth.

SMP A Symmetric MultiProcessor is a shared memory computer where: (1) every processor (or core) is treated the same by the operating system, and (2) the cost of accessing any location in memory is the same for all processors.

Speedup A ratio between some reference run time and a comparison run time. It is important when reporting speedup data to specify the reference run time. Typically, we are interested in speedup trends as additional processors are used to execute a parallel program. In this case, the reference run time should be the best serial algorithm running on one node. When the speedup equals the number of processors, we say that the program is displaying *perfect linear speedup*.

SPMD Single Program Multiple Data is a fundamental design pattern of parallel programming. Each execution entity runs the same program (Single Program) but on its own set of variables (Multiple Data). The work is managed between execution entities through the ID of each entity and the number of entities running in parallel.

Stack A contiguous block of memory managed by a process (i.e., the programmer does not explicitly allocate or free memory in the stack) and associated with any block of code (i.e., code in C placed inside "curly brackets") including threads and functions. Memory in a stack is only visible within the block it is associated with. Once a program exits a block, the data in the stack is "out of scope" and no longer available.

Structured block A block of one or more statements associated with certain OpenMP directives to define a construct. The statements in the structured block define a flow of execution. In normal operation of the program, execution enters at the top of the block and exits at the bottom. In OpenMP, the only exception to the "enter at the top and exit at the bottom" rule is an exit statement to terminate execution of the program. For C/C++, the structured block is either a single statement (including a `for` statement) or a collection of statements between curly braces ({ and }). With Fortran, OpenMP defines a directive to mark the end of the structured block (e.g., `!$OMP parallel` and `!$OMP end parallel`).

Synchronization Operations from concurrent threads are unordered with respect to each other. This means that in general, we cannot say which operations on one thread happen-before operations on other threads. Synchronization refers to ways we can insert specific ordering constraints into the execution of concurrent threads. Specifically, a synchronization event defines a synchronized-with relation between threads. Operations before the synchronized-with relation on one thread *happen-before* operations on another thread that occur after the synchronized-with relation. When the synchronization applies to the whole team of threads, such as with the barrier and the critical construct, we call it *collective synchronization*. We can also define synchronization events between pairs of threads—that is, pairwise synchronization. When synchronization refers to the order of updates to variables in memory, it is called *data synchronization*.

Task The term *task* is used informally to describe a distinct unit of work. In OpenMP, it refers to a specific instance of executable code and its data environment. A task is an *explicit* task if it is created by an OpenMP `task` construct. A task is an *implicit* task if it is implied by a construct. For example, when an OpenMP program begins execution, it is run by an initial thread that runs an implicit task known as the *initial task*. It may seem odd to define implicit tasks in OpenMP. They were added to the language to provide a consistent abstraction to be used with programs based directly on explicit threads or programs based on explicit tasks.

Thread An execution entity with its own private memory (organized as a stack) and associated static memory is called *threadprivate memory*. In a modern operating system, a program executable is launched as a single process that defines an address space and a collection of resources managed by the operating system on behalf of the process. Execution of the process occurs through one or more threads that belong to the process and share the address space and any other resources associated with the process. Threads are a general concept, and the term is used widely in computer science. Closely related to OpenMP threads are *pthreads*, which is a standard threads interface included in the IEEE POSIX standard. Unfortunately, the term *thread* is used by some GPGPU programming models, which can be confusing since a GPU thread is quite different from threads in OpenMP and POSIX. This is why in the GPGPU programming model, OpenCL, the concept of thread was dropped and instead, the more generic term *work-item* was used.

UMA The Uniform Memory Architecture is a computer system where the cost function for any memory access is the same for all processors in the system. An ideal *SMP* computer is an UMA system.

Unified shared memory On some platforms, the host and one or more devices share a single address space. In this case, a pointer accessed on the host or any device refers to the same location in memory. With Unified Shared Memory (USM), map clauses are optional on target constructs. Values stored in memory from one device are visible to all other devices (including the host) following a synchronization operation.

Worksharing A type of construct in OpenMP. A worksharing construct specifies that the team of threads will work together to carry out the work defined by the region associated with the construct. The work is divided among the threads in the team as opposed to having each thread redundantly execute the code in the region (as is done, for example, with the parallel construct). The worksharing-loop is the most commonly used worksharing construct in OpenMP. For programming a GPU with OpenMP, the loop and distribute constructs are worksharing constructs.

References

[1] E. Strohmaier, J. Dongarra, H. Simon, M. Meuer, and H. Meuer, "TOP500 November 2012." https://www.top500.org/lists/top500/2012/11/, 2012.

[2] T. G. Mattson, Y. H. He, and A. E. Koniges, *The OpenMP Common Core: Making OpenMP Simple Again*. Cambridge, MA: The MIT Press, 2019.

[3] R. van der Pas, E. Stotzer, and C. Terboven, *Using OpenMP—The Next Step: Affinity, Accelerators, Tasking, and SIMD*. Cambridge, MA: The MIT Press, 2017.

[4] J. L. Hennessy and D. A. Patterson, *Computer Architecture: A Quantitative Approach*. Cambridge, MA: Morgan Kaufmann, 6th ed., 2019.

[5] M. J. Sottile, T. G. Mattson, and C. E. Rasmussen, *Introduction to Concurrency in Programming Languages*. Boca Raton, FL: CRC Press, 2009.

[6] D. B. Kirk and W. W. Hwu, *Programming Massively Parallel Processors: A Hands-on Approach*. Waltham, MA: Morgan Kaufmann, 2010.

[7] A. Munshi, B. Gaster, T. G. Mattson, J. Fung, and D. Ginsburg, *OpenCL Programming Guide*. Boston, MA: Addison-Wesley, 2011.

[8] T. G. Mattson, B. A. Sanders, and B. L. Massingil, *Patterns for Parallel Programming*. Boston, MA: Addison-Wesley, 2005.

[9] S. Shah, G. E. Haab, P. Petersen, and J. Throop, "Flexible Control Structures for Parallelism in OpenMP," *Concurrency: Practice and Experience*, vol. 12, pp. 1219–1239, 2000.

[10] D. Knuth, "Structured Programming with *go to* Statements," *ACM Computing Surveys*, vol. 6, pp. 261–301, 1974.

[11] S. J. Pennycook, J. D. Sewall, D. W. Jacobsen, T. Deakin, and S. McIntosh-Smith, "Navigating Performance, Portability, and Productivity," *Computing in Science and Engineering, Special Issue on Performance Portability for Advanced Architectures*, vol. 23, no. 5, pp. 28–38, 2021.

[12] T. Deakin, S. McIntosh-Smith, J. Price, A. Poenaru, P. Atkinson, C. Popa, and J. Salmon, "Performance Portability across Diverse Computer Architectures," in *IEEE/ACM International Workshop on Performance, Portability, and Productivity in HPC*, P3HPC, (Piscataway, NJ), pp. 1–13, IEEE, 2019.

[13] J. Barnes and P. Hut, "A Hierarchical O(n log n) Force Calculation Algorithm," *Nature*, vol. 324, pp. 446—449, December 1986.

[14] A. Abdelfattah, T. Costa, J. Dongarra, M. Gates, A. Haidar, S. Hammarling, N. J. Higham, J. Kurzak, P. Luszczek, S. Tomov, and M. Zounon, "A Set of Batched Basic Linear Algebra Subprograms and LAPACK Routines," *ACM Transactions on Mathematical Software*, vol. 47, June 2021.

[15] T. Deakin, J. Cownie, S. McIntosh-Smith, J. Lovegrove, and R. Smedley-Stevenson, "Hostile Cache Implications for Small, Dense Linear Solves," in *2020 IEEE/ACM Workshop on Memory Centric High Performance Computing*, MCHPC, pp. 34–41, 2020.

[16] T. Deakin, J. Cownie, W.-C. Lin, and S. McIntosh-Smith, "Heterogeneous Programming for the Homogeneous Majority," in *IEEE/ACM International Workshop on Performance, Portability, and Productivity in HPC Held in Conjunction with Supercomputing*, P3HPC, (Piscataway, NJ), pp. 1–13, IEEE, 2022.

[17] A. Patel and J. Doerfert, "Remote OpenMP Offloading," in *High Performance Computing. ISC High Performance 2022* (A.-L. Varbanescu, A. Bhatele, P. Luszczek, and B. Marc, eds.), (Cham, Switzerland), pp. 315–333, Springer International, 2022.

[18] J. Kwack, "AURORA ESP Training Webinar: OpenMP 5.0." Slide presentation, https://www.alcf.anl.gov/sites/default/files/2020-01/ALCF-2019_OpenMP _Webinar-OpenMP5-v03.pdf, 2019.

[19] S. F. Antao, A. Bataev, A. C. Jacob, G.-T. Bercea, A. E. Eichenberger, G. Rokos, M. Martineau, T. Jin, G. Ozen, Z. Sura, T. Chen, H. Sung, C. Bertolli, and K. O'Brien, "Offloading Support for OpenMP in Clang and LLVM," in *Third Workshop on the LLVM Compiler Infrastructure in HPC*, LLVM-HPC, (Piscataway, NJ), IEEE, 2016.

[20] T. Deakin, J. Price, M. Martineau, and S. McIntosh-Smith, "Evaluating Attainable Memory Bandwidth of Parallel Programming Models via BabelStream," *International Journal of Computational Science and Engineering*, vol. 17, no. 3, pp. 247–262, 2018. Special issue on Novel Strategies for Programming Accelerators.

Subject Index

Scientific and Engineering Computation

William Gropp, Series Editor; Ewing Lusk and Janusz Kowalik, Previous Editors

Data-Parallel Programming on MIMD Computers, Philip J. Hatcher and Michael J. Quinn, 1991

Enterprise Integration Modeling: Proceedings of the First International Conference, edited by Charles J. Petrie, Jr., 1992

The High Performance Fortran Handbook, Charles H. Koelbel, David B. Loveman, Robert S. Schreiber, Guy L. Steele Jr. and Mary E. Zosel, 1994

PVM: A User's Guide and Tutorial for Network Parallel Computing, Al Geist, Adam Beguelin, Jack Dongarra, Weicheng Jiang, Robert Manchek, and Vaidyalingham S. Sunderam, 1994

Practical Parallel Programming, Gregory V. Wilson, 1995

Enabling Technologies for Petaflops Computing, Thomas Sterling, Paul Messina, and Paul H. Smith, 1995

An Introduction to High-Performance Scientific Computing, Lloyd D. Fosdick, Elizabeth R. Jessup, Carolyn J. C. Schauble, and Gitta Domik, 1995

Parallel Programming Using C++, edited by Gregory V. Wilson and Paul Lu, 1996

Using PLAPACK: Parallel Linear Algebra Package, Robert A. van de Geijn, 1997

Fortran 95 Handbook, Jeanne C. Adams, Walter S. Brainerd, Jeanne T. Martin, Brian T. Smith, and Jerrold L. Wagener, 1997

MPI—The Complete Reference: Volume 1, The MPI Core, Marc Snir, Steve Otto, Steven Huss-Lederman, David Walker, and Jack Dongarra, 1998

MPI—The Complete Reference: Volume 2, The MPI-2 Extensions, William Gropp, Steven Huss-Lederman, Andrew Lumsdaine, Ewing Lusk, Bill Nitzberg, William Saphir, and Marc Snir, 1998

A Programmer's Guide to ZPL, Lawrence Snyder, 1999

How to Build a Beowulf, Thomas L. Sterling, John Salmon, Donald J. Becker, and Daniel F. Savarese, 1999

Using MPI-2: Advanced Features of the Message-Passing Interface, William Gropp, Ewing Lusk, and Rajeev Thakur, 1999

Beowulf Cluster Computing with Windows, edited by Thomas Sterling, William Gropp, and Ewing Lusk, 2001

Beowulf Cluster Computing with Linux, second edition, edited by Thomas Sterling, William Gropp, and Ewing Lusk, 2003

Scalable Input/Output: Achieving System Balance, edited by Daniel A. Reed, 2003

Using OpenMP: Portable Shared Memory Parallel Programming, Barbara Chapman, Gabriele Jost, and Ruud van der Pas, 2008

Quantum Computing without Magic: Devices, Zdzislaw Meglicki, 2008

Quantum Computing: A Gentle Introduction, Eleanor G. Rieffel and Wolfgang H. Polak, 2011

Using MPI: Portable Parallel Programming with the Message-Passing Interface, third edition, William Gropp, Ewing Lusk, and Anthony Skjellum, 2015

Using Advanced MPI: Beyond the Basics, Pavan Balaji, William Gropp, Torsten Hoefler, Rajeev Thakur, and Ewing Lusk, 2015

Scientific Programming and Computer Architecture, Divakar Viswanath, 2017

Cloud Computing for Science and Engineering, Ian Foster and Dennis B. Gannon, 2017

Using OpenMP—The Next Step: Affinity, Accelerators, Tasking and SIMD, Ruud van der Pas, Eric Stotzer, and Christian Terboven, 2017

The OpenMP Common Core: Making OpenMP Simple Again, Timothy G. Mattson, Yun (Helen) He, and Alice E. Koniges, 2019

High-Performance Big Data Computing, Dhabaleswar K. Panda, Xiaoyi Lu, and Dipti Shankar, 2022

Programming Your GPU with OpenMP: Performance Portability for GPUs, Tom Deakin and Timothy G. Mattson, 2023